Gender and Society in Renaissance Italy

THE UNIVERSITY OF
WINCHESTER

Martial Rose Library
Tel: 01962 827306

SEVEN DAY LOAN ITEM

To be returned on or before the day marked above, subject to recall.

This series, published for students, scholars and interested general readers, will tackle themes in gender history from the early medieval period through to the present day. Gender issues are now an integral part of all history courses and yet many traditional text books do not reflect this change. Much exciting work is now being done to redress the gender imbalances of the past, and we hope that these books will make their own substantial contribution to that process. This is an open-ended series, which means that many new titles can be included. We hope that these will both synthesise and shape future developments in gender studies.

The General Editors of the series are *Patricia Skinner* (University of Southampton) for the medieval period; *Pamela Sharpe* (University of Bristol) for the early modern period; and *Penny Summerfield* (University of Lancaster) for the modern period. *Margaret Walsh* (University of Nottingham) was the Founding Editor of the series.

Published books:

Gender, Church, and State in Early Modern Germany:
    Essays by Merry E. Wiesner
Merry E. Wiesner

Gender and Society in Renaissance Italy
Judith C. Brown and Robert C. Davis (eds)

Women and Work in Russia, 1880–1930:
    A Study in Continuity through Change
Jane McDermid and Anna Hillyar

Gender and Society in Renaissance Italy

Edited by
JUDITH C. BROWN
and
ROBERT C. DAVIS

Longman
London and New York

Addison Wesley Longman Limited
Edinburgh Gate,
Harlow, Essex CM20 2JE,
United Kingdom
and Associated Companies throughout the world

*Published in the United States of America
by Addison Wesley Longman Inc., New York*

© Addison Wesley Longman Limited 1998

First published 1998

ISBN 0 582 29326X PPR
ISBN 0 582 293251 CSD

British Library Cataloguing in Publication Data

A catalogue record for this book is available from the British Library

Library of Congress Cataloging-in-Publication Data

Gender and society in Renaissance Italy / edited by Judith C. Brown
and Robert C. Davis.
p. cm. — (Women and men in history)
Includes bibliographical references and index.
ISBN 0–582–29326–X (PPR). — ISBN 0–582–29325–1 (CSD)
1. Women—Italy—History—Renaissance, 1450–1600. 2. Sex role—
Italy—History. 3. Social structure—Italy—History. 4. Women—
Religious life—Italy—History. I. Brown, Judith C. II. Davis,
Robert C. (Robert Charles), 1948- . III. Series.
HQ1149.I8G46 1998
305.3'0945—dc21
97–42981
CIP

Set by 35 in 10/12pt Baskerville
Printed and bound by Antony Rowe Ltd,

Contents

List of Abbreviations

ASB	Archivio di Stato di Bologna
ASF	Archivio di Stato di Firenze
AMS	Arte dei Medici e Speziali
Dipl.	Diplomatico
OBGR	Otto di guardia e balìa, Repubblica
Osp.	Ospedale del
PR	Provvisioni registri
UN	Ufficiali di notte e conservatori dei monasteri
ASPi	Archivio di Stato di Pisa
ASPr	Archivio di Stato di Prato
Datini CP	Archivio Datini, Carteggio privato
ASPg	Archivio di Stato di Perugia
ASR	Archivio di Stato di Roma
ASV	Archivio di Stato di Venezia
ASVa	Archivio Segreto Vaticano
BAV	Biblioteca Apostolica Vaticana
DIP	*Dizionario degli Istituti di Perfezione*, G. Pelliccia and G. Rocca, eds.

List of Contributors

KAREN-EDIS BARZMAN, assistant professor of art history at Cornell University, has recently completed *The Discipline of "Disegno": the Florentine Academy and the Early Modern State* (Cambridge, MA, forthcoming). She has also published articles and reviews on critical theory, feminist art history, sacred imagery and devotional practice in *The Journal of Aesthetics and Art Criticism, Art History, Woman's Art Journal*, and in the anthology *Donne e fede. Santità e vita religiosa in Italia*, L. Scaraffia and G. Zarri, eds (Rome–Bari, 1994).

DANIEL BORNSTEIN is associate professor of history at Texas A&M University. He is the author of a score of articles on popular religion and female spirituality in the Middle Ages. He has written *The Bianchi of 1399: Popular Devotion in Late Medieval Italy* (Ithaca, NY, 1993), and is co-editor, with Roberto Rusconi, of *Mistiche e devote nell'Italia tardomedievale* (Naples, 1992), translated as *Women and Religion in Medieval and Renaissance Italy* (Chicago, IL, 1996). Bornstein has also translated, edited and annotated two important medieval Italian texts, published as *Dino Compagni's Chronicle of Florence* (Philadelphia, PA, 1995) and Bartolomea Riccoboni's *The Chronicle and Necrology of Corpus Domini: Life and Death in a Venetian Convent, 1395–1436* (Chicago, IL, forthcoming).

JUDITH C. BROWN is dean of the School of Humanities at Rice University. She has been director of the Institute for Research in Women and Gender at Stanford University and a fellow at Villa I Tatti, the Stanford Humanities Center and the Center for Advanced Study in the Behavioral Sciences. She has published two books, *In the Shadow of Florence: Provincial Society in Renaissance Pescia* (Oxford, 1985) and *Immodest Acts: The Life of a Lesbian Nun in Renaissance Italy* (Oxford, 1985), as well as articles on gender in journals such as *Renaissance Quarterly* and *Quaderni Storici* and in such anthologies as *Rewriting the Renaissance: The Discourses of Sexual Difference in Early Modern Europe*, M. Ferguson et al, eds (Chicago, IL, 1986).

STANLEY CHOJNACKI is professor of history at the University of North Carolina, Chapel Hill. He is the author of numerous articles, including publications in *The Journal of Family History*, *Renaissance Quarterly*, *The American Historical Review*, *Renaissance Studies*, and *The Journal of Interdisciplinary History*, and essays in anthologies including *Renaissance Venice*, J.R. Hale, ed. (London, 1973), *Women and Power in the Middle Ages*, M. Erler and M. Kowaleski, eds (Athens, Ga., 1988), and *Medieval Masculinities: Regarding Men in the Middle Ages*, C. Lees, ed. (Minneapolis, MN, 1994). His current project is a book on marriage in Venice from the mid thirteenth to the early sixteenth century.

SAMUEL K. COHN, JR is professor of medieval history at the University of Glasgow, Scotland. He has published many articles and four books: *The Laboring Classes in Renaissance Florence* (New York, 1980), *Death and Property in Siena 1205–1800: Strategies for the Afterlife* (Baltimore, MD, 1988), *The Cult of Remembrance and the Black Death: Six Renaissance Cities in Central Italy* (Baltimore, MD, 1992), and *Women in the Streets: Essays on Sex and Power in Renaissance Italy* (Baltimore, MD, 1996). He has also edited two collections: *David Herlihy, The Black Death and the Transformation of the West* (Cambridge, MA, 1997), and with S. Epstein, *Portraits of Medieval and Renaissance Living* (Ann Arbor, MI, 1996).

ROBERT C. DAVIS is associate professor of history at the Ohio State University and has been a fellow at the Institute for Advanced Study in Princeton NJ, and at the American Academy in Rome. He is the author of *Shipbuilders of the Venetian Arsenal: Workers and Workplace in the Preindustrial City* (Baltimore, MD, 1991) and *The War of the Fists: Popular Culture and Public Violence in Late Renaissance Venice* (Oxford, 1994). He has published various articles on popular customs and culture in early-modern Italy and is editor of *News on the Rialto*, a newsletter for Venetian studies.

THOMAS J. KUEHN is professor of history at Clemson University. He is author of the monographs *Emancipation in Late Medieval Florence* (New Brunswick, 1982) and *Law, Family, and Women: Toward a Legal Anthropology of Renaissance Italy* (Chicago, IL, 1991), as well as editor, with Richard Golden, of the source book *Western Societies: Primary Sources in Social History*, 2 vols (New York, NY, 1993).

KATHARINE PARK is professor of the History of Science and of Women's Studies at Harvard University. She is author of *Doctors and*

Medicine in Early Renaissance Florence (Princeton, NJ, 1985) and, with
L. Daston, of *Wonder and the Orders of Nature, 1150–1750* (New York,
1998). Her articles have appeared in publications such as *Renaissance Quarterly* and in anthologies such as *Medicine in Society*, A.
Wear, ed. (Cambridge, 1991), and *Medicine and Charity before the
Welfare State*, J. Barry and C. Jones, eds (London, 1991).

MICHAEL ROCKE is adjunct processor at Syracuse University in
Florence and acting director of the Biblioteca Berenson at Villa I
Tatti in Florence. He has published the monograph *Forbidden Friendships: Homosexuality and Male Culture in Renaissance Florence* (New
York, 1996), and is the author of articles in the *Journal of Homosexuality* and *Quaderni Storici*, and in the collection *Infanzie. Funzioni di
un gruppo liminale dal mondo classico all'Età moderna*, O. Niccoli, ed.
(Florence, 1993).

SHARON STROCCHIA is associate professor of history at Emory
University. She has published the monograph *Death and Ritual in
Renaissance Florence* (Baltimore, MD, 1992), as well as articles in the
Renaissance Quarterly and in the collections, *Life and Death in Fifteenth-
Century Florence*, M. Tetel, R. Witt and R. Goffen, eds (Durham,
NC, 1989) and *Refiguring Woman: Perspectives on Gender and the Italian
Renaissance*, M. Migiel and J. Schiesari, eds (Ithaca, NY, 1991).

GABRIELLA ZARRI is professor of modern history at the University of Florence. She is author of numerous articles and book chapters as well as the monograph *Le Sante vive. Cultura e religiosità
femminile nella prima età moderna* (Turin: Rosenberg & Sellier, 1990).
She has edited the collection *Finzione e santità tra medioevo ed età
moderna* (Turin, 1991) and *Donne, discipline, creanza cristiana tra XV
e XVII secolo. Studi e Testi a stampa* (Rome, 1996) and has co-edited
with Lucetta Scaraffia the anthology *Donne e fede. Santità e vita religiosa
in Italia* (Rome–Bari, 1994).

Glossary of Terms

aditio haereditatis: the act of accepting an inheritance.

agnation: a relation through male descent or on the father's side.

battagliola: a mock or play battle, often fought by artisans armed with wooden swords, sticks, rocks, or fists.

broglio: the area in Venice adjacent to the Ducal Palace that was set aside for the city's noble men to meet and politick.

cacce dei tori: literally a 'hunt of the bulls'. A popular entertainment in pre-modern Italy, something between the Spanish *corrida* and bull-baiting with dogs.

catasto: a census; in particular, the Florentine *catasto* of 1427 was an especial survey of the population of the city and its territories, compiled for fiscal purposes. It contains information on wealth, household structure, and other social variables.

contado: that area of the countryside legally subject to a nearby town.

empiric: a person who relies on practical experience rather than on scientific principles.

estimo: a form of tax survey, common in late medieval and Renaissance Italy, whereby the value of a taxpayer's properties was estimated for tax purposes.

fideicommissum: a legally binding restriction that prevented the inheritor from alienating property outside the family.

ius commune: common law, primarily civil and canon law, but also including academic feudal law and even Lombard law, generally accepted and used with some variations throughout most of Italy.

miles Christi: soldier of Christ.

monte: the public debt in Florence and other Italian cities, often funded by 'forced loans' from the richer citizens.

mundualdus/mundium: a male legal guardian who possessed the power (mundium) to act on behalf of a woman in a legal transaction.

patria potestas: legal control by the father.

ricordi/ricordanze: the combination family diary and household account book kept by many Florentine fathers and husbands during the Renaissance.

scorreria: in military terms, a raid or forray.

spousa Christi: bride of Christ.

xi

Introduction

JUDITH C. BROWN

Modern conceptions of the Renaissance begin with the 1860 publication of Jacob Burckhardt's *The Civilization of the Renaissance in Italy*. For Burckhardt, Italians were the 'first-born among the sons of Europe'.[1] Breaking the veil of faith and illusion under which Europeans had slumbered half awake for more than a millennium, they emerged as self-conscious individuals – they were the first modern people. Despite the gendered metaphor used by Burckhardt, in this process of self-discovery, as in other aspects of Renaissance life, 'women stood on a footing of perfect equality with men'.[2] The discovery of 'man' also meant the discovery of 'woman'.

Just over a century after Burckhardt developed this conception of the Renaissance, Joan Kelly fired the opening salvo of the critiques mounted by women's history.[3] 'One of the tasks of women's history', she argued, 'is to call into question accepted schemes of periodization. ... The Renaissance is a good case in point.' The economic and political developments 'that reorganized Italian society along modern lines and opened the possibilities for the social and cultural expression for which the age is known ... affected women adversely, so much so that there was no renaissance for women – at least not during the Renaissance'.[4] For Kelly, the two

1. Jacob Burckhardt, *The Civilization of the Renaissance in Italy* (London, 1990; orig. 1860), p. 98.

2. Ibid., p. 250.

3. Joan Kelly, 'Did women have a Renaissance?', in Renate Bridenthal and Claudia Koonz, eds, *Becoming Visible: Women in European History* (Boston, 1977), pp. 137–64; reprinted in *Women, History, and Theory: The Essays of Joan Kelly* (Chicago, 1984; hereafter the edition cited), pp. 19–50. Burckhardt's thesis had been criticized before from other points of view by medievalists, economic historians, historians of science and historians of religion, to name a few. For a useful summary, see, Gene A. Brucker, *Renaissance Italy: Was It the Birthplace of the Modern World?* (New York, 1965).

4. Kelly, 'Did women have a Renaissance?', p. 19.

sides of the Renaissance, male and female, were causally connected. The development of the modern state and the emergence of capitalism, which were essential for the creation of a larger range of opportunities for men, necessarily had a negative effect on women.

In the twenty years since Kelly's challenge to reconceptualize the way we organize history and evaluate historical periods, historians have confirmed, refuted, and modified different aspects of her thesis. In a powerful series of essays, Christiane Klapisch-Zuber has painted a bleak picture of the restrictions imposed on patrician women in Florence by a patriarchal system intent on the preservation of male lineage.[5] To the contrary, Stanley Chojnacki has observed that some of the same phenomena that appear to have had a negative impact on the lives of Florentine women, such as the increasing importance of ever-larger dowries, gave Venetian women power they had not had before the Renaissance.[6] Similarly, while David Herlihy and Christiane Klapisch-Zuber have argued that in Renaissance Italy there was a progressive exclusion of women from the labour force, Isabel Chabot, Samuel Kline Cohn, and others have shown that women participated in the economy in larger numbers and more diverse ways than had been previously thought.[7] In an interesting and probably unintended 'synthesis', one historian has claimed, in keeping with Kelly, that the deteriorating social and economic conditions faced by upper-class women in sixteenth-century Italy, led, in keeping with Burckhardt, to the emergence of the first modern, self-conscious women. According to this view, Lucrezia Marinella and Modesta Pozzo wrote the first truly feminist tracts in European history as a reaction against the narrowing of options available to women in the sixteenth century. The former, sounding curiously Burckhardtian, argued that 'if women, as I hope, will wake themselves from the long slumber that has oppressed them, their ungrateful and proud oppressors will be

---

5. Christiane Klapisch-Zuber, *Women, Family, and Ritual in Renaissance Italy* (Chicago, 1985).

6. Stanley Chojnacki, 'Dowries and kinsmen in early Renaissance Venice', *Journal of Interdisciplinary History*, 5, 1975 (571–600); and 'The power of love: wives and husbands in late medieval Venice', in Mary Erler and Maryanne Kowaleski, eds, *Women and Power in the Middle Ages* (Athens, GA, 1988).

7. David Herlihy and Christiane Klapisch-Zuber, *Les toscans et leurs familles: une étude du catasto florentin de 1427* (Paris, 1978), pp. 582–83. Isabel Chabot, 'La reconnaissance du travail des femmes dans la Florence du bas Moyen Age: contexte idéologique et réalité', in S. Cavaciocchi, ed., *La donna nelleconomia sec. XIII–XVIII* (Florence, 1990), pp. 563–76; Samuel Kline Cohn in his chapter in this volume.

humbled and tamed'.[8] Being realistic, and not wanting to rely only on moral persuasion, however, Lucrezia also counselled women to arm themselves like the Amazons of antiquity and to battle men in order to achieve the degree of economic and political independence they needed and wanted.

At first, the implicit or explicit dialogue with Kelly's work proceeded along the lines of women's history, whose goal was to restore women to historical accounts. In a sense, this was an archeological approach – to uncover from the rubble of history the lives of women who had been buried or consigned to the margins by historians of earlier generations. At its simplest, this meant uncovering the lives of a small number of famous women – Caterina Sforza, Isabella d'Este, St Catherine of Siena, Vittoria Colonna and others – who, by virtue of their role in political circles, as patrons of the arts, or as well-known religious figures, were able to influence society. Extending outward from this small circle, the project required finding worthy women writers or artists who might be brought into the illustrious company of great men. Finally, it required combing the historical documents – tax records, notarial contracts, family diaries, etc. – for the telltale signs of the activities of everyday women – the bakers, seamstresses, innkeepers, and others whose work and social contributions enabled ordinary people to survive.

On the heels of these efforts to discover the range of women's activities and influence, historians also began to concern themselves with the more complicated issue of the legal, political, economic, and social conditions that governed the lives of the vast majority of women. If most of the wealth, for example, was in the hands of men, what legal restrictions on inheritance or property ownership contributed to this unequal distribution? If there were few women artists, what barriers kept women from receiving professional training and status? What educational opportunities were available to women? Did guild regulations limit the range of occupational choices available to them? If so, how did these vary from one Renaissance city to another and from one century to the next?

In the course of finding the answers to such questions, it became clear that historians needed new theoretical categories to approach the issue of the relation between the sexes and new conceptions of the self. Women's history at its best could help us discover aspects

8. Virginia Cox, 'The single self: feminist thought and the marriage market in early modern Venice', *Renaissance Quarterly*, 48:3 (Autumn 1995), p. 521.

of women's lives that were hidden from history. But if not handled well, it could also isolate the history of women in an anachronistic separate sphere. It could dehistoricize women's past, turning it into an unchanging landscape of victimization. 'Woman', timeless and classless, could thus become the object of history rather than its subject.

Historians instead wanted to examine the ways in which women and men interpreted the meaning of being male and female, of what characteristics men and women in the past attached to what they considered 'feminine', and 'masculine', how those attributes varied by time and place, and how both women and men could appropriate these categories for different purposes. If in some places in Italy men allowed women to be guardians of their children, why did they not allow them to represent themselves in a court of law? What was 'male' and what was 'female' about these two powerful functions that women could and could not practise in one and the same place? Indeed, why could they do so in some Italian cities but not in others? Why, in the absence of obvious barriers in the law, did women in some cities, even in the same region, exercise greater independence in disposing of their property compared to women in neighbouring cities? Given the theoretical equality of the spirit between men and women in Christian thought, why was it that the ceremonies of women's consecration to the religious life increasingly resembled nuptial rites as opposed to the rites of military obligation in men's consecration? In short, what cultural constructs allowed women and men in the past to attach different meaning to similar circumstances?

The answers to these questions undermine any timeless and essentializing notion of 'woman'. They lead us instead to the category of 'gender', which enables scholars to examine the social construction of male and female identities and of the meaning attached to different social roles assumed by women and men, depending on age, social class, and other social rather than biological characteristics. Gender can also point us in the direction of examining aspects of life – of which politics is perhaps the most obvious – from which women were excluded but which were based on strong conceptions of gender that had powerful effects on both women and men. Last but not least, gender leads us in the direction of analysing the construction of male identity rather than taking men as the undifferentiated norm and women as the other. One might say that the discovery of 'woman' has led to the discovery of 'man'. With this, the tight coupling of sex and gender has come undone; binary oppositions have weakened and it has become possible to examine gender as a process in which women and men situate themselves and are situated by others along a shifting continuum that varies according to several characteristics, among them age, class, region, and even, but by no means only, sex.[9]

Gender as a category of historical analysis is by no means beyond criticism. Judith Bennett has warned that by intellectualizing the inequality of the sexes it can gloss over past injustices. By emphasizing the agency of both women and men, it can elide the powerlessness of women in the face of patriarchy. And by its concern with meaning and metaphor, it can steer historians away from the hard realities of social history.[10] At the other end of the spectrum, Thomas Kuehn, one of the contributors to this volume, argues for 'social personhood' as a more useful conceptual tool than gender. Overly neutral though gender may sound to scholars like Bennett, Kuehn feels that it cannot escape the limitations of 'natural' sexual imagery. 'Social personhood instead points to relations between individuals, or even between parts of an individual.'[11]

The advantages and limitations of gender as an analytical tool for understanding the society of Renaissance Italy may be explored by readers in the following chapters. The contributors have sought, where possible, to transcend the limitations of women's history and to address issues of gender in order to historicize the conditions of both women and men as actors on the historical stage.

The other limitation the authors have sought to overcome is the local particularism that characterizes most scholarly work on Renaissance Italy. Because the Italian archives are generally organized according to the jurisdiction of governmental institutions in the Renaissance and since Renaissance states were organized according to cities, historians have concentrated on historical developments in one particular place, most often Florence, and secondarily Venice. After nearly three decades of research on women's history, however, it is clear that to understand the gender dimensions behind specific local variations one must look at local experiences in a comparative framework. It is also important to be attentive to temporal changes. Social history's emphasis on structure over events has tended to obscure change over time. As a consequence, the

---

9. Joan W. Scott, 'Gender: a useful category of historical analysis', *American Historical Review*, 91 (December 1986), pp. 1053–75.

10. Judith M. Bennett, 'Feminism and history', *Gender and History*, 1:3 (Autumn 1989), pp. 258–9.

11. Thomas Kuehn, see Chapter 4 below.

history of women and of gender relations has sometimes appeared static, lending credence to those who would argue that women have no history. The chapters in this volume seek to address the issue of change over time. What was new about gender relations in the Renaissance compared to earlier periods? How did notions about gender-appropriate behaviour change in Renaissance Italy and in response to the currents of religious reform that emanated from northern Europe in the sixteenth century? Finally, many of these authors are attentive to issues of class and ask in what ways the changes observed in the relations between men and women of the elite differ from those of the lower classes?

Part One of this volume focuses on some of these questions with regard to urban geography and ritual life. As Robert Davis shows, urban spaces were gendered. Newly constituted Renaissance governments made them so through the passage and implementation of laws that reinforced notions of public spaces as male and private spaces as female. Most public rituals involving the installation of governments or the celebration of public events brought out processions of councillors, guildsmen, noblemen and rulers who were invariably male. Their ritual walks through the city proclaimed the theoretical masculinity of public spaces and of the law. Yet other forces were also at work to undermine this partnership between government and gendered geography. Class figured prominently in this. The gender of public space was not a constant, but was tested frequently and required repeated reaffirmation. Throughout the cities of the Italian peninsula, lower-class youths, often in defiance of government orders, though sometimes in tacit connivance with government officials, engaged in contests to prove their physical prowess through bullchasing, wars of the fists, stone-throwing contests, etc. These masculinized public space in ways that disrupted public order. Of necessity, working-class women ventured out more often into this dangerous public sphere than did their elite sisters. Prostitutes in particular tested the restrictions imposed by governments on the use of the streets and courtesans sometimes controlled entire neighbourhoods. Yet at the same time the transgressions of these last two groups reinforced the notion that the streets were for those women with less honour or those whose honour had been depleted altogether. Elite women ventured out less frequently, and when they did so, they often walked on enormously high platform shoes that made it impossible for them to move about unaided by a large corps of female servants. Such visible, accompanied displays would have left no doubt that the honour of these women was unassailable and also that, at least fleetingly, they were reclaiming the streets, as passersby tried futilely to get around these slow-moving retinues.

According to Sharon Strocchia, women of the middling and upper classes had once been more visible in the streets of late medieval and early Renaissance Italy. The rituals of marriage and corporate groups had allowed women greater participation in public life. Yet as the fifteenth century wore on, nuptial rites increasingly highlighted the honour and public recognition of grooms and their families. Corporate groups also developed rites that made it more difficult for women to partake in common public ceremonies. Strocchia argues, for example, that as the flagellant movement made inroads in religious confraternities, females were increasingly excluded. The issue was not flagellation *per se*, which women and men had practised in solitude for centuries; it was not even the unseemly exposure of the bleeding bare backs of anonymous confraternal members; rather, the problem was the inversion of gender roles by self-abasing men. The patriarchal ideal placed the confident male at the top of the social hierarchy. The spectacle of men flagellating themselves would have undermined the confidence of women in the social pyramid that placed them towards the bottom.

Yet the self-same forces that served to masculinize public life, in the end worked to feminize it as well. Strocchia speaks about the 'civilizing' efforts of the state. As Renaissance governments tried to tame the disruptive behaviour of male youths and nobles, they spread the ethos of restraint and polite behaviour. In the course of the sixteenth century, in most places in Italy, loud public insults and vendettas gave way to courtly manners and duels. Males may have had greater access to public places but the new codes of behaviour to which they were expected to adhere were, by earlier standards, distinctly 'feminine'.

The importance of the state in gender relations, evident in the work of Davis and Strocchia, becomes one of the primary themes in Part Two of this volume, which focuses on the state, the law, and the economy. Stanley Chojnacki advances a new interpretation of the centrality of gender for the formation of the Renaissance state. As elites throughout the Italian peninsula tried to set themselves apart and to establish themselves above the rest of society, the state developed as an instrument for the consolidation and regulation of oligarchic hegemony. The state both represented and disciplined their efforts, and in so doing, extended its regulatory tentacles into areas of social life that had previously been the province of the family. Indeed, it could be said that by creating a public sphere, the Renaissance state also created a 'private' one. The principal means through which this new institution, the state, confirmed the public roles and confronted the private interests of the elites was gender. New magistracies and new laws, starting in the late fourteenth century, asserted the prerogatives of patriarchy as a way to represent the state and control the behaviour of individuals within the family. Patriarchy, that is what it meant to be a male capable of holding authority, was defined in these centuries. In the process, the divide between men and women widened, with the latter increasingly relegated to the private sphere. But the distance between males who were deemed fit to rule and those who were not by virtue of their class, age, or position within the family also widened, and for some of the same reasons. The result was that the conflicts revealed by state efforts to mediate between these different interests created the room that enabled women to manoeuvre more effectively as notable agents in the social landscape. The Renaissance state, for Chojnacki, marks a decisive turning point in the creation of notions about the public and the private; gender lines were the contested boundaries around which these notions developed.

Thomas Kuehn examines the role played by law in this process. Legal scholarship has often portrayed the law in Renaissance Italy as a prison for women. Kuehn concludes that if it was a prison, it was not an effective one; moreover, it was also increasingly one for men, as local statutes elaborated new sets of laws to complement, supplant, or deal with new developments that had not been covered in the common law (*ius commune*) that was the legal inheritance of the Roman and the medieval worlds. It was these new local statutes, not common law, that 'detracted most from the legal condition of women in the Renaissance'. Kuehn examines two types of statutes that clashed with common law – those governing inheritance and those imposing male guardianship over women's property rights. While Renaissance lawmakers may have wanted to depart from *ius commune* and to limit inheritance to agnates, that is those relatives whose kinship was traceable exclusively through male lines, the reality of family life often dictated that property move through women. Similarly, in cities like Florence, where male guardianship (*mundualdus*) over women was most pronounced, women could be required to have a *mundualdus* in court while at the same time having the right of principal guardianship over their children as long as there was a male co-guardian somewhere in the scene.

This was a right that they had not had in Roman law. Kuehn argues that because there was no single, uniform body of law, the discrepancies between common law and local statutes led to a growing number of legal disputes and court cases in which women asserted their agency. Women, like some categories of men, may have had a limited persona in common law, but they did have personhood and legal rights they could assert. In this they were often aided by male relatives – husbands, fathers, or children – whose interests lined up with theirs. Thus women and men were able to manoeuvre around some of the legal barriers that went up around them. The plurality of law, both according to type of law and according to place, resulted in considerable flexibility. The one common denominator was that women could not have *patria potestas* (paternal legal control), but neither could certain categories of males. The study of gender in Renaissance law reveals that clear-cut dichotomies between male and female did not exist either in legal theory or in everyday practice.

The absence of rigid boundaries also extended to the world of work. Samuel Kline Cohn finds that the distribution of men and women in the labour force depended on notions of gender-appropriate work, not on biology. The historical documents that bear on the question conceal as much as they reveal; however, they do show women in occupations requiring heavy physical exertions, such as skinners, carders, and stretchers in the wool industry. The documents also show women in occupations, such as sheep-herding over long distances, which put them away from home and in potentially risky situations that had previously been thought closed to them. Whether such activities were common for both women and men, or whether the sexual division of labour varied by region or time, is not yet clear, but what Cohn argues convincingly is that the chronology, geography and causes behind the shifts in labour-force gender patterns are far from being understood. Some historians have posited a demographic model of labour participation, with women driven out of the labour force during periods of population growth. When such patterns are shown to have persisted after the cataclysmic contractions of population brought on by the Black Death, others have focused on the consolidation of guilds as the primary determinant for the exclusion of women from the paid labour force. When this explanation seemed inadequate, yet others turned to economic expansion as the key. But when this too failed to explain the ratio of male and female workers in different cities of the Italian Renaissance or in certain occupations, some turned to a 'Mediterranean' model. According to this explanation, women were kept out of the work place because of notions of honour and shame that had deleterious effects not only for women but for the Italian economy, which lost ground to the burgeoning economies of northern Europe. Cohn's survey of the experience of different parts of Italy, however, suggests that there was no such single model. Not only was there no steady deterioration in the participation of women in the world of work, as the Mediterranean model or the model proposed by Joan Kelly posit, but cycles of participation varied considerably from one place to another, from one set of decades to the next, and even from one stage in women's lives to another. Much more detailed research will need to be done before we understand the reasons for these patterns.

Renaissance notions of what was masculine and what was feminine were to a large extent rooted in Renaissance notions about human biology. Part Three of this volume, 'The Social Body', explores some of these ideas. Katharine Park notes that while many anatomists and natural philosophers adhered to the Aristotelians' conceptions of women as defective males, whose colder and moister humours affected everything from menstruation to intelligence to sexual behaviour, most medical practitioners and their patients held a variety of opinions that were more gender-neutral. The emphasis of medical practice was on evacuating the substances that impacted and corrupted the humours. This could be accomplished through urination, menstruation, bleeding, sweating, and so on, with the process being analogous in men and women. Indeed, so close were these systems that some physicians discussed them with reference to 'menstruating men'. Because physicians did not have a clearly dichotomous view of the bodies of women and men, they tended to interpret female inferiority to behaviour patterns rather than to corporeal imperatives.

If in everyday practice, views of the human body were less gendered than the theoretical literature suggests, gender nonetheless figured prominently in the practice of medicine. Women healers did not exclusively treat women patients, as conventional wisdom would have it, but they tended to rely on different types of healing methods. Women medical practitioners and magical healers relied more heavily than their male counterparts on bodily fluids to compose medicines for their patients. Male healers, perhaps because they had a greater level of education, tended to rely more frequently on the written word to compose remedies and amulets.

Women practitioners also clustered more frequently in the ranks of empirics and magical healers. Much has been made in modern scholarship about Renaissance women being edged out of the medical and other professions that they had practised in the Middle Ages. Park argues that while there is some truth in this, the reason was not that women were excluded from medical practice as such, but that the professionalization of medicine, with its emphasis on university-trained and learned physicians, worked against informal practitioners and magical healers where women figured prominently. The professionalization of medicine and the increasing concern of the Church with establishing the limits of orthodoxy in the sixteenth century undoubtedly had a negative effect, and in the case of sorcerers an even lethal effect on women. Yet the essence of Park's analysis suggests a greater degree of flexibility in Renaissance beliefs, a plurality of medical approaches, an eclectic set of ideas about the effects of sexual difference on the body, and a need for greater subtlety in the interpretation of the evidence.

This call for a more nuanced interpretation is echoed in Michael Rocke's chapter on sexuality. Rocke looks at how gender differences entered into the prescriptive discourse about sexual behaviour and how gender ideology shaped the sexual behaviour of men and women in a range of cross-sex and same-sex activities. As in many of the other chapters in this volume, Rocke finds that social reality departs considerably from prescriptive statements. While sex outside marriage was in theory proscribed to men and women alike, there was greater flexibility and toleration towards it on the part of men than of women. Chastity was the central component of women's honour and its loss had serious social consequences. The difficulty was that women were less prone to reason and hence more vulnerable to sexual temptations. A lot rested on a very weak base. This may be one reason that male adulterers were hardly ever punished, whereas females were prosecuted and punished publicly. Public shaming may have been seen as a preventive measure for women in the audience who may have been contemplating similar transgressions.

Within marriage, both partners were supposed to render the conjugal debt, but here again there were contradictions. On the one hand, women were subject to the authority of their husbands; on the other, they were supposed to be informed about and refuse illicit, that is non-procreative, sexual acts considered sinful by the Church. As Rocke points out, Renaissance moralists tended to disempower women as autonomous sexual subjects and to place greater responsibility on them to act as guardians not only of their chastity, but of the sexual morality of their husbands as well.[12]

For Rocke, same-sex relations between males are a particularly useful vantage point from which to examine the construction of gendered identities in Renaissance Italy because they so clearly separate notions of gender from the sex of the body. Same-sex erotic activities among males were quite widespread and frequently punished. In Florence alone, between 1432 and 1502 roughly 3,000 males were convicted and more than five times that many were incriminated for such behaviour. Homosexual acts, however, were not related to any sense of homosexual identity, but rather were part of a common life stage that saw young males taking on 'passive', receiving sexual roles *vis-à-vis* older men as part of a wider set of social relations. In these exchanges, the passive partner was seen as feminine, and what made him so was not his appearance, but his receptive role in the sexual act. 'Sodomite', a term that did not have gendered connotations, was reserved for the 'active' partner who penetrated his younger companion. Most youths made the transition from one role to the other around the age of eighteen. Once they became adults, most of these men, even those who engaged in same-sex erotic relations with younger males, also had sexual relations with women. Because diminished capacity was in a sense associated with women and the young, opprobrium was attached, not to passive young males, but to the few older men who did not manage to cross over into accepted roles. Gender identity then was not fixed, but was constructed along age and behaviour patterns. The sex of the body had little to do with it.

Nothing would seem more removed from the body than questions of spirituality. Yet the chapters in Part Four reveal the strong links as well as the affinities in the handling of gender issues. Daniel Bornstein examines the tensions between the religious ideal of celibacy and the social pressures to reproduce in an age haunted by the ravages of the Black Death. In trying to negotiate these tensions, individuals did not remain quietly and passively in their predicted roles. While male theologians, preachers and humanists increasingly wrote about family and the religious life in tracts addressed to women, it is clear that their audience, in the process of assimilating their messages, really modified them and often reversed the roles assigned to them. Catherine of Siena is perhaps the most famous example of this. Bornstein shows how she 'turned

12. See below, pp. 155–6.

her family home into a sacred place' and how she replaced her biological family with a spiritual one. In this new environment, a convicted young nobleman becomes a 'bride' of Christ and her father confessor becomes her son and spiritual spouse.

Role reversal was not confined to women. Bornstein also examines the experience of men, such as the friar Giovanni Dominici, born less than a decade after the Black Death. Although Giovanni was the sole surviving son of a widowed mother and joined the religious life against her wishes, thus dooming the family line to extinction, he did not hesitate to counsel secular women to serve God outside the monastic life, thus fulfilling their obligations simultaneously to God and their families. Neither did he hesitate to offer them advice about childrearing, even though as a celibate friar, he had no experience in the matter. In turn, however, the Florentine housewife to whom he proffered the advice did not hesitate to offer spiritual counsel in return. While his letters were full of the details of the domestic life, hers sounded like the products of the male spiritual adviser of a convent. Neither biology nor family ties seemed to keep men or women in their place.

The kind of gender continuum and role reversal observed by nearly all the contributors to this volume became more difficult to maintain in many areas of social life after the mid-sixteenth century. Gabriella Zarri explores efforts to impose gendered social discipline in religious life in the wake of pressures brought about by the Protestant Reformation and by internal reform currents within the Catholic Church. The new norms focused on the reform of religious orders in general but they had different effects on men and women. The metaphor of spiritual marriage that had shaped the life of nuns and the military metaphor that had influenced the life of monks grew in importance and were now exemplified by new types of religious orders, the Ursulines and the Jesuits. Marriage became the unifying status for women, both inside and outside the convent. With this came a heightened sense that women needed to submit to male authority – the father, the husband, the confessor, or the bishop. After the Council of Trent in the mid-sixteenth century, women's independence was also curbed by stricter rules of enclosure in convents. This affected a growing proportion of women as more of them were sent to convents by their families, which were intent on keeping the family patrimony intact rather than dividing it up into multiple dowries. To be sure, priests and monks were also held to tighter standards than before but the latter could leave the monastery for cause. As soldiers of

Christ, engaged in missionary activity, many men did just that, experiencing the freedom (and the hardship) of spreading the gospel to parts of the world that were far removed from the restraints and the comforts of European society.

Yet even within the confines of the convent, women were producers of culture. In the last chapter of this volume, the art historian Karen-edis Barzman examines how gender affected cultural production. She begins with the question that animated Linda Nochlin's essay, 'Why Have There Been No Great Women Artists?' She goes on to explore the scholarship on women as artists and patrons of the arts and the gendered institutional limitations on both. She also examines the meaning of images of women for men and women and the problematics of looking at Renaissance art as a timeless aesthetic contribution to culture. More importantly, she broadens the focus from art, as traditionally defined (painting, sculpture, architecture), to 'cultural production', that is the production, use and appropriation of meaning in images and everyday objects. Barzman uses as her example the life of the sixteenth-century Florentine nun, Maria Maddalena de' Pazzi, who used the religious images that were the common currency of her time to fashion herself as a work of art. Her self-fashioning gave her an authoritative voice that at times subverted the intent of the images and that made her the kind of Renaissance woman that Lucrezia Marinella and Modesta Pozzo may have had in mind.

To conclude, the chapters that follow challenge us with a more complex view of the interplay between gender and society than was possible to imagine when women's studies began several decades ago. All of the authors suggest that the relationships between men and women in the society of Renaissance Italy do not fit dichotomous categorizations. Because the meaning of gender was culturally produced, it had no fixed boundaries; classifications of gender had to be constantly reinvented and reinforced. To be sure, some clear patterns emerge. In the course of the Renaissance, the state, religious institutions and the professionalization of knowledge all worked to harden gender categories. The emergence of capitalism, on the other hand, had no such obvious results. There were also enormous regional variations whose causes and ramifications need to be explored further. Most important, the men and women of Renaissance Italy found ways to undermine the social restrictions imposed on them by custom and by the emergence of new sets of beliefs. Their ability to do so often required them to marshal all their imaginative capacities and to incur considerable risks. Nothing better illustrates their achievements and the price paid for them than the ambiguous praise heaped by Lauro Querini on the learned Isotta Nogarola: 'The greatest praise is justly bestowed upon you, Illustrious Isotta, since you have ... overcome your own nature. For you have sought with singular zeal that true virtue, which is essentially male ... as befits the whole and perfect wisdom that men attain.'[13] In short, by overcoming the limitations of her sex, Isotta had constructed herself and was perceived by others as a male intellectual. Her predicament encapsulates the complications of gender in the society of Renaissance Italy.

13. Cited in Margaret L. King, 'Book-lined cells: women and humanism in the early Italian Renaissance', in Patricia Labalme, ed., *Beyond their Sex: Learned Women of the European Past* (New York, 1980), pp. 76, 89.

PART ONE

The Gendered City in Renaissance Italy

CHAPTER ONE

The Geography of Gender in the Renaissance[1]

ROBERT C. DAVIS

Students of the Italian Renaissance have long since learned to pay close attention to what happened in the city streets and piazzas of these intensely public, human-scale societies. It was here, as much as in the writings of the humanists or the art of the masters, that Italians expressed who they were, to themselves and to the outside world: whether in their carefully staged ceremonials or in the everyday allocations that they made of their limited public spaces to competing groups and classes. Some areas were designated for making money and others for making things; some were reserved for the nobility, others the preserve of commoners. Space was also set aside and embellished for ceremony and devotion, some in homage to the state and some to the Church, though in the Renaissance both forms of worship might well be mixed, in spirit as much as in location.

More recently, scholars have become interested in the gendered nature of urban space in the Italian Renaissance. As much as certain areas of these cities were consecrated to the prerogatives of commerce, ceremony, and class, so too, it is now recognized, were some places considered more masculine and others more feminine. Linked with an enduring 'Mediterranean' culture whose roots reached back to well before classical Athens, such social traditions in Renaissance Italy saw the public realm – the guild halls and taverns, the main streets and piazzas – as the appropriate male sphere; while to women were allotted the household, local neighbourhoods and parish churches, and the convent – all of those urban areas most 'identified with the private, domestic, and sacred

1. My thanks to Cynthia H. Davis and Stefany Dal Mina, without whom this chapter could not have been written.

19

roles that women were expected to play in society'. As the source of the 'strong symbolic and moral associations that helped define gender roles and determine relations between the sexes', the sex-based cityscape can offer an excellent point of departure for this volume: the silent background, it might be said, of the fundamental interplay between gender and society in the Italian Renaissance.[2]

Social historians have seen this gender bipolarity as the direct consequence of a strongly patriarchal culture, in which ruling male elites sought to protect patrilineal interests, masculine honour and political power by 'defining urban space in gender terms'. As we shall see elsewhere in this volume, the isolation and enclosure of women played a crucial role in promoting these goals. This chapter, however, will focus less on the goals underlying a sex-based urban geography than on how the geography itself was experienced by Renaissance men and women. We shall see, in fact, that the gendered valence of urban space was not only 'defined' though the edicts of male elites, but was also the result of an ongoing process, a continuing social interplay between the sexes and between social groups that helped maintain, extend or challenge prevailing notions that certain areas of the city should be reserved for men and others for women.[3]

To better chart the dynamics of Italy's gendered geography, it is useful to turn to a source that even today still captures some of the immediacy of the experience – the writings of foreign visitors to the peninsula between the fifteenth and eighteenth centuries. As they flocked to Italy to make and write about what would eventually be known as the Grand Tour, these visitors and amateur authors from France, Germany, and above all Britain tried to bring alive for their readers (the 'many that neither have beene there, nor ever intend to go thither while they live') the exotic and sophisticated societies through which they were travelling.[4] Hampered, however, by their own linguistic timidity and the often ferocious agendas of cultural enrichment that kept many of them endlessly scurrying from one church or monument to another, few of these Grand Tourists ever

    2. Dennis Romano, 'Gender and the urban geography of Renaissance Venice', *Journal of Social History*, 23 (1989), pp. 339–53.
    3. Dennis Romano, *Patricians and Popolani: The Social Foundations of the Venetian Renaissance State* (Baltimore, 1987), esp. pp. 131–40; and Romano, 'Gender and the urban geography', p. 348; Diane Owen Hughes, 'Invisible Madonnas? The Italian historiographical tradition and the women of medieval Italy', in Susan M. Stuard, ed., *Women in Medieval History and Historiography* (Philadelphia, 1987), pp. 25–57; Richard C. Trexler, *Public Life in Renaissance Florence* (New York, 1980), pp. 358–61.
    4. Thomas Coryat, *Crudities* (Glasgow, 1905), vol. 1, p. 256.

had much time to actually meet any Italians, much less penetrate very deeply into these often dauntingly complex societies. Yet even the most tenaciously ethnocentric of them found the time to convey to their readers the actual experience of walking the streets of the cities they visited, and it is this aspect of an otherwise often highly subjective source that can prove so useful in recapturing the visual sense of urban space in Renaissance and early-modern Italian cities.

Thus, travellers to Venice – which was, along with Rome, Italy's most popular destination – have left us with portraits of how the money changers did business at the Rialto, how gondoliers signalled to avoid hitting one another, and the way in which gentlemen managed to keep walking side-by-side, despite the narrow streets. Determined to see as much of the public city as possible, visitors gawked at passing processions, invaded the Greek churches and Jewish synagogues, and gazed with admiring envy at the *broglio*, that special space set aside for the Venetian nobility, where neither they nor the city's commoners were allowed to intrude. When there was seemingly nothing else around to describe, they even wrote about the paving stones that covered the Piazza San Marco.

But few things evidently struck them as more worthy of note than the dearth of Venetian women in the public spaces they were writing about. 'Woemen . . . if they be chast, [are] rather locked up at home, as it were in prison', observed Fynes Moryson, the sixteenth-century Scottish traveller. Philip Skippon would later note much the same thing: 'All the young women (except the ordinary common whores) are close kept within . . . [for] Few women walk the streets besides the old bawds.' Even what few women there were to be seen were hardly to be recognized as such, for they moved from home to church (the only public place they were seemingly allowed to frequent) bundled from head to foot in such heavy wraps and veils that, as Pietro Casola said in 1494, 'I do not know how they can see where to go in the street'.[5]

Why the women of Venice (but also other Italian cities, where 'the wemen . . . [were] locked up at home and covered with vayles when they goe abroad') ventured out so much less in public than did those back home in London, Paris, or Amsterdam was the cause of much speculation. Nearly all the Grand Tourists were men, after all, and they would have dearly liked to meet some of these

5. Fynes Moryson, *An Itinerary* (Glasgow, 1907), vol. 1, p. 70; Philip Skippon, *An Account of a Journey Made thro' the Low-Countries, Germany, Italy and France*, in A. Churchill and J. Churchill, eds, *Voyages* (London, 1746), vol. 6, p. 533; Pietro Casola, *Viaggio di Pietro Casola a Gerusalemme* (Milan, 1855), p. 15.

elusive females. Many, like Skippon, blamed 'jealous husbands and parents', who, it was said, abhorred above all else that 'they should be capricornified' – with 'the fatall hornes they so much detest'. As a result, daughters were bundled off out of the reach of other males: 'sent to nunneries in their infancy, from whence they do not stir till they married, or take the veil'. Some men supposedly tried to lock their wives up as well, in the depths of their homes; those who felt forced, out of respect for religious observances, to let their wives out to go to church, made sure that they were always 'attended by old women, who observe their behavior; the old woman being one of the first things the husband provides after he is marry'd'. There were, it seems, no other reasons for Italian women to go out in any case: 'they never, or very rarely visit each other, and if they happen to meet any where, they do not converse together'. They did not even have to worry about the shopping, because 'onely men, and the Masters of the family, goe into the market and buy the victuals, for servants are never sent to that purpose, much lesse woemen'.[6]

Though they painted a bleak picture of women's public lives in Italy, these Grand Tourists were, in fact, only lamenting the absence from view of that ten or fifteen per cent of the females who made up their own class – the gentry, the nobility, the well-to-do. Back in England, one might mistake a duchess for a common whore,[7] but these travellers seemed quite capable of recognizing 'women of quality' (or the lack of them) once they went abroad. If the public space in Italian cities was gendered, it was done so selectively, on a class basis, for unlike the patriciate, urban workers could simply not afford the luxury of locking up half their numbers at home. Though few visitors bothered to record the fact, market stalls, outdoor workshops, and local piazzas were certainly occupied by women of modest means, going about the various activities necessary for their families' survival. Even these, however, seem to have exercised a certain reticence when out in such public spaces, a fact that was recorded by some of the more discerning foreign observers, who noted that 'The ordinary Women cover themselves with a great Scarf, which opens only a little before their Eyes ['. . . just

6. Fynes Moryson *Shakespeare's Europe: Unpublished Chapters of Fynes Moryson's 'Itinerary'* (London, 1903), pp. 409–11; Moryson, *An Itinerary*, vol. 2, p. 70; Coryat, *Crudities*, vol. 2, p. 403; Skippon, *A Journey*, p. 533; Alexandre Saint Disdier, *The City and Republick of Venice* (Paris, 1680; trans., London, 1699), vol. 3, p. 18; Thomas Nugent, *The Grand Tour* (London, 1756), vol. 1, p. 87.
7. At least, such was reported in Thomas Broderick, *Travels* (London, 1754), vol. 1, p. 330.

as much as is necessary to see their way'] and they go abroad but rarely'.[8]

That working-class women in a cosmopolitan centre like Venice were so reluctant to expose themselves in the streets is not so easily explained by ascribing to them the same causes that kept elite women indoors: with 'those of inferior rank' there were no patrician men hovering in the background, fretting that the presence of wife or daughters in public might prove a threat to the honour of the lineage or its marriage strategies. These women made up that great mass of those without a family name or inheritence to defend, without an obsessive concern for personal or ancestral honour, but also with an acute awareness of how important it was for simple family survival that everyone – men, women and children – be out and about to earn their share of the daily bread. One reason they tended to keep inside, of course, was that the streets and alleys of Renaissance Italy could be dangerous places for women, who, unlike most men, did not apparently go about the city armed (a sword for patricians, a dagger or staff for ordinary men). Where the streets were narrow and unlit, the police often far from efficient, and unknown persons lurking around every corner, a solitary female was always at risk of robbery or sexual assault. Interestingly, the tourists who wrote of women scurrying past without making eye contact never wondered if this might have in good part been due to their own – foreign – presence. Some did, however, remark on the risks to female virtue in a city like Venice: 'the frequent Attempts, that were daily made upon the Persons of these Modest Women; for even the most Sacred Places could not be esteem'd as assur'd Sanctuaries, and in which the Chastity of the Women were out of all danger'. Alexandre Saint-Disdier thought that 'the Young Nobility Living in Idleness . . . [and] being addicted to the pursuit of their Pleasures' was responsible for many such assaults, although he also added wryly that, 'the *Republick* seem'd to believe that the Sea-Air render'd this Disorder habitual and without remedy . . .'.[9]

Making the streets male

Beyond any physical danger that streets and piazzas may have represented for Renaissance women (and, in fact, the judicial records

8. F.M. Misson, *A New Voyage to Italy* (trans., London, 1699), vol. 1, p. 195; Nugent, *The Grand Tour*, vol. 1, p. 87.

9. Saint Disdier, *The City and Republick of Venice*, vol. 3, pp. 48–9; also Pietro Molmenti, *Venice, Its Individual Growth from the Earliest Beginnings to the Fall of the Republic*, Horatio Brown, trans. (Chicago, 1907), vol. 4, p. 178.

do not especially support Saint Disdier's assertion), there was also the intrinsic masculinity that characterized most public space in Italian cities and made it implicitly alien or even hostile to females. The public arena was, after all, repeatedly consecrated as male space by the ruling regimes themselves, as they demonstrated their dominance to their rivals and subjects, through such overwhelmingly male-oriented rituals as guild or confraternal processions, patrician games and contests, and state ceremonials. Yet what might be termed the day-to-day business of keeping public space in Italian cities masculine – that continual reassertion of male prerogatives to ensure that women would never feel completely comfortable on the streets of their own cities – certainly fell less to elites than to ordinary, working-class men and youths. As often as not, these commoners, far from publicly asserting their masculinity in concert with the patriarchal state, did so in defiance of government edicts, sometimes at considerable risk to themselves.

In Venice, where both horses and carriages were unknown and where elites had largely opted for the waterways, travelling about in their private gondolas, the thoroughfares and piazzas on land seem to have been the particular preserve of 'those of inferior rank'. Perhaps as a result, Venetian artisans and workers seem to have developed an especially elaborate repertoire for their competitive forms of virile display.[10] Certainly the most overtly masculine of these (though by its nature not especially threatening) was the so-called *forza d'ercole*, in which groups of men from opposing factions contended to see which side could build the tallest human pyramid. Some of the strongest and most agile groups were able to arrange themselves in an acrobatic spectacle that was eight men (about forty feet) high, usually with a young boy at the top, waving a flag and an open bottle of spumante. Other competitive games had the potential for much more manly disruption and display, however. The most notorious of these in Venice were the *guerre dei pugni*, or wars of the fists, where anywhere from several dozen to two thousand of the city's toughest men would meet to battle in huge mobs for temporary, symbolic possession of one of the city's bridges. When the passion to 'get up on the bridges' (*montar sui ponti*) ran hot among Venetian workers, these encounters would be staged virtually every Sunday and holiday for months at a time, often in direct defiance of the ruling elite and its police. In fact, the Venetian

10. For the following discussion, see Robert C. Davis, *The War of the Fists: Popular Culture and Public Violence in Late Renaissance Venice* (Oxford, 1994).

state often seemed of two minds about these popular eruptions: on the one side, nervous about the potential for damage and disorder represented by so many young men, crazed with excitement, drink and aggression; on the other, content that its ordinary working men might have such opportunities to show off their manly qualities, to each other and (not coincidentally) to any representatives of foreign governments who might be present.

When major *guerre di pugni* were staged in Venice, large swaths of the city were, in effect, turned into fairs of masculinity. Here, male domination of the streets and piazzas was complete: one long binge of challenges, muscular displays, arguments, knife fights, wagering, speech-making, processions of boxers, and military-style drills – all leading up to the actual cataclysm of battle, and then slowly tapering off in a week or more of celebratory (or consolatory) festivals. In all of this, Venetian women had a very limited role. They would apparently follow the fighters to the battle site: '[in a] great swarm of women, cheering them from behind, giving support to their Brigades, some to their husband, some to their brother, and some to their son or relative'. On the other hand, there is not much evidence that they joined in the actual press of spectators along the canal bank: since those in the audience were tightly packed, highly emotional, and often armed, women – except for those *zentildonne* who could afford to rent themselves a spot safely removed on a nearby balcony – seemed willing to consider the watching of the *guerre di pugni* as much the business of men as was the fighting in them.[11]

Moreover, local youths had their own ways of purging the streets and public spaces of women, as part of getting their neighbours in an appropriately aggressive state of mind, in the days before a battle. Typically, those of one parish would stage a raid, or *scorreria*, on the territory of a neighbouring, rival parish. Shouting and singing as they charged up and down the alleys, they would attempt to gain the centre of their rival's territory – usually the parish church or a central bridge – banging on shutters with rocks as they ran, or fixing lighted brands in doorways. Such attacks were meant to provoke enemy youths to some reaction, but they also had the effect of clearing the streets and alleys of anyone not physically able or

11. Venice, Museo Correr, Codici Cicogna (MCCC) 3161, 1633/3, 1639/19. That women were not so much among the spectators can be deduced by the events of 5 September 1611, when a panic rush among onlookers caused twenty-eight of their number to be drowned or trampled. Of these, none were women: ASV, Sanità-Necrologie, buste 842 and 843.

well enough armed to resist them. This especially applied to women, about whom the young men would brag, 'just at our appearance, they would lock the doors and the balconies, not knowing in what hole to hide themselves'. Sometimes, to make their riotous message of dominance even clearer, these youths would include in their raid a bull (or, more precisely, an ox), driving it before them by means of enormous dogs that snapped at its ears and heels, and with exploding fireworks tied to its horns. Thus panicked, the hapless and bellowing beast and its masculine retinue plunged through the crowded, residential streets, purging them of every trace of tranquil domesticity.[12]

The bull/ox figured in another Venetian ritual in which men demonstrated their dominance over the city's public spaces. This was the so-called *caccia dei tori*, or baiting of the bulls, in which butchers' boys, dockers and gondoliers, with the support of some local worthy, would 'rent' a dozen or more oxen from the city slaughterhouse, for a celebration in their local piazza.[13] Here, the animals would be baited – attacked by large, specially trained dogs that tried to bite off their ears, while one or two youths struggled to keep them under control by means of ropes tied to their horns. The successful *tiratori*, as they were known, showed off their strength and finesse by the way they controlled their animal, keeping it from bolting and, with a few well-timed tugs, eventually bringing it to its knees, under a pile of dogs. Once the unfortunate ox was sufficiently bled and battered to be manageable (and assuming he could still walk), his tormentors would take him from the piazza and parade him about the local streets. Having made their mark, with trails of blood, all around the parish, they would complete the spectacle by 'presenting' their animal, in a series of skits and bravados, before the balcony of their wives or sweethearts, who applauded this display of masculine dominance from the windows that connected the two gendered realms.

Different versions of the *caccia dei tori* were also held in other Italian Renaissance cities, and though the details of the events might vary – many used real bulls, and occasionally patricians or peasants

12. MCCC 3161, 1632/7, 1633/5, 1634/6; on shaming races more generally, see Richard Trexler, 'Correre la terra: collective insults in the Late Middle Ages', in *Mélanges de l'École Française de Rome, Moyen Age-Temps Modernes*, 96 (1984), pp. 845–902.

13. See Robert C. Davis, 'The trouble with bulls: how to stage a *caccia dei tori* in early-modern Venice', in *Histoire sociale/Social History*, (forthcoming, late 1997); cf. Asa Boholm, 'The *Caccia di tori*. Regeneration in the Venetian carnival', in *Journal of Mediterranean Studies*, 3 (1993), pp. 46–61.

might also join in the fray – their structure and import was inevitably similar. Men brought this large and (if still sexually intact) potentially dangerous symbol of the countryside into the heart of their city, so that they might test and display their own manhood by dominating, humiliating and eventually slaughtering it. They used their city's own piazzas and thoroughfares as staging grounds for these male rituals: in Siena, the Piazza del Campo was favoured; in Rome, the via del Corso. Probably this rather amateurish approach to the complex business of bull-fighting may have prevented Italian men from ever reaching the same elaborate combination of ritual and sport that was evolving at just about this time in the specially built *Plazas de toros* in Spain. It did, however, provide another, recurring means for them to assert the force and importance of masculinity in the public space of their cities.[14]

This working out and display of public masculinity was not limited to such relatively large-scale spectacles as the *cacce*, however. Mature youths and even rather young boys, when first leaving the female and domestic space of the household and entering into the male domains of the city at large, sought to magnify and broadcast their own virile claims. One way they did so was simply 'to show without respect [their] shameful parts . . . say bad words and commit wicked acts . . . bringing scandal to the women . . . who . . . pass on the streets nearby them or who go to do the laundry or other necessary things'. They also competed with other boys for dominance in the public arena, although less as individuals than as gangs, based either on a shared neighbourhood or work place. While scholars since Jakob Burckhardt have evaluated the political implications of the violence and vendetta generated by packs of elite youths, working-class youth gangs in Italian Renaissance society are far less well understood. It is at least certain, however, that they both abounded and left their own particular mark of belligerent masculinity on the public spaces of the cities where they lived.[15] This can best be seen in rock throwing, a form of interaction and contention which can be equally identified with both plebeian youths and city space during the Italian Renaissance.

The staged fight with rocks and stones, or *sassaiola*, seems to have been especially popular in central Italy, though it had its

14. Mario Verdone, 'Cacce e giostre taurine nelle città italiane', in *Lares*, 29 (1963), pp. 176–88; Garry Marvin, *Bullfight* (Oxford, 1988).

15. BAV, Arm. V, tome 225, f. 88, 7 June 1599; Jakob Burckhardt, *The Civilization of the Renaissance in Italy* (New York, 1954), pp. 25–7, 323–6; cf. Elizabeth S. Cohen, 'Honor and gender in the streets of early modern Rome', in *Journal of Interdisciplinary History*, 22 (1992), pp. 597–625.

enthusiasts from Venice down at least as far south as Rome.[16] In their more formal moments, rock battles somewhat resembled the *guerre dei pugni*, at least in that two opposing teams of youths might battle over a piece of contested terrain. Combatants fought at a distance and usually defended themselves by wrapping a coat or cloak around the arm they were not using for throwing, unless they were using both hands for operating some form of slingshot or catapult (*fionda* or *frombola*). But most rock fights actually had very little structure, and could take place anywhere and at any time, between two youths or between hundreds, swirling into existence in seconds and often disappearing just as fast (especially with the appearance of the police). Such noisy encounters between boys made it a trial for anyone who was intent on just using the streets for his or her business: stray rocks flying everywhere meant bystanders could easily be injured, and perhaps permanently scarred by a chance hit.[17]

Just how tenacious and disruptive the *sassaiole* could be is amply demonstrated by the centuries-long campaign waged against them in the Umbrian city of Perugia. Starting in the 1480s and continuing though the seventeenth century, a long line of local elites and cardinal legates sent from Rome issued edicts against those who would 'play at stones' (*jocar a saxi*). That boys were involved here was in no doubt, for even the very first proclamation, of 24 November 1487, was directed against 'any lad [*mamolo*] of eight years and up who from bad upbringing would dare or presume to throw rocks'. Subsequent legates would lower the supposed 'age of discretion and capacity for malice' down as low as seven. They created four different gradations of punishments, intensified according to the age of the miscreant (with the younger boys tied to the city's celebrated *Fontana Maggiore* for a caning). Relatives of participants, the doctors who treated the wounded, and even boys on the opposing side were charged with turning in those who threw the stones. Yet, it was all to little effect. Year after year (often several times a year) the edicts were reissued, sometimes beginning with such pathetic preambles as that on 8 December 1578: 'Although [we] have other times prohibited rock fighting [*il fare a sassi*], both within

16. William Heywood, *Palio and Ponte: An Account of the Sports of Central Italy from the Age of Dante to the Twentieth Century*, 2nd edn (New York, 1969), pp. 138–96.
17. A facial 'scar . . . from a rock fight' might well be bad enough to provide an identifying mark later on: ASVa, Arciconfraternita del Gonfalone, busta 8, filza 14; such disfigurement was especially repellant to gentlemen and to women of all classes, and a good reason to stay out of the streets.

and outside the city, nevertheless, [we] have understood that many, without the slightest respect, have not stopped throwing rocks in many areas. . . .'[18]

And so, the streets of Perugia still remained in the hands of its young males, whose battles erupted in virtually every corner of the city. The edicts lamented that even right under the walls of the papal fortress (the *Rocca Paolina*) youth gangs throwing rocks at each other had grown so bold that they 'impeded people who usually pass that place . . . from going about their business'. Perched as it was on a hilltop, with steep cliffs on several sides, Perugia also had a topography that proved particularly inviting to youths looking for other targets than just one another, and many complaints were lodged about those who persisted in raining stones on buildings down below. Boys particularly took aim at the roofs of monasteries and convents, bringing the chaos of the streets right into some of Perugia's most protected interior space, 'impeding the orations of the Reverend Fathers' and 'with great disturbance to those Venerable Sisters'.[19]

In the much larger and more cosmopolitan city of Rome, the *sassaiole* developed into the direction of a sporting event, even taking on political overtones, without, however, losing any of its disruptive character. Gangs of hundreds of boys (sometimes joined by 'bearded men') from opposite sides of the river fought on behalf of *Trastevere* or *I Monti*, staging their encounters in every corner of the city, from Piazza Navonna to the Esqualine, and down to the Aventine and Testaccio (a trash mountain from classical times, composed of millions of handy chunks of pottery). Jews and Christians would also meet in large- or small-scale battles, as would supporters of the 'French' and 'Spanish' interests that struggled for influence over the papacy in the sixteenth and seventeenth centuries. As in Perugia, boys also liked to toss stones at buildings and public monuments: in Rome, the statue of Marcus Aurelius on the Campidoglio was an especially popular target, evidently because of the loud clang when a rock hit the emperor's bronze horse. The effect of all these encounters on the tenor of public life, even in a major centre like Rome, was unmistakable. Police reports from the late sixteenth and early seventeenth centuries indicate that, even in

18. ASPu, Editti e bandi, busta 2, 24 November 1487; busta 3, 1 November 1538; busta 6, 8 November 1563; busta 8A, 8 December 1578; busta 12, 14 November 1611.
19. ASPu Editti e bandi, busta 8A, 27 November 1578; busta 9A, 18 November 1603; busta 9, 13 April 1604.

broad daylight, 'one could not pass, for the stones' being thrown in the streets around Campo de' Fiori, Piazza Navonna or San Giacomo degli Incurabili.[20]

Perhaps more significantly, when youths were not throwing rocks at each other, they often targeted those they considered vulnerable outsiders, in the age-old tradition of the *charivari* and *mattinata* throughout Europe: peasants visiting town, Jews, foreigners of every stripe, and women – especially prostitutes without a protector (*ruffiano*) – who might linger too long in the street.[21] In times of famine (increasingly common in the later sixteenth century), elites themselves might come under attack, and many a bread riot cul-minated with a full-scale rock war, directed against the soldiers of the state or sometimes the rulers themselves. Even in periods of relative calm, too ostentatious a display by wealthier members of society – distinguished clerics, noblemen and women, and high-class courtesans – could provoke a *sassata* by gangs of poor boys. Particularly attractive targets were private carriages, much in fash-ion in the larger cities like Rome by the sixteenth century: seeking to elevate themselves above the pedestrian mob, elites instead often found themselves in traffic jams, stuck in the narrow streets and subjected to humiliating showers of rocks launched by anonymous urchins on every side.[22]

The use of city streets and piazzas by working-class youth as an arena both for competitive encounters and for their coming-of-age activities thus insured, as much as did the more formal efforts of male elites, that public space in Renaissance Italian cities would be continuously 'masculated': that is, repeatedly reconsecrated as gender-appropriate territory for men. Washerwomen, who typically had to do their work at the wells located right in the middle of this public space, could find themselves regularly caught in the crossfire of such masculine contention, at the risk of serious injury

20. ASV, Arm. V, tome 233, p. 20; ASR, Governatore, Relazioni di Birri, busta 97, 31 December 1594; busta 100, 23 May 1600; busta 104, 30 March 1611, 8 January 1612, 10 February 1612; Editti e bandi, vol. 21, tome 1, p. 61: 5 September 1656.

21. Thus, one 'picked up a rock to throw at [a] dog': ASR, Governatore, Costituti, busta 779, 21 March 1623; Relazioni dei Birri, busta 104, 20 January 1611, 8 April 1611, 23 September 1611. The legate of Perugia issued edicts to protect 'the poor peasants' from being assaulted by city children – with snowballs, however: ASPu Editti e bandi, busta 11, 8 March 1604.

22. As Sharon Strocchia explores in Chapter 2 in this volume, the houses of prostitutes were especially common targets for those (usually somewhat older youths) wishing anonymously to attack and publicly shame these marginal members of Roman society; also Giovanni Battista Crispolti, *Cronaca di Perugia, 1578–1586*, in A. Fabretti, *Cronache dell citta' di Perugia*, 4 vols (Turin, 1887–1892), Vol. 4, p. 283.

or even death.[23] To allow these *lavandiere* to carry out their work in peace, cities like Perugia built special, enclosed wash-houses, from which were banned teasing, provocative youths and men who would stop by to water their horses. In Rome the authorities furnished some of the city's many fountains with special wash facilities, but still complained about the 'Insolent youths [who] come to the wash area to molest the women with words, signs and dishonest acts . . . without any regard for public honour or the privacy of the women who gather there, including many spinsters and married women'.[24]

The feminine response

Yet no amount of male display and aggression could guarantee that all public space in Renaissance Italian cities would remain forever masculine, unchallenged by the slightest feminine response. Two areas in particular seem to have remained as contested and ambiguous gender territory, although for very different reasons. The first and certainly the more striking were the special districts where courtesans lived and street prostitutes plied their trade. These 'whore towns' were the creation of local governments, often following, as we will see elsewhere in this volume, their own agendas of social control. All major cities had one and sometimes several such centres for the flesh trade: fifteenth-century Florence established its public bordello right in the heart of town, between the Old Market and the Cathedral Baptistry; in Renaissance Rome, the prostitution quarter was along the Via Giulia and near the mausoleum of Augustus, in an area called the 'Ortaccio'. In Venice there were four or five such districts, both centrally located near the Rialto exchange and also out on the edge of the city, along the waterfront and the Arsenal.[25]

23. As happened in 1626 to Giovanna di Stefano Gasparini, hit on the temple and killed by a stray rock thrown by some mule drivers who were 'playing at stones' near where she was washing her laundry at Porto Portese, in Rome: ASR, Tribunale del Governatore di Roma, Processi, busta 210, f. 840.

24. ASP, Editti e bandi, busta 9, 31 August 1589; busta 11, 19 January 1603; busta 12, 15 December 1614; quote of Sebastiano Varo, in Pecchiai, *Acquedotti e Fontane di Roma nel Cinquecento* (Rome, 1944), pp. 41–2: my particular thanks to Katherine W. Rinne for bringing this to my attention.

25. Richard C. Trexler, 'Florentine prostitution in the fifteenth century: patrons and clients', in *The Women of Renaissance Florence*, vol. 2, *Power and Dependence in Renaissance Florence* (Binghamton, NY, 1993), pp. 41–6; Elizabeth Cohen, 'Seen and known: prostitutes in the cityscape of late sixteenth century Rome', forthcoming in *Renaissance Studies* (1998); Romano, 'Gender and urban geography', p. 345; Robert C. Davis, *Shipbuilders of the Venetian Arsenal: Workers and Workplace in the Preindustrial City* (Baltimore, 1991), pp. 106–7, 115–16.

Of all Italian cities of the time, Venice's 'whore towns' certainly seemed to have made the greatest impression on foreign visitors. No doubt this had much to do with the sheer number of women who sold themselves there for a living – some ten to twelve thousand according to tourist lore – and the contrast with the city's otherwise almost oriental customs of female seclusion.[26] At the same time, in Venice the sex trade was run far more by 'olde bauds' than by male protectors, making these districts all the more strikingly female territory, alien and rather threatening to those men who, 'feel[ing] Nature begin to work', were attracted within their confines. Even if many Grand Tourists (overwhelmingly male, after all) clearly came to Venice to sample its sex trade, not a few still seem to have been unnerved at actually entering a world so dominated by women. They remarked on its contrast with the enforced sobriety and masculinity prevailing in Venice's other public spaces: 'as the habits of other people are black and dismal, these [courtesans] dress in the gayest colours, with their breasts open, and their faces bedaubed with paint, standing ... at the doors and windows to invite their Customers'. It was like stepping into a casbah, at once alluring and alarming, where 'the Streets and Canals are abundantly supplied with these sorts of Ladies; who commonly stand at their Windows and Balconies set out with a mighty profusion of Ribbons ...', and where men found themselves curiously under threat from those '... drest in red and yellow, like Tulips; with their Breasts open, and their Faces painted a Foot deep, always a Nosegay above their Ears: you may see them standing by Dozens at the Doors or Windows; and the Passersby seldom 'scape without torn Sleeves'.[27]

Moreover, following the logic of the marketplace, the 'whore towns' of Renaissance Italian cities constantly threatened to expand and intrude into space which should have otherwise been masculine, as prostitutes continually probed the borders of their ghetto in search of new custom. From the original enclave that the government had set aside for them, Florence's prostitutes had within a few generations initiated new centres of trade, both north towards the Palazzo Medici and east behind the modern Uffizi Gallery. Roman whores were also soon colonizing new territories that ran along the

---

26. '... it is thought there are of them in the whole City and other adjacent places, as Murano, Malamocco, etc., at least twenty thousand', Coryat, *Crudities*, p. 402.

27. Nugent, *The Grand Tour*, vol. 1, p. 88; Skippon, *A Journey*, p. 533; Saint Disdier, *The City and Republick of Venice*, vol. 3, p. 48; Misson, *A New Voyage to Italy*, p. 197.

present-day Tridente, and if the crack-downs sponsored in these cities by preaching friars or reforming popes occasionally rolled back their gains, their testing of male territorial claims never wholly ceased. In Venice, by the eighteenth century, street-walkers were invading Piazza San Marco, traditionally perhaps the most masculine space in the city, long consecrated to male business, display and ritual. Threats to shave off the hair of these invasive *fille de joie* or brand them between the eyebrows seems to have had little effect. Indeed, during the Ascension Week fair Venetian prostitutes can be found holding a virtual whores' market right in the Piazza, with mothers offering their daughters to the highest bidders, in what appears as a grotesque parody of the notorious auctions of Christian slaves that took place during these same years in Algiers and Tunis.[28]

The other zone of contention between the sexes can be found in parish and convent churches, whose public space was by both doctrine and tradition made equally accessible to men and women.[29] In Venice, the females who challenged men over territory in this context were, perhaps surprisingly, patrician women, those same *zentledonne* who, once married, were supposedly 'shut up so close, that you can scarcely see their Face; not even in the Churches, which are the only places where they usually appear in Publick. When they go abroad, they are shut up in their *Gondolas*'. Yet if Venetian ladies were rarely seen in the city's public spaces, when they did make their appearance it was in style, outfitted with enormously high platform shoes known as *zoccoli* (or to the English, *chappines* or *croponi*). Thomas Coryat described these at some length:

> [It is] a thing made of wood, and covered with leather of sundry colors, some with white, some redde, some yellow. It is called a Chapiney, which they weare under their shoes. Many of them are curiously painted; some also I have seen fairly gilt ... many of these Chapineys [are] of a great height, even half a yard high.[30]

It was a sight that never failed to provoke a response from those who visted Venice, and their reactions ranged from sympathy to loud contempt. In the 1490s, Pietro Casola compared the custom to Chinese foot-binding, and Arnold von Harff wrote that 'women

28. Lady Ann Miller, *Letters from Italy* (Dublin, 1776), vol. 3, p. 211; Jean du Mont, *A New Voyage to the Levant* (English trans., London, 1696), pp. 401–3.

29. John J. Martin, 'Out of the shadow: heretical and Catholic women in Renaissance Venice', in *Journal of Family History* 10 (1985), pp. 21–32.

30. Coryat, *Crudities*, p. 400; Misson, *A New Voyage to Italy*, vol. 1, p. 195.

walk on great high soles covered with cloth, three of my fists high,
which cause them to walk with such difficulty that one pities them'.
On the other hand, John Evelyn sneered about the sight of 'Ladys
on *Choppines* about 10 foote high from the ground ... stalking
together', while Thomas Coryat termed them 'frivolous and ...
ridiculous instruments ... [at which] both I my selfe and many
other strangers (as I have observed in Venice) have often laughed'.[31]

Zoccoli in some form or other had a long history among Italian
women: legislators in Genoa and Siena were complaining about
them as early as the fourteenth century. Clogs of varying height
had been commonplace implements throughout medieval and early
Renaissance Italy, presumably as a way for women to avoid soiling
their dresses in the muddy and garbage-strewn city streets. Only by
the sixteenth century did the practice apparently die out (or at
least modify) in most Italian cities – perhaps because upper-class
women were increasingly moving about their cities in carriages or
sedan chairs, and perhaps also because they caused a woman wearing them to mince as she walked, which made them seem more
appropriate gear for prostitutes. In Venice and (to a lesser extent)
its dominion cities, by contrast, *zoccoli* not only persisted but
actually grew, until by the seventeenth century they had reached
heights (one might say) that were positively baroque. Whereas the
clogs that von Harff had estimated in 1496 as 'three of my fists
high' (perhaps nine inches) might have just been on the edge of
functional, by the mid-1600s *zoccoli* had grown to wildly impractical
dimensions – 'at least Two Foot high', according to Saint Disdier.[32]

Mounted on such 'extravagant Engines', Venetian patrician
women were apparently almost helpless on their own. ''Tis very
ridiculous to see how these Ladys crawle in & out of their *Gondolas*
by reason of their Choppines', and once on dry land they walked
'with such a hobbling gate' that they were 'not ... able to set one
Foot before the other without ...' 'set[ting] their hands on the
heads of two Matron-like servants or old women to support them,
who are mumbling their beades'. Without her servants at her side,
a noblewoman so equipped ran considerable risks of tumbling right
over, on Venice's stone-paved lanes and humped-back, stone bridges.
As Coryat noted, 'I saw a woman fall a very dangerous fall, as

31. Arnold von Harff, *Pilgrimage*, Malcolm Letts, ed. (London, Hakluyt Society,
1946), series II, v. 94, p. 65; John Evelyn, *Diary*, E.S. de Beer, ed. (London, 1959),
p. 227; Coryat, *Crudities*, vol. 2, p. 400.

32. Moryson, *An Itinerary*, vol. 2, p. 168; Coryat, *Crudities*, vol. 2, p. 400; Saint
Disdier, *The City and Republick of Venice*, vol. 3, p. 23.

she was going down the staires of one of the little stone bridges with her high Chapineys alone by her self: but I did nothing pitty her . . . .'.[33]

As to why Venetian patrician women sported these 'prodigious high Shooes', it is difficult to agree with William Hazlitt, who argued that *zoccoli* were simply extreme versions of medieval clogs, to help a Venetian lady keep her dress tidy while 'traversing the kennels and alleys' of the city. In fact, Venice's public spaces were exceptionally clean for the times (something Hazlitt himself had to admit), and far from requiring such outlandish adaptive measures, the city had 'dainty smooth neat streets, whereon you may walk most days in a silk stocking and satin slippers, without soiling them, nor can the streets of Paris be so foul, as these are so fair'. That anyone could wade through mud or water on platforms as 'high as a mans legg', must have seemed absurd to visitors in any case, and many concluded that instead *zoccoli* represented yet another example of the Venetian nobleman's extreme jealousy and insecurity with regards to his wife: '. . . a pretty ingenious way', as Richard Lassels put it, 'either to clog Women at Home by such heavy shoes . . . or at least to make them not able to go either far or alone, or invisibly'.[34]

In the context of the gendering of public space, however, it may be nearer the mark to give much of the credit for the persistence (and exaggeration) of the fashion of *zoccoli* in Venice to the noblewomen themselves, as Diane Hughes has done in her study of sumptuary legislation in Renaissance Italian cities more generally. If the clogs hobbled a woman, they also (as those who wrote the sumptuary laws were well aware) allowed her to wear a much longer dress, and thereby put on a more extensive and extravagant public display of satins, silks, brocades and trimmings than if she were of normal stature. With her halting progress from home to church and back again, she presented her neighbours with a maximized, walking exhibit not only of the wealth realized in her own dowry and her husband's subsequent largess, but also in the Venetian patriciate as a special, privileged caste. More implements of class than of fashion, it is not surprising, as the Grand Tourists observed, that

33. Evelyn, *Diary*, p. 228; Nugent, *The Grand Tour*, vol. 2, p. 87; Saint Disdier, *The City and Republick of Venice*, vol. 3, p. 23; Coryat, *Crudities*, p. 400.
34. William C. Hazlitt, *The Venetian Republic: Its Rise, its Growth, and its Fall, A.D. 409–1797* (London, 1915), p. 935; Edmund Warcupp, *Italy, in its Original Glory, Ruine, and Revival* (London, 1660), p. 273; James Howell, *Familiar Letters* (London, 1903), pp. 75–6; Richard Lassels, *An Italian Voyage* (London, 1698), vol. 2, p. 235.

the wearing of these torturous devices were the special prerogative of the Venetian *zentildonne*, 'to distinguish themselves from the Courtezans', 'the many Common *Misses* or Whores' who had otherwise so completely usurped the city's public space from its ladies of quality.[35]

And yet these aristocratic women were not simply mannequins, completely oblivious to the exhilarating and unnerving experience of venturing out into the city while 'taller by the Head than any Man'. However absurd, *zoccoli* were nevertheless marvellous instruments of self-promotion for women brought up with few social graces and restricted to little more human contact than that of their serving maids, yet still possessed of an inherent pride that demanded a public stage on which to show off and compete for honour. 'I have heard that this is observed amongst them', said Coryat, 'that by how nobler a woman is, by so much higher are her Chapineys', and there is little doubt that 'these proude dames' looked down on the world around them – figuratively, as well as literally. In this sense, the 'neare 30' that Evelyn saw 'together stalking, halfe as high or more, as the rest of their world', were no doubt carrying out the same rituals of competitive self-display as were the Roman women who took their carriages to the Corso every evening.

When, in the course of these studied forays, these women actually arrived at church ('which is one of the greatest Diversions they enjoy, and they stay there as long as they can, before they return') it must have been a full-blown spectacle, designed not only to command public attention, but also to reassert the preeminence of female space within the church itself. Teetering along on their *zoccoli*, arrayed in a 'Gown [that] is very long and large, training upon the Ground', and moving so slowly as to seriously block pedestrian traffic inside and outside church, they brought with them 'as many Waiting Women as they have (part of whom being hired only for Days of Ceremony), who do not usually stir one step from their Mistresses, for they usually stand in the greatest Crowds both before and behind their Ladies . . .'. Saint Disdier complained that 'Nothing can be more inconvenient than these Troops of Waiting Women, in such great Crowds', and went on to marvel how, at the helm of her female entourage, the *zentildonna* would proceed to

35. Diane Owen Hughes, 'Sumptuary Law and Social Relations in Renaissance Italy', in John Bossy, ed., *Disputes and Settlements: Law and Human Relations in the West* (Cambridge, UK, 1983), pp. 88–96; Evelyn, *Diary*, p. 228; Warcupp, *Italy, in its Original Glory*, p. 273.

'choose her own place [to sit], which she does with the greatest Air of Haughtiness, dispossessing both Citizen and Gentleman, without shewing any Demonstration of Civility for the Place she takes from either'.[36]

Urban space may well have been more obsessively gendered in Renaissance Venice than in most other Italian cities, and perhaps just for this reason these eruptions of patrician ladies into the public realm of parish and conventual churches took on such an extravagant form. Their message, in any case, seems to have been clear: at least in these very limited areas to which they retained some customary access, these women were not about to cede to the notion that all their city's public spaces should be consecrated as masculine. Indeed, with their gendered 'gangs' of serving maids, the Venetian *zentildonne* were feminizing the public space of churches very much in the same manner that working-class youths 'masculated' the public streets with their *scorrerie*. Each combined extravagant display with sheer numbers to block out, intimidate, frighten away, or dispossess those of the opposite sex – in the process reconfirming the gendering of a particular space to the advantage of their own sex.

Conclusion

The few examples of social interaction that it has been possible to examine here can offer only limited insight into the dynamic and often highly complex ways in which urban space was gendered on a daily basis during the Italian Renaissance. For most citizens, most of the time, the experience of gendered geography was an ongoing process, a day-to-day pushing-and-pulling, provocation-and-retaliation that for many was an invitation to a very Renaissance sort of creativity. Still to be explored, however, are the creative tensions that we might very reasonably expect to find flourishing within the other, much more hidden half of the Italian city's gendered geography – the realm of the household. The tenacity and aggressiveness with which women – whether prostitute or patrician – sought to feminize those few public spaces that social and religious custom had left to them, would seem to call into question any notions of the passivity of women at home, that supposedly most feminine of

36. Lassels, *An Italian Voyage*, vol. 2, p. 234; Coryat, *Crudities*, vol. 2, p. 400; Saint Disdier, *The City and Republick of Venice*, vol. 3, pp. 19–22.

territories.[37] Nor do we really understand all that lay behind the eventual emergence of women into the public arena in Italian cities, except that it certainly occurred, and rather suddenly. By the later 1700s tourists were enthusing that 'Instead of the confinement in which women were formerly kept at Venice, they now enjoy a degree of freedom unknown even at Paris'. No doubt decreasing urban violence, improved lighting and policing, changing legal norms, and a wider awareness of social customs elsewhere in Europe all combined to produce this seismic cultural shift. Yet it also seems fair to conclude that the continuous, often ritualized contention that we have examined here also played its part, keeping open to interpretation and negotiation a gendered world-view that tradition might have sanctified as invariable and eternal as the sexes themselves, but which in fact turned out to be as fleeting as fashion.

37. And yet, the household can hardly be termed the womanly version of the piazza: while the streets were public and implicitly open to all but closed to women by the custom of Mediterranean culture, the household was private (often male-owned) property, where access and interaction with outsiders were controlled, not only by such custom, but also by the wider imperatives associated with property ownership. See, however, Elizabeth Cohen and Thomas V. Cohen, 'Camilla the go-between: the politics of gender in a Roman household (1559)', in *Continuity and Change*, 4 (1989), pp. 53–77.

CHAPTER TWO

Gender and the Rites of Honour in Italian Renaissance Cities

SHARON T. STROCCHIA

The study of honour in Italian Renaissance cities presents an intriguing paradox. On the one hand, honour seemed 'more dear than life itself' to many Italians,[1] and provided one of the essential values that shaped the daily lives of urban elites and ordinary cityfolk. For wealthy merchants and aspiring artisans, honour established a code of accepted conduct against which an individual's actions were measured by his or her peers, subordinates and social superiors. Possessing honour helped to locate a person in the social hierarchy and endowed one with a sense of personal worth. Recent work has demonstrated that the culture of honour, which originated with the medieval aristocracy, directed the everyday activities of Italian urban-dwellers of virtually all social groups from at least the fourteenth century on.[2] The complex code of honour offers scholars a key to understanding many different social practices in the intense urban theatres of Renaissance Italy.

At the same time, honour – whether of one's self, family or neighbourhood – hinged on a publicly bestowed evaluation over which individuals had only limited control. 'Honor was at once individual and collective ... [representing] the summation of

1. The phrase is taken from Guido Ruggiero, '"Più che la vita caro": onore, matrimonio, e reputazione femminile nel tardo rinascimento', *Quaderni storici*, 16 (1987), pp. 753–75.
2. See especially Robert C. Davis, *The War of the Fists: Popular Culture and Public Violence in Late Renaissance Venice* (New York, 1994); Elizabeth S. Cohen, 'Honor and gender in the streets of early modern Rome', *Journal of Interdisciplinary History*, 22 (1992), pp. 597–625; Lucia Ferrante, 'Honor regained: women in the Casa del Soccorso di San Paolo in sixteenth-century Bologna', in Edward Muir and Guido Ruggiero, eds, *Sex and Gender in Historical Perspective* (Baltimore, 1990), pp. 46–72; and James R. Farr, *Hands of Honor: Artisans and their World in Dijon, 1550–1650* (Ithaca, NY and London, 1988), esp. pp. 150–95.

social worth, as seen by others.'[3] To regain lost honour required not only the exertion of personal agency but also the intervention and re-evaluation of others in the community. Within the fray of every-day life one's personal or family honour was subject to repeated attacks and might be won, lost or exchanged with remarkable speed. Hence honour, despite its immense and pervasive value, was para-doxically neither a static nor an absolute possession. Rather, for Renaissance Italians it functioned as an important yet intangible resource that figured in social transactions between people who might have competing property claims, divergent political or mar-ital aspirations, patronage ties, class differences, or simply grudges against each other.

Although honour acted as a primary driving force in Italian urban culture, its precise expressions and meanings varied accord-ing to social group, local political structure and era. While duty and revenge stood at the heart of an enduring code of honour, the actual behaviours that expressed these values depended on par-ticular historical circumstances for their strategies and success. For example, the avenues to both honour and material rewards for the elites of ducal Milan derived primarily from the preferment of the prince, especially as the Milanese court expanded in size and splendour under Galeazzo Maria Sforza (1466–76).[4] By contrast, in republics like Florence, honour derived from multiple criteria such as wealth, office-holding, ancestry, personal networks and correct social behaviour. Yet even in republican Florence, broad political changes reshaped the path to honour as the guild republic gave way to Medici domination by the early sixteenth century.

One of the main factors differentiating the precise currency of honour at work in Renaissance Italy, whether in a principality or republic, was gender. That is, the social and symbolic practices of honour defined, defended and restored honour in different ways for women and men. The multiple ways that men and women laid claim to honour, whether through word or deed, converged to form a rich, interwoven set of cultural values and shared interests. Yet at the same time, considerations of honour also point to par-ticular disjunctures between the ways that women and men lived their lives as gendered beings. The code and ethics of honour caught men and women in different kinds of situations and cultural

3. Thomas V. Cohen, 'The lay liturgy of affront in sixteenth-century Italy', *Journal of Social History*, 25 (1992), pp. 857–77, at p. 862.

4. Gregory Lubkin, *A Renaissance Court: Milan under Galeazzo Maria Sforza* (Berkeley and Los Angeles, 1994), esp. pp. 153–84.

binds, particularly as social institutions and conceptions of civility changed over time.[5] At present, historians lack a systematic under-standing of these distinctions, although we have a growing number of studies that document the intersections of honour and gender in specific early modern settings. Still at issue is the extent to which a woman's public reputation and standing in a community hinged on her adherence to sexual norms, especially to concepts of chastity and sexual fidelity.[6]

Here we will approach the gendered construction of honour through the evidence of ritual activities, which offer a useful point of entry into this problem for several reasons. First, Italian street life bustled with an assortment of ritual enactments that afforded numerous opportunities for assertions of honour, animating the rhythms of daily affairs in the process. These rites ranged from well-orchestrated familial occasions such as weddings and funerals, to more loosely organized or improvised events such as corporate competitions, to personal insults that sometimes erupted into out-right violence. Public ritual performances had a double edge: they communicated broad conceptions of power and hierarchy among urban-dwellers, while at the same time offering participants a means to stake out their own specific claims to honour within the bounds of social conventions.

It is also useful to study gender and honour through the lens of ritual activities because these occasions pulled into their orbit such a broad array of participants, including those who followed norm-ative behaviours as well as those who deviated from them. Mature, established men and women of urban elites played their parts in various rites, just as did robust youth gangs who occasionally got in trouble with their elders, if not the law, for their disorderly actions. Artisans, tradesmen, and still more socially marginal people such as prostitutes and domestic servants, who traditionally have been placed outside the sphere of honour concerns, frequently engaged in ritualized verbal exchanges with neighbours who affronted them, thereby adopting some of the conventional postures that allowed them to claim a share of honour. The wide array of ritual behaviours in word and deed reveals both the creativity of those who

5. Edward Muir, 'The double binds of manly revenge in Renaissance Italy', in Richard C. Trexler, ed., *Gender Rhetorics: Postures of Dominance and Submission in History* (Binghamton, NY, 1994), pp. 65–82; Sandra Cavallo and Simona Cerutti, 'Female honor and the social control of reproduction in Piedmont between 1600 and 1800', in Muir and Ruggiero, eds, *Sex and Gender*, pp. 73–109.

6. See Lyndal Roper, 'Will and honour: sex, words and power in Augsburg crim-inal trials', *Radical History Review*, 43 (1989), pp. 45–71.

had different lines of access to honour resources, as well as the conditionality of the code of honour itself.

Finally, rituals marked important sites for the creation of gender identity. Ritual activities provided the stage settings for women and men to carry out socially appropriate behaviours marking key points along the moving edge of their life course. In the process, rituals posited a set of gender expectations that were complicated by the realities of everyday life, for ritual practices embodying definitions of masculinity and femininity were alive to other variables such as age, class, personal circumstances or changing political relationships. Studying Italian urban rites helps us to move away from an older, binary view of gender, or even a more recent one of the repressive gendering of early modern culture, to see how actual men and women constructed both each other's honour and gender identity by means of a complicated 'network of oppositions and dependencies'.[7] In this way we can view prescriptive gender constructs alongside the practical relationships and tasks that bound men and women together. In particular, we can see a certain malleability in contemporary notions of female honour, especially in regard to sexuality.

Drawing on the rich secondary literature for Florence, Venice, Rome, Bologna and other north-central Italian locales, this chapter will map out some of the changing markers and meanings of gender for inhabitants of Italian Renaissance cities. It is divided into three parts based on types of ritual activity, each of which inflected the relationship between gender and honour in different ways and involved different sets of participants. The first part treats the way honour was gendered in rites of passage rooted in kinship, specifically nuptial rites – events that helped anchor a family's reputation in the community, while also stabilizing gender assignments for society at large. The second section focuses on rites celebrating forms of corporate association outside the family, which gives us a wider source base to explore the gendering of honour in groups below the level of the urban elite. Here we will consider such festivities as the Venetian *battagliole* – the mock battles staged between masses of working men intent on vaunting both honour and masculinity – as well as the more formal rituals of religious confraternities.

---

7. The quote is from Thelma Fenster, 'Why men?', in Clare A. Lees, ed., *Medieval Masculinities: Regarding Men in the Middle Ages* (Minneapolis, MN, 1994), pp. ix–xiii, at p. xii. See also the excellent formulation of gender relationality by Stanley Chojnacki, 'Subaltern patriarchs: patrician bachelors in Renaissance Venice', in ibid., pp. 73–90.

The final part turns to encounters of interpersonal conflict: the rites of insults and affronts where we can see the greatest fluidity of social exchange between persons, and the most direct, dramatic challenges posed to an individual's honour, manhood, or reputation as a respectable woman.

Gender, family and life-cycle rites

The cluster of rituals surrounding birth, marriage and death marked key events in the lives of individuals and their families. Renaissance Italians bestowed on these occasions tremendous social and symbolic weight, as well as considerable material resources. It was through birth rites, for example, that infants were first integrated into their local and Christian communities through baptism, acquiring the beginnings of their social identities and networks through godparentage and the symbolism of a name.[8]

No less critical for determining personal relationships and social identity in the Renaissance was marriage, as Italians themselves were well aware. 'Tell me whom you marry and I'll tell you who you are', runs an old Italian proverb; and, indeed, it would be difficult to overstate the centrality of marriage as a Renaissance institution, not only for reproducing families biologically, but also for creating webs of familial alliance, especially within the middle and upper classes.[9] Among propertied Florentines, who did not shy away from an unabashedly pragmatic view of the institution, marriage alliances expedited strategies for social advancement, exchanges of material resources and the circulation of both persons and reputations. The prospective bride played an even more marginal role in the matchmaking than did her future husband. Both were conditioned by longstanding social norms to recognize that familial rather than personal interests governed marriage, but their likely disparity in ages – at first marriage, girls were typically sixteen to eighteen, while their husbands were thirty to thirty-two – meant that each

8. On godparents, see Christiane Klapisch-Zuber, 'Parrains et filleuls. Une approche comparée de la France, l'Angleterre et l'Italie médiévales', *Medieval Prosopography*, 6 (1985), pp. 51–77; idem, 'Au péril des commères. L'alliance spirituelle par les femmes à Florence', in *Femmes. Mariages-Lignages XIIe–XIVe siècles. Mélanges offerts à Georges Duby* (Brussels, 1992), pp. 215–32; and Louis Haas, 'Il mio buono compare: choosing godparents and the uses of baptismal kinship in Renaissance Florence', *Journal of Social History*, 29 (1995), pp. 341–56.

9. Quoted in Anthony Molho, *Marriage Alliance in Late Medieval Florence* (Cambridge, MA, 1994), p. 13.

would approach marriage from very different perspectives. It also meant that many women would be widowed while still under forty; thus re-marriageable, they could find themselves still pawns in family marital strategies, subjecting them at times to situations of profound emotional conflict between their natal and marriage families.[10]

In fourteenth- and fifteenth-century Florence, the marriage ritual proceeded in several distinct phases, rather than being embodied in a single act.[11] Marriage was an entirely secular affair, divided into contractual and festive stages that nowhere required the intervention of clergy. The initial step was to conduct informal negotiations between the interested families, by means of intermediaries or marriage brokers. At the centre of the eventual prenuptial agreement was the dowry: its size, terms and payment schedule.

The twin sister of marriage, the dowry was the money, land or goods given by the bride's family to the groom for the duration of the union. In Renaissance Italy, where arranged marriages were the rule, there could be no marriage without a dowry, regardless of class. The dowry provided the economic means for a new couple to begin its livelihood together: a young labourer might use his wife's dowry to purchase tools, a master artisan might buy his own shop, or a merchant establish a new business venture. No matter how small the exchange, labourers such as wool workers, weavers, and even sharecroppers contracted dowry agreements using the same formulaic language as important patrician families. The dowry also carried the significant social and symbolic functions of guaranteeing the honour due the prospective bride and her family, while proclaiming, through its size, the rank of the marrying couple. This linking of dowry size with family status inflated the threshold of what was considered an 'honourable' dowry. By the 1470s the well-born Alessandra Macinghi Strozzi could belittle 1,000 florins – a sum that would have been treated as an attractive offer fifty years earlier – as a 'mere artisan's dowry'. Ironically, the municipal dowry fund established by the Florentine government in 1425 as an

10. On Florentine marriage ages, see David Herlihy and Christiane Klapisch-Zuber, *Tuscans and their Families: A Study of the Florentine Catasto of 1427* (New Haven and London, 1985), pp. 210–11; for the conflicts faced by Florentine widows, see Christiane Klapisch-Zuber, 'The "cruel mother": maternity, widowhood, and dowry in Florence in the fourteenth and fifteenth centuries', in her *Women, Family, and Ritual in Renaissance Italy*, trans. Lydia G. Cochrane (Chicago and London, 1985), pp. 117–31.

11. The following discussion is based on Christiane Klapisch-Zuber, 'Zacharias, or the Ousted Father: nuptial rites in Tuscany between Giotto and the Council of Trent', and 'The Griselda complex: dowry and marriage gifts in the quattrocento', in her *Women, Family, and Ritual*, pp. 178–212, 213–46.

innovative approach to curb this problem only fuelled the inflation further. Through the Renaissance and beyond, dowries continued to entangle families in complex and unpredictable ways, even after the death of one partner dissolved the union, as the return of dotal goods frequently gave rise to legal conflicts sometimes lasting for generations.[12]

Once a preliminary agreement had been reached, the actors in the nuptial drama could proceed with the three main ritual episodes that gave a marriage its social and legal legitimacy. The first scene in this ceremonial triptych was the public meeting between the future groom, accompanied by his kinsmen and male friends, and the male guardians, kin and friends of the prospective bride. At this meeting the respective parties exchanged ritual handshakes or kisses that pledged their good faith and agreement; the dowry terms were legally notarized and the engagement given a binding public character.

Beginning their nuptial rites with an all-male ceremony, where even the bride-to-be was absent, Florentines thus made no secret of the asymmetrical terms in which they cast honour and gender in this supreme act of familial alliance. The second stage in the process, however, emphasized exchange and incorporation to a much greater extent, as if by way of compensation. The locus of honour shifted to the girl's house, where her kin and familial allies, both male and female, gathered, along with the groom's much smaller party. With the assistance of a notary, the groom placed the nuptial ring on the bride's finger, giving rise to the name of 'ring day' for this ceremony. Then the husband offered gifts, the so-called 'counter dowry', to his new wife and in-laws, who in turn provided a festive banquet for the entire group. These series of exchanges, both material and symbolic in nature, sealed the alliance and established a network of interdependency within the newly enlarged kin group.

The objects exchanged in this second ritual moment did more than restore a sense of social equilibrium and reciprocal family honour. Nuptial gifts – jewels and clothing for the more affluent, more marginal gifts like a length of cloth or small household items

12. On dowries, dowry inflation and the Florentine dowry fund, see Molho, *Marriage Alliance*; Stanley Chojnacki, 'Dowries and kinsmen in early Renaissance Venice', *Journal of Interdisciplinary History*, 5 (1975), pp. 571–600; idem, 'Marriage legislation and patrician society in fifteenth-century Venice', in Bernard S. Bacharach and David Nichols, eds, *Law, Custom, and the Social Fabric in Medieval Europe: Essays in Honor of Bryce Lyon*, (Kalamazoo, MI, 1990), pp. 163–84; Samuel K. Cohn, Jr, *The Laboring Classes in Renaissance Florence* (New York, 1980), pp. 16–25.

for artisans and labourers – offered by husband to wife also helped disguise the fundamental imbalance between the economic burden of the dowry that separated a woman from her family and the much lower cost of aggregating her into a new family. While some grooms were extremely generous in providing clothes, jewels and bedroom furnishings for their brides, most Tuscan husbands, rich or poor, urban or rural, spent only one- to two-thirds of the promised dowry on such gifts. Moreover, this counter-dowry was only temporary, for husbands retained ownership of these goods and frequently reclaimed them once they had fulfilled their ritual purpose.[13]

Although at the end of the ring day the couple was considered to be husband and wife, the process of marriage was not truly completed until the union was announced to the community at large, and then physically consummated. This third stage of the nuptial scenario began with a highly public transfer of the bride to her husband's residence. Dressed in finery, she was led on horseback by his friends and family to her new home, in a procession as marked by the ostentatious transport of her trousseau goods as of her person. After more feasting and gift-giving, the couple was led to the bridal chamber to consummate their union. In more modest, less affluent circles the bride followed her husband home as soon as the ring ceremony ended, assuming the dowry had been paid.

In this third segment, the accent shifted once again to the groom, who took full possession of his wife's person and goods, along with her virginal or sexual honour. Over the course of time this emphasis on the husband and his honour became more pronounced, a process marked by modifications to the ritual transfer of goods that tipped the ceremonial balance away from complementary linkages and towards the groom's role as a new proprietor. In the fourteenth and early fifteenth centuries, the bride had made her triumphal nuptial entry into her husband's house accompanied by painted wooden coffers (*forzieri*) containing her trousseau. Considered a 'woman's' object, these coffers reflected the double honour of both her and her family. By the late fifteenth century, however, such 'women's' objects had vanished from the public wedding parade. Instead, the trousseau was sent on beforehand, to be stored in the large, beautifully painted chests (*cassoni*) that the husband provided to help furnish the bridal chamber, an obligation for which

13. Isabelle Chabot, '"La sposa in nero": la ritualizzazione del lutto delle vedove fiorentine (secoli XIV–XV)', *Quaderni storici*, 86 (1994), pp. 421–62; Klapisch-Zuber, 'Griselda complex', pp. 220–1, 225, 227–8.

he became entirely responsible. A bride's coffer now also remained in her husband's house after her death, whereas a fourteenth-century widower typically restored his dead wife's goods to her natal family.[14]

Nuptial rites thus began and ended with ceremonies that increasingly accentuated the honour of the groom and his family, even while retaining an interlocking character in order to create alliances. By 1500 Florentines, like other Italians, were moving towards more sumptuous display in more than just life-cycle rites such as weddings, funerals and baptisms.[15] Their nobilization of cultural representations of all kinds was accompanied by a parallel tendency to highlight male honour and patrilineage over older forms of reciprocity and familial authority. The consequence, over the course of the Renaissance, was a widening of the gendered asymmetry of honour that these rites embodied.

Persons and gender in corporate groups

Beyond the household and family ties that formed the core of their social world, Renaissance Italians enjoyed numerous forms of corporate sociability that brought them together for purposes of work, prayer and play. Guilds, neighbourhood festive groups, parish associations, lay confraternities and consororities, and political factions all provided regular opportunities for townsfolk to engage in common projects and to pool their collective resources and energies in a structured fashion. Corporate groups played a central role in shaping an individual's public associations and organizing social life more generally. Yet in Italian Renaissance cities most formally organized corporations were composed solely of men, rather than including both sexes. While an individual man, whether artisan or patrician, might enjoy multiple memberships in various occupational, religious and political groups, his wife, daughter, mother or sister typically belonged to no such aggregate of organizations. Although women participated in the urban work force in many capacities, it is doubtful that they matriculated as full guild members in any significant numbers. It is even less likely that women engaged in such guild rites as the festive processions intended to

14. Chabot, '"Sposa in nero"', pp. 429, 445.

15. On this point, see Sharon T. Strocchia, *Death and Ritual in Renaissance Florence* (Baltimore, 1992), and Samuel K. Cohn, *The Cult of Remembrance and the Black Death: Six Renaissance Cities in Central Italy* (Baltimore, 1992).

foster a common work identity and sense of male brotherhood. Of course, formal associations by no means exhausted the potential social bonds based on personal friendships or patronage that both women and men might enjoy. Still, the fact that male sociability lay at the heart of public culture throughout the Renaissance gave men's honour a corporate dimension that its female counterpart lacked.

Because of their institutional record-keeping practices, we know far more about organized corporate groups like guilds and confraternities than we do about the informal and often intimate contacts that made up the bulk of social interactions for both sexes but have left fewer documentary traces. Nonetheless, we can turn this imbalance in the evidence to our advantage by using it to explore the meanings of masculinity celebrated in group ritual. The rites enacted by the various corporate groupings to which men belonged portrayed masculinity less as a single, unified construct or behavioural system than as a complex code beset by profound tensions. Models of masculinity were always plural in number and were related to one's class and household position, age and marital status, local political setting, as well as the historical moment.

One important strand of masculine behaviour was that portrayed in the corporate rites of confraternities, the religious brotherhoods designed for collective worship. Confraternities were self-governing congregations of lay Christians who gathered for collective prayer and devotion, and they were among the most popular voluntary associations across the Italian peninsula from the thirteenth century on. Yet these pious groups were not easily accessible to women. Bologna, for example, with a population of 50,000, boasted over eighty active confraternities and their subgroups in the mid-sixteenth century; of these only twelve definitely enrolled women.[16] Much of this gender imbalance stemmed from the rise of flagellant confraternities, whose popularity surpassed the older types of hymn-singing and charitable brotherhoods over the course of the fifteenth century, and whose particular ritual practices further diminished women's participation. Thus, in fourteenth- and early fifteenth-century Bologna, women drawn mainly from the artisan class had

16. Nicholas Terpstra, 'Women in the Brotherhood: gender, class, and politics in Renaissance Bolognese confraternities', *Renaissance and Reformation*, 26 (1990), pp. 193–211, at p. 194. On confraternities, see also James R. Banker, *Death in the Community: Memorialization and Confraternities in an Italian Commune of the Late Middle Ages* (Athens, GA and London, 1988); John Henderson, *Piety and Charity in Late Medieval Florence* (Oxford, 1994); Ronald F.E. Weissman, *Ritual Brotherhood in Renaissance Florence* (New York, 1982).

joined hymn-singing groups and engaged in their corporate charit-able work. The fact that they were barred from holding administrat-ive positions in such confraternities led to poor female retention rates, but it was particularly the spread of self-flagellation as a pop-ular penitential practice in confraternities of the later fifteenth century that seems to have squeezed women out of these corporations. Self-flagellation with corded ropes performed in a group setting promoted a strong sense of fraternity, as small clusters of participants dramatically imitated the sufferings of Christ and together expiated their sins. The collective practice of flagellation on a weekly basis established a resilient bond between members that probably helped to assuage whatever conflicts arose outside communal worship. It also stressed a concept of masculinity based on self-imposed humil-ity and discipline: a rite of self-abasement from which a member derived his sense of belonging to a harmonious brotherhood of Christ's disciples.

As confraternal flagellation grew in popularity, it increasingly challenged women's claims to corporate membership and corres-ponding participation in group rites. At issue was not the practice of flagellation itself, since Italian women had long exercised this form of penance in private. Rather, it was their participation in the collective practice of flagellation – either in processions or in confraternal devotions – that met resistance from ecclesiastical authorities and ritual brothers alike, and that ultimately led to the barring of women from confraternal membership. It was more than simply the shame of having women expose their naked backs in mixed company, since flagellants commonly wore robes and hoods that hid their identities. Instead, as Nicholas Terpstra has observed, '[t]he consistency and completeness of the exclusion suggests that collective flagellation was seen as a distinctly male ritual'.[17] Although a rationale was never articulated in confraternal records, it may have been that men were unwilling to humiliate themselves pub-licly in such an intimate setting before members of the subordinate sex, who could hold no positions of authority and whose corporate membership was considered to be ancillary at best. Such perform-ances would effectively surrender social power, erode the gender hierarchy and diminish the opportunity to create deeper ties of male brotherhood.

Ironically, while Bolognese women were pushed out of artisanal confraternities because of these shifts in devotional practices in the

17. Terpstra, 'Women in the Brotherhood', p. 196.

fifteenth century, their male brethren would themselves soon be marginalized in their own confraternities, by political developments in the next century that emphasized social hierarchy and class distinctions. In the new political atmosphere of patrician dominance that characterized sixteenth-century Italy, both patrician and artisan women in Bologna regained some limited participation in organized piety through the advent of all-female consororities. These new consororities were generally each attached to a male company and stressed their members' role as spiritual and political subordinates to their male counterparts. Unlike those in Roman consororities, however, sixteenth-century Bolognese women did not join in public confraternal processions, anniversary masses or other corporate feasts. Their most visible public role was to dress a deceased sister in the robes of the men's company and accompany her to the confraternal tomb.[18] Although the gender relations celebrated in Bolognese confraternal rites had shifted by the mid-sixteenth century from a model of familial patriarchy to one of political hierarchy, the principle of corporate sexual segregation remained unchallenged.

The male-defined piety embodied in ritual brotherhoods had its mirror image in forms of aggressive violence that were also particularly masculine in nature. The amount and form of violence acceptable in Italian male culture was determined by many factors, with age norms playing a critical role. The public behaviour of the mature political leaders of, for example, fifteenth-century Florence or Venice, while appropriately masculine, was also decidedly different from that of boys and young men of the same class and locale, who 'lacked the gravity, the dispassionate reason, and the controlled sexuality that were the necessary moral qualities of governors'.[19] One of the hallmarks of youthful masculinity was its sheer disruptiveness,[20] and boys in Florence threatened the peace and social order with their fisticuffs, carnival misrule, rock throwing and gang activities; older adolescents consciously mocked the order of society created by their political elders through charivaris, noise-making,

18. Nicholas Terpstra, *Lay Confraternities and Civic Religion in Renaissance Bologna* (Cambridge, UK, 1995), p. 126.

19. Richard C. Trexler, *Public Life in Renaissance Florence* (Ithaca, NY and London, 1980), p. 367.

20. Lyndal Roper, *Oedipus and the Devil: Witchcraft, Sexuality and Religion in Early Modern Europe* (London and New York, 1994), p. 115, argues that even though German town councils sought to identify a 'rough' culture with youth, 'experience did not confirm such a comforting view of masculine excess as no more than a passing adolescent phase'.

and crude parades, just as did their French counterparts. Richard Trexler has argued that the ruling regime of late fifteenth-century Florence succeeded in part because it ritually absorbed (and subsequently transformed) unruly boys and adolescents into the public processional life of the city. This placing of male youth at the city's charismatic centre was not to last long, however, for with the advent of the Medici principate in 1530 such an accommodation came to an abrupt end.[21]

In fact, young men almost seemed to have been culturally compelled to undertake both routine and ritualized forms of disruption precisely to demonstrate that they had achieved the manliness considered appropriate to that particular stage in their life cycle. In such behaviour Italian youths resembled their counterparts in German towns, who were expected to establish themselves publicly as potential civic protectors by fighting, whether over a point of honour or simply showing off their prowess. During their prolonged adolescence, created by the custom of men marrying late, Italian youths also exhibited their virility for public confirmation by indulging in excesses of 'drinking, whoring, and gorging'.[22]

Class as well as age figured in Italian notions of masculinity and male honour, a complicating factor made evident in Venice's popular *guerre dei pugni*, or the 'wars of the fists'.[23] As rival squads of young Venetian workers battled bloodily as members of one of two great city-wide factions, they were also seeking to win personal glory and reputation in one of the few public arenas available to them for asserting their honour and public status. For a young fighter, skilful conduct in the war of the fists won him acclaim at the public fountain of honour, in the form of crowd applause and peer recognition. Even though the honours won in such battles might be fleeting, they nevertheless excited the passions of participants and viewers alike, in part because they accentuated a youth's masculinity: his prowess, aggressiveness and adherence to the ritualized codes of the contest. As Robert Davis remarks, in these ways a young man won a place for himself in the world of men, for: 'to celebrate the *pugni* was to celebrate being male, to assert not only

21. Trexler, *Public Life*, pp. 367–547. On French youth abbeys, see Natalie Zemon Davis, 'The reasons of misrule', in her *Society and Culture in Early Modern France* (Stanford, CA, 1975), pp. 97–123; for the Italian version of charivaris, see Christiane Klapisch-Zuber, 'The "Mattinata" in Medieval Italy', in her *Women, Family, and Ritual*, pp. 261–82.

22. Roper, *Oedipus*, p. 145.

23. The following discussion is based on Davis, *War of the Fists*; see also pp. 24–6 in Chapter 1 of this volume.

the strength, endurance, and aggression that were proper to men, but also to proclaim how this maleness differed from the female and the childish'.[24]

What was at stake in these rough encounters was a young worker's relatively fragile sense of manhood, further diminished by his low place in the social hierarchy. Yet violence and aggressive masculinity were not confined to workingmen by any means. At the opposite end of the social scale, many Venetian patricians freely asserted their own, elite prerogatives of maleness by preying on young, lower-class women through rape or false promises of marriage. Not all patrician men, of course, engaged in such activities, if only because more than a few preferred those of their own sex. Nevertheless, demographic, economic and family pressures forced many patricians to remain life-long bachelors, with all the potential for social destabilization that this implied.[25] Throughout the fifteenth and sixteenth centuries the effects of aggressive masculinity dominated the agendas of municipal governments, which sought to control disruptive behaviours that threatened public order at numerous levels. To do so, however, meant confronting head on deeply rooted social and cultural definitions of manhood. Even in this age of patriarchal dominance, masculinity still contained within itself conflicting imperatives and multiple, often ambivalent strands that confused gender relations and thwarted moves towards greater order and discipline throughout the Renaissance and beyond.

Gender and rites of interpersonal conflict

In addition to claiming and displaying honour in ritual activities, Renaissance Italians also negotiated the tensions and interpersonal conflicts of daily life through a well-developed rhetoric of honour. Like other early modern Europeans, they believed in the power of words to make or break reputations in the community. Injurious words, insults and slurs were symbolic assaults on honour that could not go unanswered, without inviting loss of social standing and self-esteem. In pre-modern communities, where social relations were both dense and intense, insults and defamation were 'a primary

---

24. Ibid., p. 109.
25. Guido Ruggiero, *The Boundaries of Eros: Sex Crime and Sexuality in Renaissance Venice* (New York, 1985); Chojnacki, 'Subaltern patriarchs'.

means of conducting the small politics of everyday life', and Italians had at their disposal a whole 'insult system' that formed an important part of their transactional habits and social exchanges.[26]

The use of this ritualized vocabulary of vilification was neither haphazard nor random. Such verbal assaults aimed at influencing friends, neighbours or relatives in the community, setting in motion a spreading cycle of gossip that gave the insulter increased leverage over his or her victim, however temporary its effects. Spoken insults also figured in the renegotiation of a dispute already under way, with injurious words both signalling and sealing the rupture of an economic, social or sexual relationship. For example, in sixteenth-century Rome, 'the response to "I want my money" was often a slur on the character of the asker', who might be called a spy, a scoundrel or a slut, depending on who was making the request. This tactic shifted the onus from the debtor to the creditor, whose honour and reputation were now called into question, probably undeservedly.[27] Such counter-attacks had the added advantage of demonstrating the quick, often witty or biting verbal skills so highly prized in Italian Renaissance culture. While heated exchange of insults might easily lead to blows, effective threats and responses could also stave off violence, by allowing participants to make verbal reparation to their honour before the tribunal of public opinion.[28]

Insults, slander or even outright lies could only achieve their objectives to the extent that they resonated with community values and opinions. Their effectiveness lay in providing the inverse definition of what were considered the essential characteristics of respectable men and women in a given context. It was less the insult itself, as Lawrence Poos remarks, than 'its transmission, reception, and normative evaluation [that] comprised its power to injure'.[29]

Ritualized verbal assaults were particularly important for women in pre-modern communities. Insults and gossip gave women of virtually all classes 'a major, albeit highly informal, means of influencing or shaping "public opinion" in a society in which males controlled all formal political activity'.[30] Injurious words or retorts provided

26. Daniel R. Lesnick, 'Insults and threats in medieval Todi', *Journal of Medieval History*, 17 (1991), pp. 71–89, at p. 72; Peter Burke, *The Historical Anthropology of Early Modern Italy: Essays on Perception and Communication* (Cambridge, UK, 1987), p. 96.

27. E.S. Cohen, 'Honor and gender', p. 601.

28. Farr, *Hands of Honor*, pp. 179–86.

29. L.R. Poos, 'Sex, lies, and the Church courts of Pre-Reformation England', *Journal of Interdisciplinary History*, 25 (1995), pp. 585–607, at p. 601.

30. Lesnick, 'Insults', p. 76.

an especially powerful tool for women seeking to defend their honour, given their problematic relationship to physical violence in the early modern period.[31] In Italy as throughout Europe, women were quite ready to turn the language of insult against others, including other women. The sixteenth-century art historian Giorgio Vasari, for example, tells of the passionate insults hurled by Margharita Acciaiuoli Borgherini, the well-born wife of a leading Florentine citizen, at a petty merchant who had criticized the quality of her marriage bed decorations. Criminal records in such Italian cities as late medieval Todi reveal that defamation of character was a distinctly female form of crime, just as in fifteenth-century England women were tried for defamation slightly more often than were men.[32] Records of verbal assaults that were litigated in court present only a small fraction of a hidden history of social interaction and conflict at the most basic level of everyday life.

The lexicon of insults in Renaissance Italy drew from a stereotyped, gender-loaded stockpile of invective which both women and men adapted creatively, according to the needs of the situation. The most common epithets hurled at a woman concerned her sexual integrity, impugning her as some variant of a whore, adulteress or procuress, 'with various unpleasant adjectives such as "dirty" or "poxy" tacked on'. These slurs indicate that defamation of a woman's character, and hence her honour and social position, turned rather narrowly on sexual concerns: chastity and fidelity in marriage, preceded by virginity or at least a promise of marriage in exchange for its surrender.[33] In Todi, for example, thirty-two per cent of insults identifiable in the criminal records between 1275 and 1280 either attacked a woman's sexual integrity directly, by calling her a whore or adulteress, or indirectly, as when a man was termed a bastard. Roman records from a later period demonstrate how frequently the term 'cuckold' was used against men.[34] In either case, the very vocabulary of sexual insult was female-centred, either assailing a woman for failing to adhere to sexual mores or indicting a man as the product or victim of illicit sexual relations.

31. On this problematic relationship, see Natalie Zemon Davis, *Fiction in the Archives: Pardon Tales and Their Tellers in Sixteenth-Century France* (Stanford, CA, 1987), pp. 77–103.
32. Cited in Patricia Lee Rubin, *Giorgio Vasari: Art and History* (New Haven and London, 1995), p. 160; for the Todi records, see Lesnick, 'Insults', p. 76; for the English cases, see Poos, 'Sex, lies and Church courts', p. 596.
33. Burke, *Historical Anthropology*, p. 97; Guido Ruggiero, *Binding Passions: Tales of Magic, Marriage, and Power at the End of the Renaissance* (New York, 1993), p. 59.
34. Lesnick, 'Insults', p. 76; Burke, *Historical Anthropology*, p. 96.

While such ritualized insults no doubt exaggerated the real importance of a woman's sexuality in determining her identity and life experience, they certainly made it clear that, ironically, her sexual honour was never solely her personal possession, especially if she belonged to the middle or upper classes. Instead, a woman's sexual honour was intricately bound up with the honour of her family and its dominant males. Daniel Lesnick argues that in late medieval Todi, 'sexual reputation was immeasurably more important to married women than to unmarried women' because of the concerns it raised about the legitimate transmission of wealth and property. Yet for respectable, unmarried urban girls the stakes were also high, since the very definition of marriage was so ambiguous in the pre-Tridentine period.[35] The promise of marriage was often enough to initiate sexual relations between prospective marriage partners outside the urban elite, since prior to the Council of Trent the canonical definition of marriage involved simply the exchange of consent between partners. When a man subsequently rejected his promise, it was not only the girl's honour that was violated but that of her whole family.

As many fathers found out, the cunning that brought honour to a young man who 'fooled' or 'tricked' a young girl into sexual relations brought only dishonour to them and their daughters. Fathers and male guardians so wronged sought to rehabilitate their lost honour by pressuring the offender to make good on his promises, either through family or community networks or through formal litigation in ecclesiastical or civil courts, although the shameful publicity resulting from such trials probably kept many families out of court. If such attempts failed, honour might still be salvaged by placing the girl in a monastic-like custodial institution.[36] Whatever the prescriptions about premarital chastity in Italian Renaissance communities, virginity was a negotiable commodity, which poorer girls occasionally attempted to use to contract a marriage promise. Once lost, however, its social counterpart – honour – had to be reclaimed before social reintegration could take place.[37]

35. Lesnick, 'Insults', p. 76. For an interesting case history of the ambiguity surrounding marriage before Trent, see Gene Brucker, *Giovanni and Lusanna: Love and Marriage in Renaissance Florence* (Berkeley and Los Angeles, 1986).

36. Ruggiero, *Binding Passions*, esp. pp. 57–69; Ferrante, 'Honor regained'; Cavallo and Cerutti, 'Female Honor'; Sherrill Cohen, *The Evolution of Women's Asylums since 1500: From Refuges for Ex-prostitutes to Shelters for Battered Women* (Oxford, 1992).

37. Elizabeth S. Cohen, 'No longer virgins: self-presentation by young women in late Renaissance Rome', in Marilyn Migiel and Juliana Schiesari, eds, *Refiguring Woman: Perspectives on Gender and the Italian Renaissance* (Ithaca, NY, 1991), pp. 169–91.

Ritualized insults also tell us that women's sexual conduct, whether real or alleged, was not solely the concern of men but figured as a source of contention between women as well. Sixteenth-century French pardon tales report all-female quarrels where women shouted the same sexual slurs against other women as did men. Whenever early modern townspeople spoke about sex, as Lyndal Roper reminds us, they were 'inevitably speaking about position, class, and honour', an assertion that is amply corroborated by the rich verbal testimonies preserved in the era's civil and criminal court records.[38]

So Thomas and Elizabeth Cohen have demonstrated in the Roman domestic case of 1559 that they have labelled 'Camilla the Go-Between'. Here, the unhappy wife, Giulia, caught in the act with her noble lover by her repressive notary husband Gieronimo Piccardi, soon tried to excuse her own adultery by casting a large part of the blame on her serving woman, Camilla. Although Camilla had acted as the go-between in an illicit love affair between two apparently willing individuals, making the initial contacts, carrying their amorous messages back and forth, and counselling Giulia in the arts of deception necessary for an adulterous relationship, Giulia had no compunction about denouncing her helper to the judges as a seductive procuress. 'If I had been a saint', Giulia maintained, 'this bawd of a Camilla would have made me break my neck as she did with her pretty sweet-talk and with all the persuading she did.' In fact, the two women shared a complementary bond in which each needed the other to keep their conspiracy alive. Giulia's high status and corresponding low freedom of action was balanced by Camilla's apparent social weakness. From her scant honour this ordinary maid-servant had forged some considerable strengths: her liberty of movement that she used to create networks of the men and women for whom she performed favours; her savviness in the ways of love; and her first-hand knowledge of her mistress's transgressions, should the need for blackmail ever arise. When, under the pressure of formal male power, this bond dissolved, Camilla and Giulia could only turn on each other, with sexual insults and innuendos that gained extra force from their overtones of class and honour.[39]

In contrast to the sexual slurs typically used against women, insults aimed at men were more economic in nature. The men of

38. N.Z. Davis, *Fiction in the Archives*, p. 101; Roper, *Oedipus*, p. 56.

39. The trial transcript is translated and printed in Thomas V. Cohen and Elizabeth S. Cohen, *Words and Deeds in Renaissance Rome: Trials before the Papal Magistrates* (Toronto, 1993), pp. 159–87, quote at p. 166.

Todi were frequently defamed as liars or thieves, charges that undermined their credibility in business transactions. Accusations of dishonesty directly attacked the honour which mediated a man's business and social relationships, and hence called into question his success and stature as a merchant, tradesman, artisan or labourer. Allegations of economic and sexual illegitimacy commonly went together, however, as when one Todi wife called her local priest a 'thieving bastard'. A political dimension might be added to the repertoire of abuse, as in seventeenth-century Rome, where the slur of 'thief' could be complemented with those of 'traitor' and 'spy', reflecting an awareness of the papacy's increasing administrative intrusiveness.

Yet if such insults reveal male honour to be economically and politically based, they still often carried a strong sexual import. Thus, since one's masculinity was 'guaranteed' when he took up arms and defended his city, calling a citizen a traitor aimed a devastating blow at both his honour and his manhood.[40] Sexual slurs also called into doubt a man's virility relative to the behaviour of women. Being termed a cuckold questioned a husband's ability to control or satisfy his wife, thus robbing him of an important component of his manhood. In the case of Camilla the Go-Between, the honour of the injured husband Gieronimo had been tainted through the behaviour of his wife, who thwarted his vigilance and proved him incapable of protecting the integrity of either his dwelling or his marriage. Even accusations of male homosexuality, turning on the highly loaded term 'bugger', symbolically placed a man in the position of a woman, thus threatening both his honour and his gender identity.[41]

Like rites of passage, insults thus cast the notion of honour asymmetrically along gendered lines, and in Italy as elsewhere in early modern Europe, each sex bore a different yet interdependent relationship to the linguistic codes of honour.[42] In addition to verbal abuse, Renaissance Italians also had at their disposal a rich range of physical gestures that formed part of their insult system and code of honour. These included sticking out one's tongue at an enemy, pulling a man's beard or a woman's hair, singing lewd songs in front of an enemy's house, spitting in someone's face,

40. Burke, *Historical Anthropology*, p. 96; Roper, *Oedipus*, p. 108.
41. Burke, *Historical Anthropology*, p. 97; N.Z. Davis, *Fiction in the Archives*, p. 97.
42. Lesnick, 'Insults', p. 77; Poos, 'Sex, lies and Church courts', p. 586; Farr, *Hands of Honor*, pp. 185–6.

knocking off his hat, and making insulting hand gestures that implied someone to be a cuckold, whore or bugger.

One of the more elaborate of these gestural rituals of contempt was the system of affronts from sixteenth-century Rome that has been termed 'house-scorning', where persons aggrieved in their honour retaliated by assaulting the house of their offender, usually as part of an escalating quarrel.[43] A scorner typically raised a ruckus outside the house, often under cover of darkness, threw stones or ink at windows or shutters, and smeared the doorways and walls of the dwelling with mud or excrement. Such insults affronted the honour of victims in both their person and in the symbolically charged personal space in which they dwelt. House-scornings were especially effective modes of insult because of their highly public nature, since even after the event itself, which disturbed a peaceful night's sleep, there were left visible or pungent traces that continued to attract the attention of neighbours and passersby. As with verbal abuse, the trigger for such ritual assaults was the breakdown in an economic, social or sexual relationship. When the Roman Anello Palumbo found his front door befouled with excrement in 1602, for example, he blamed his wife's brother Pietro Poggio, with whom he had a longstanding grudge and who, after numerous quarrels, had not been invited to a dinner party for two of Anello's nephews. Anello seemingly had no doubt that Pietro, as a close kinsman, would feel that his exclusion from the family fold was a matter of dishonour sufficiently cutting to precipitate his alleged retaliation against Anello's house.

Just as with verbal slurs, what lay at the root of many house-scornings was tension over the entangling sexual conduct of women. Rejected suitors were among the most common performers of scornings, as they sought to ease the sting of rejection while restoring their public face. A disproportionate number of house-scornings in late sixteenth-century Rome concerned prostitutes or courtesans, whose dwellings were also assailed by rejected lovers or clients. The fact that numerous Roman prostitutes chose to prosecute their offenders in court argues strongly that in their own eyes they possessed a sense of honour in need of defence and revenge, despite their seemingly shameful profession. The social identity of many men accused of house-scorning – bachelors, immigrants, temporary residents – also shows marginalized men beyond the conventional

43. The term is taken from E.S. Cohen, 'Honor and gender', upon which the following discussion is based.

domains of honour absorbing and adapting the language and gesture of honour to their own purposes. Yet the gender lines of house-scorning were not neatly drawn, for women occasionally participated in, and at times orchestrated, the ritual derision of other women with whom they were at odds. For instance, in 1607 the Roman courtesan Agnese de Incoronatis responded to the sexual insults of her neighbour, Domitilla Corvina, by having her male friends put on two separate house-scornings and she even participated in the second one herself. In sum, the public ritual of house-scorning in the late Renaissance shows how both sexes, including those on the margins of society, used the discourse of honour to negotiate personal disputes and interpret the intimate and public events of their lives.

Although the litany of insults and gestures itself may have altered little with the passage of time, historians have detected an evolution in the ways in which honour, particularly that of males, was defended from such attacks. In tandem with the new standards of civility emerging between the fourteenth and seventeenth centuries, many northern Italian upper-class men began to embrace new strategies to limit and focus the violence required to protect their honour and masculinity from insult. Duelling, with its elaborate rules, became more common than vendetta and revenge killing among aristocrats by the mid-sixteenth century and greatly diminished violent incidents because of the long delays in acting on and accepting a challenge. Moreover, the expansion of judicial authority by regional states substantially increased the use of law courts by those seeking to resolve disputes over honour, despite the potential for shameful disclosure inherent in such a move.[44]

Yet the inroads made by the 'civilizing process' caught men in a complex gender dilemma, as Edward Muir has suggested. To accept new standards of honour that prized restraint and greater control of emotions placed Italian gentlemen in an ambivalent moral and social position as to whether they had fully discharged their debt of honour as men. The spread of good manners and courtly behaviour and the corresponding abandonment of rougher revenge practices was viewed by some traditionalists as 'unmanly', while to others it even signalled 'the beginnings of a feminization of public life'.[45] Given the difficulty of the situation, the best a well-mannered

44. Muir, 'Double binds', p. 66; Burke, *Historical Anthropology*, p. 103.
45. Muir, 'Double binds', p. 80.

sixteenth-century gentleman could do was to deflect an insult and orchestrate the impressions around it.

Despite the interdependence of honour practices, notions of honour in the Renaissance turn out to have been distinctly asymmetrical for women and men. This was as true for fifteenth-century Florentine nuptial rites, with their highly structured and idealized gender roles, as it was for the much earthier Roman insults and gestures of contempt of the late sixteenth century. The resulting gender norms for both sexes were complex and often problematic. Its gendered asymmetry did not prevent Italian women from laying claim to honour as aggressively as did men, while the relationship of sexuality to women's social identity proves to have been an intricate one. If sexuality was planted at the very core of Renaissance definitions of womanhood, the extent to which sexual behaviours determined female honour was situational and must be located in a larger historical matrix of power, persons and institutions. Likewise, the many strands of masculinity produced many practical conflicts – not only for regional states seeking to impose a higher degree of social control, but also for individual men striving to protect a changing sense of manhood. Scholars are only starting to understand how gender norms and behaviours moved in relationship to each other, but we have already begun to appreciate the subtleties inherent in this research.

PART TWO

The Social Foundations of Gender

CHAPTER THREE

Daughters and Oligarchs: Gender and the Early Renaissance State*

STANLEY CHOJNACKI

From the enduring image of Machiavelli's cunning prince to Jacob Burckhardt's mid-nineteenth-century depiction of 'the state as a work of art', historians have continued to be fascinated by innovations in government and statecraft as prominent features of the Italian Renaissance. Since the 1970s, however, a new dimension has been added to these traditional interests, and that is a concern with gender and the political structures that influenced women's lives. Was the Italian Renaissance state concerned with gender? Are gender and politics related parts of a historical process? I will argue that the answer to both questions is 'yes', and that in Renaissance Italy, government and gender converged in the uncharted terrain between the public and private interests of the ruling classes. Since the publication in 1977 of Joan Kelly's germinal essay, 'Did Woman have a Renaissance?', scholars have substantiated her negative response to her question by documenting women's subordinate status in the patriarchal societies of the Italian cities. A landmark of that scholarship was the 1985 publication of Christiane Klapisch-Zuber's collected essays, in which she described with poignant eloquence how Florentine patrician women were exploited for the purposes of their menfolk.[1] Like most scholars in the field, Klapisch-Zuber emphasized the implications for women of the politics of family and lineage. That focus has highlighted the pivotal role of

* This chapter owes much to discussions in the seminar on 'Men, women, and the state in Renaissance Europe' at the Folger Shakespeare Library in Spring 1996. I gratefully acknowledge my debt to its members. I also wish to thank Barbara J. Harris for her valuable suggestions.
1. Joan Kelly-Gadol, 'Did women have a Renaissance?', in Renate Bridenthal and Claudia Koonz, eds, *Becoming Visible: Women in European History* (Boston, 1977), pp. 137–64; Christiane Klapisch-Zuber, *Women, Family, and Ritual in Renaissance Italy* (Chicago, 1985).

women in the marriage strategies devised by men in pursuit of their families' social, economic and political objectives.[2]

Those objectives are the link between the new scholarship on gender and the perennial interest in the state. The intricate meshings of family, gender and government in Italy's political development are captured in the very title of Giorgio Chittolini's contribution to a recent symposium on *The Origins of the State in Italy*: 'The "private", the "public", the state'. Chittolini deftly outlines the reciprocal dynamic of state and family. From one perspective, the state is 'a system of institutions that operates like an underlying web in which diverse forces [such as 'families, kin groups and factions'] and purposes are interwoven in mutual interdependence': that is, government institutions shaping the dealings of private interests. But from another, it can be imagined as 'a political structure formulated in terms of lineages, factions, and groups, organized on the basis of systems of relations and mechanisms of power that are private in nature': private interests shaping government. Although for Chittolini these are alternative perspectives, they can also be complementary sides of a single phenomenon. In either case, 'it is essential to keep constantly in mind the structures of association, the intentions, and the formal and informal uses of power generated by society in that interplay between "public" and "private" . . .'.[3]

The families best positioned to impose their private interests on the functioning of government or, alternatively, to adapt their private aims to the state's policies, were the members of the oligarchical elites. In the activity of urban patriciates and feudal/courtly aristocracies, government and private life overlapped in a zone of uncertain boundaries where families, lineages and factions colluded and collided. The policies of regimes show the effects of the elites' grip on government or princely favour; the sociocultural complexions of the various states reflect the distinctions fashioned by oligarchies to mark themselves off from the rest of society. But political and social hegemony was not a permanent achievement but the object, continually redefined, of unceasing effort by families to

2. For similar findings, see Diane Owen Hughes, 'Representing the family: portraits and purposes in early modern Italy', *Journal of Interdisciplinary History*, 17 (1986), pp. 7–38; Julius Kirshner, 'Pursuing honor while avoiding sin: the Monte delle Doti of Florence', *Quaderni di Studi Senesi*, 41 (Milan, 1978); and Anthony Molho, 'Deception and marriage strategy in Renaissance Florence: the case of women's ages', *Renaissance Quarterly*, 41 (1988), pp. 193–217.

3. Giorgio Chittolini, 'The "private", the "public", the state', in *The Origins of the State in Italy, 1300–1600*, supplementary issue of the *Journal of Modern History*, 67 (1995), pp. S53–S56; interpolation from p. S52.

gain or keep it amid the turbulence of the fourteenth-sixteenth centuries.[4] To do so required demonstrating it on two fronts: the political, by taking part in government; and the social, by cultivating the behaviour and associations befitting members of a ruling class. Those two requirements often blended but were often at odds, as individual families balanced the demands of political ascendancy against the prerogatives of social distinction. The tension between public discipline and private privilege set the state on a new course, that of regulating relationships within and between families, as governing elites sought to secure their status by enacting rules for male behaviour, female behaviour, and relations between men and women. The state was both the instrument and the regulator of oligarchy, and gender was the medium with which it confronted the private interests of families. In the following pages, we explore this confrontation, chiefly in the well-studied cases of Florence and Venice but with occasional reference to other states as it was played out in the charting of the destinies of women.

The state and male identity

Sustained interaction between public authority and private life dates from the first great turning point in Renaissance Italy's political history, the late fourteenth and early fifteenth centuries. This was the formative period of the territorial states, but it also saw a burst of new magistracies and regulations aimed at entrenching regimes by assigning identities, roles and behaviour to age and gender categories. The first step was to define the elites themselves. Starting in the late fourteenth century, humanist writers added to the two traditional criteria of nobility, heredity and virtue, a third: government attribution, based on service to the state. This theoretical innovation coincided with new efforts by regimes to shore up their dominance in the aftermath of the crises of the fourteenth century. Mercantile ruling classes, especially those of Venice and Florence, devised an ideology of oligarchy to counter the enduring claims of the older nobility.[5] Elsewhere, an updated feudalism complemented

---

4. In the changing concept of nobility, see Claudio Donati, *L'idea di nobiltà in Italia: secoli XIV–XVIII* (Bari, 1988), chapters 1–3.
5. Donati, *L'idea di nobiltà*, pp. 4–15, 22, n. 24. On the quest for a non-feudal claim to honour in republican Florence, see Richard C. Trexler, *Public Life in Renaissance Florence* (New York, 1980), pp. 16–30, 223–4.

republican elitism. In Ferrara, the Este marquesses used the venerable practice of conferring fiefs to neutralize resistance from the old Ferrarese nobility and rivalry within their own family, by fashioning a new feudal/courtly nobility out of nobles attracted from elsewhere and Ferraresi of obscure origins rewarded for loyal service to the Este.[6] The Ferrarese example, like those of Milan, Venice, Florence, and other states, underscores the interdependence between the new territorial regimes and the elites that increased their wealth and status by participating in the governing of them.[7]

That mutual dependence also influenced the articulation of a new sociopolitical order within cities, as nascent and established elites alike found new ways to entrench themselves. While the supporters of the Este were gaining the distinction and material benefits of vassalage, the Milanese nobility was being inscribed in an official register, a step in the princely–feudal collaboration then being developed by the Visconti *signori* and later followed by the Sforza dukes.[8] Florence's oligarchy strengthened its political dominance after the Ciompi revolt in 1378 by enacting electoral reforms guaranteeing control of the most powerful offices by the traditionally dominant families and their clients while giving a broad population of lesser guildsmen the illusion of political franchise, thereby achieving 'a separation between participation and power', between 'ruling group and ruling class'.[9] In Venice, too, in the years around 1400, the ruling patriciate widened the gap between itself and the populace, culminating a century-long evolution 'from community to hierarchy'.[10] This has been associated with the entrenchment, as in Florence, of a small ruling coterie within the patriciate, but there

6. Trevor Dean, *Land and Power in Late Medieval Ferrara: The Rule of the Este, 1350–1450* (Cambridge, UK, 1988), pp. 77–91.

7. For overviews, see Giorgio Chittolini, 'Introduzione' to idem, ed., *La crisi degli ordinamenti comunali e le origini dello stato del Rinascimento* (Bologna, 1979), pp. 7–50, esp. pp. 26–40; and Elena Fasano Guarini, 'Center and periphery', in *The Origins of the State in Italy*, pp. S74–S96.

8. James S. Grubb, 'Memory and identity: why Venetians didn't keep ricordanze', *Renaissance Studies*, 8 (1994), p. 382; see Giorgio Chittolini, 'Infeudazione e politica feudale nel ducato visconteo-sforzesco', in a collection of his essays, *La formazione dello stato regionale e le istituzioni del contado: Secoli XIV–XV* (Turin, 1979), pp. 36–100.

9. Gene Brucker, *The Civic World of Early Renaissance Florence* (Princeton, NJ, 1977), pp. 60–101, 254–79; Samuel K. Cohn, Jr, *The Laboring Classes of Renaissance Florence* (New York, 1980), pp. 65–115; Dale Kent, 'The Florentine reggimento in the fifteenth century', *Renaissance Quarterly*, 28 (1975), pp. 577–84; quotation from John Najemy, 'Guild republicanism in trecento Florence: the successes and ultimate failure of corporate politics', *American Historical Review*, 84 (1979), pp. 70–1.

10. Dennis Romano, *Patricians and Popolani: The Social Foundations of the Venetian Renaissance State* (Baltimore, 1987), esp. pp 152–8.

is ample evidence that the patrician rank and file enthusiastically supported measures to reinforce their class's exclusiveness and to replace ancient prominence with official procedures as the determinant of patrician status.[11] As in Florence, these developments were in reaction to crisis. Massive levies of forced loans during the war of Chioggia (1378–81) had devastated the fortunes of many 'noble' families (as patricians called themselves) and simultaneously enriched *popolani*, some of whom were subsequently ennobled. The government's response was a combination of new programmes to provide public employment for needy nobles and tough new tests of patrician credentials, in order to prevent diffusion of the new prerogatives and a cheapening of noble status by more additions to the patriciate.[12]

In both Venice and Florence, the hegemony of an exclusive ruling class was bolstered by legislation authorizing the state to regulate social identity by age and gender. Venetian laws of 1414 and 1430, designed to keep usurpers out of the patriciate, focused on the transition from youth to adulthood, setting up official procedures in which young claimants to noble status documented their fathers' patrician credentials, the marital and social condition of their mothers, and their own attainment of the requisite age. This information was entered into ledgers which thenceforth served as a continually updated, official registry of the patriciate.[13] In Florence, too, the government's 'tenacious reorganizing penchant' during the period 1382–1433 'insinuated itself into ... the most private realms of citizens' and subjects' social lives', and, as in Venice, new record-keeping practices were set up to create an 'institutionalized and government-controlled memory of families' wealth [which] enhanced the government's ability to intervene in the private affairs of its citizens'.[14] The Florentine initiatives resembled the Venetian ones in making checks of men's ages the occasion of

11. Giorgio Cracco, 'Patriziato e oligarchia a Venezia nel Tre-Quattrocento', in Sergio Bertelli et al., eds, *Florence and Venice: Comparisons and Relations*, Vol. I, *Quattrocento* (Florence, 1979), pp. 71–98; and Stanley Chojnacki, 'Social identity in renaissance Venice: the second *serrata*', *Renaissance Studies*, 8 (1994), pp. 341–58.

12. On ennoblement of commoners and noble-assistance programmes, see Stanley Chojnacki, 'Famiglie e schieramenti sociali nel Trecento: la costituzione della nobiltà dopo la Serrata', in Girolamo Arnaldi et al., eds, *La Storia di Venezia*, Vol. III, *La formazione dello stato patrizio*, (Rome, forthcoming), sections 8–9. On tests of credentials, see Chojnacki, 'Social identity', pp. 343–8.

13. Ibid.

14. Anthony Molho, 'The state and public finance: a hypothesis based on the history of late medieval Florence', in *The Origins of the State in Italy, 1300–1600*, pp. S114–S116.

state acknowledgment of their families' status, further bringing private relationships under the government's documentary purview. In 1429, in an effort to counteract widespread lying about their ages by men eager for the offices on which Florentine patricians, like their Venetian counterparts, increasingly depended for their livelihoods, a law was enacted requiring all candidates for government office to prove their ages by presenting the family *ricordi*. As in Venice, the age proofs were entered into official registers, creating a constantly updated official census of the political class.[15]

In both republics, the state's initiatives pivoted on male identity: that of sons laying claim to the oligarchy's governmental franchise and that of fathers transmitting it. The Venetian law of 1430 required documentation of the identity of the mothers of would-be nobles as well as their fathers, but the chief emphasis was on the patrilineal basis of roles reserved to men. Patriarchy was the principle that linked governmental and private spheres in securing elite hegemony. The ideology of Florence's increasingly aristocratic government after 1382 was modelled on the patriarchal family; in Venice the authority of fathers was enhanced by their inscription as channels of government authority to the family.[16] The new documentary initiatives reinforced patriarchy not just for the ruling class but for all fathers, whose status as family heads was enhanced by the official recognition it received from registration in fiscal censuses.[17]

New definitions of male roles inevitably involved new definitions of female ones. Around 1400, the campaign to consolidate oligarchy led regimes to give serious consideration to women's participation in the social order. Dennis Romano and Elisabeth Crouzet-Pavan have shown how in Venice the government tried to restrict women's presence in urban space as a way of promoting stability.[18] But there and in Florence the state's regulation of women went much further, addressing their vocations, property and behaviour.

15. David Herlihy, 'Age, property, and career in medieval society', in his *Women, Family and Society in Medieval Europe: Historical Essays, 1978–1991* (Providence, RI, and London, 1995), pp. 263–5.

16. Najemy, 'Guild republicanism', p. 69; Stanley Chojnacki, 'Subaltern patriarchs: patrician bachelors in Renaissance Venice', in Claire A. Lees, ed., *Medieval Masculinities: Regarding Men in the Middle Ages* (Minneapolis, MN, 1994), pp. 74–7.

17. David Herlihy and Christiane Klapisch-Zuber, *Tuscans and Their Families: A Study of The Florentine Catasto of 1427* (New Haven, CT, 1985), pp. 9–10, 299–301.

18. Dennis Romano, 'Gender and the urban geography of Renaissance Venice', *Journal of Social History*, 23 (1989), pp. 339–55; Elisabeth Crouzet-Pavan, *'Sopra le acque salse': espaces, pouvoir et société à Venise à la fin du Moyen Age*, 2 vols (Rome, 1992), Vol. II, pp. 799–876, *passim*.

Since those matters lay at the very heart of family interest, the stage was set for intense jockeying between oligarchs in their private dimension and the interests of the oligarchical state. One of the most sensitive issues was government policy aimed at controlling nuns and their sacred spaces.

The state and religious women

Religious women were objects of state concern in two main ways, behavioural and ideological. The most anxious issue was the moral tone of convents. Already in 1349, in the climate of devout terror following the Black Death, Venice's government reacted to the 'abominable frequency with which the crime of fornication is committed in convents', by taking upon itself responsibility for regulating religious communities.[19] The problem persisted, however, and the government responded with steadily escalating penalties. A measure of 1382 prescribed three years in prison for raping a nun, two years for intercourse with a willing nun, and one year for merely entering a monastery; by 1486 a fine of 1,000 lire had been added to the prison term for consensual intercourse, one of 600 lire for unauthorized entry into a convent, six months in prison and 100 lire for disorderly conduct in the vicinity of a monastery, and a draconian three years in prison and 1,500 lire for persuading a nun to leave her convent.[20] The sanctions were unavailing. In 1497 a Franciscan preacher blamed a current outbreak of plague on a catalogue of Venetians' sins, of which 'worst of all, whenever a foreign dignitary comes to Venice, they give him a tour of the city's convents, which in reality are not convents but public bordellos'.[21]

The progressive harshening of the penalties for heterosexual activity in convents documents a perennial problem rooted in the social practices of ruling-class families. Many nuns had no motivation to observe the vow of chastity; they dwelt in convents not in response to spiritual callings but because physical or economic

19. ASV, Maggior Consiglio, Reg. 21, Leona, f. 176r., ibid., Avogaria di Comun, Reg. 2, Capitolare, cap. 289, f. 106v; Guido Ruggiero, *The Boundaries of Eros: Sex Crime and Sexuality in Renaissance Venice* (New York, 1985), pp. 77–84.

20. ASV, Maggior Consiglio, Deliberazioni, Reg. 20, Novella (copy), ff. 410v–411r; Giovanni Scarabello, 'Devianza sessuale ed interventi di giustizia a Venezia nella prima metà del XVI secolo', in *Tiziano e Venezia: Convegno internazionale di studi, Venezia 1976* (Vicenza, 1980), p. 78, n. 9.

21. Rinaldo Fulin et al., eds, *I diarii di Marino Sanuto*, 58 vols (Venice, 1879–1903), Vol. I, col. 836.

obstacles prevented them from marrying. The most important was the relentless rise in dowries during the fifteenth and sixteenth centuries. A growing percentage of girls were taken off the marriage market by a widespread family strategy of marrying off one or two daughters with large marriage portions rather than a larger number with mediocre ones.[22] Because a sexually mature unmarried daughter was regarded as a menace to family honour, it was better to consign her to a convent where at least the fiction of chastity would shield her family from the risk of sexual disgrace.[23] The result was forced vocations. A Venetian law of 1420 noted the 'tears and wailing' of girls 'imprisoned' within convent walls, and a Bolognese writer of the mid-sixteenth century described women 'forced by their fathers and brothers into convents with meager allowances, not to pray and bestow blessings, but to blaspheme and curse the bodies and souls of their parents and relatives, and to indict God for letting them be born'. In the early 1600s the Venetian feminist writer Arcangela Tarabotti, herself a nun, condemned with fierce eloquence the matrimonial system in which fathers, 'motivated purely by worldly pride and the desire to pile up riches', forced daughters into convents in order to funnel family wealth into dowries for one or two of their sisters. By Tarabotti's time the practice had grown so outrageous that the patriarch (archbishop) of Venice, claiming that 2,000 noblewomen were stored in convents 'as though in a public warehouse', actually proposed relaxing the rules governing convent discipline.[24] But his voice was lost in the noise of state efforts, however unavailing, to enforce strict moral behaviour in convents.

The practice of forcing unmarriageable girls into convents highlights the tension between the private interests and the governmental role of elites in matters concerning women. In 1421, to put

22. Anthony Molho, 'Tamquam vere mortua: le professioni religiose-femminili nella Firenze del tardo medioevo', *Società e storia*, 43 (1989), pp. 22–32 and *passim*; and Richard C. Trexler, 'Celibacy in the Renaissance: the nuns of Florence', in idem, *Power and Dependence in Renaissance Florence*, 3 vols (Binghamton, NY, 1993), Vol. II, *The Women of Renaissance Florence*, pp. 17–20, 26–7.

23. Kirshner, 'Pursuing honor while avoiding sin', pp. 8–15; Molho, 'Deception and marriage strategy in Renaissance Florence', pp. 204–12 and *passim*; Christiane Klapisch-Zuber, 'The "cruel mother": maternity, widowhood, and dowry in Florence in the fourteenth and fifteenth centuries', in her *Women, Family, and Ritual*, pp. 119–20.

24. Virginia Cox, 'The single self: feminist thought and the marriage market in early modern Venice', *Renaissance Quarterly*, 48 (1995), pp. 536, 540; Giulio Bistort, *Il Magistrato alle Pompe nella Repubblica di Venezia* (1912; reprinted Bologna, 1969), p. 107. Gabriella Zarri, 'Monasteri femminili e città (secoli XV–XVIII)', in Giorgio Chittolini and Giovanni Miccoli, eds, *La chiesa e il potere politico dal medioevo all'età contemporanea, Storia d'Italia: Annali* (Turin, 1986), Vol. IX, p. 365.

an end to what Archbishop Antoninus called a '*scandalum populorum*', the oligarchs of Florence created a magistracy to 'conserve the morality' of the city's convents, but it was in vain for they continued to fill convents to bursting with their vocationless daughters.[25] The percentage of Florence's female population living in convents, a mere 1.2 per cent in 1336, had risen by 1427 to 6.7 per cent overall, 20 per cent for daughters of the elite; in sheer numbers, the total convent population rose from 906 in 1427 to 2,000 in 1500 and to 2,500 in 1515. The number of convents also climbed steadily, from sixteen in 1368 to twenty-six in 1415, to thirty in 1470; as did the average number of nuns in each, from 14.5 in 1377 to twenty in 1428, to 32.8 in 1478. In Venice, there were thirty-one convents in the 1490s, and, just as in Florence, the patricians who in the council hall legislated stern penalties for seducers of nuns nonetheless forced ever larger numbers of their daughters into the unhappy claustration that fostered seduction. It is estimated that by 1581 no less than three-fifths of all patrician women were in convents, causing an awkward problem for the government: in 1553 the magistracy that supervised nuns went unfilled because of the impossibility of finding a patrician who could meet the requirement of having no daughters, sisters, nieces or cousins in convents.[26]

However, the sexual fallout of marriage strategies was not the only stimulus to the state's interest in religious women. The special charisma associated with female religiosity made them focal points of governmental ideology. A fifteenth-century Florentine declared that the nuns of his city 'spend day and night praying for the most worthy Signoria of Florence', and an abbess in the same city argued for her convent's continued tax exemption by claiming that those prayers, 'coming as they do from persons of such great religion, are more useful than two thousand cavalry'. The government showed

25. Gene Brucker, 'Monasteries, friaries, and nunneries in Quattrocento Florence', in Timothy Verdon and John Henderson, eds, *Christianity and the Renaissance: Image and Religious Imagination in the Quattrocento* (Syracuse, NY, 1990), p. 55; Andrea Zorzi, 'The judicial system in Florence in the fourteenth and fifteenth centuries', in Trevor Dean and K.J.P. Lowe, eds, *Crime, Society and the Law in Renaissance Italy* (Cambridge, UK, 1994), p. 43. The quotation from St Antoninus is in Roberto Bizzocchi, *Chiesa e potere nella Toscana del Quattrocento* (Bologna, 1987), pp. 31–2.

26. Judith C. Brown, 'Monache a Firenze all'inizio dell'età moderna. Un'analisi demografica', *Quaderni storici*, 85 (1994), p. 119; Trexler, 'The nuns of Florence', pp. 10, 12, 16; Brucker, 'Monasteries, friaries, and nunneries', pp. 46–8; Marino Sanudo il giovane, *De origine, situ et magistratibus urbis Venetae ovvero la città di Venetia*, Angela Caracciolo Aricò ed. (Milan, 1980), p. 45; Ruggiero, *Boundaries of Eros*, pp. 76–84; Jutta Sperling, 'Convents and the body politic in late Renaissance Venice' (PhD dissertation, Stanford University, CA, 1995), pp. 12, 16.

its appreciation by subsidizing the construction costs of convents.[27] In 1398 the doge of Venice rewarded the nuns of the convent of Corpus Christi for their prayers for Venice's civic well-being by interceding personally on their behalf in a property dispute with the marquess of Ferrara. The civic importance of nuns in Venice was most solemnly displayed at the convent of the Vergini, where the doge, the convent's official patron, accompanied by the entire executive council (Signoria) as well as other patricians, symbolically married each newly consecrated abbess in an elaborate ceremony, complete with rings and presided over by the patriarch of Venice. The diarist Marino Sanuto's account of the ceremony in 1506 reveals that it had special significance for patrician women; afterwards, he reported, there was a banquet in the convent's refectory for 500 women, 'and few men'.[28]

For republican and princely states alike, the charisma of holy women was a talisman providing protection and moral validation for the regimes that harboured them, especially amid the wars and political upheavals of the years around 1500. Duke Ercole I of Ferrara wrote in 1500 that in those tormented times God had provided 'many spiritual, pious, and religious persons, especially of the female sex, in order that [Italians] might rise from ruin to sublimity'. The sublimity was made concrete by saintly women like Caterina of Bologna, whose prayers were credited with 'the deliverance of the city of Bologna from a seige by a Milanese army', and Osanna of Mantua, who declared herself ready 'to be chopped into morsels and roasted in order to save the city of Mantua'.[29] Princes exerted strenuous efforts to bring such 'living saints' to their courts and to promote due piety in convents, as a way of gaining moral legitimation and popular support. In 1497, Duke Ercole resolved to attract to Ferrara the saintly Lucia di Narni, then living in Viterbo. When the Ferrarese ambassador arrived there to convey his duke's offer, more than 1,000 women crowded the city square to protest, and the leading citizens sent their overlord, the pope, a letter arguing that if Lucia's protective sanctity left Viterbo the city 'would be

27. David Herlihy, 'Did women have a Renaissance? A reconsideration', *Medievalia et Humanistica*, n.s., 13 (1985), pp. 1–22. Brucker, 'Monasteries, friaries, and nunneries', p. 54; Trexler, 'The nuns of Florence', p. 6.
28. *Diarii di Marino Sanuto*, VI, col. 353; Zarri, 'Monasteri femminili e città', p. 375; Daniel Bornstein, 'Giovanni Dominici, the Bianchi, and Venice: symbolic action and interpretive grids', *Journal of Medieval and Renaissance Studies*, 23 (1993), pp. 156–7, n. 42.
29. Zarri, 'Monasteri femminili e città', p. 273.

destroyed to its very foundations'. But Duke Ercole would not be denied. He offered to found a new monastery for Lucia with accommodations for 100 other holy women, who would join with her in praying for the Ferrarese state. In the end his recruitment efforts were successful, but it took two years of negotiations to get Lucia to Ferrara.[30]

The veneration of religious women as essential to civic well-being inspired governmental initiatives for convent reform in places as varied as Mantua, Milan, Brescia, Mirandola, Perugia, Venice, Carpi, Modena, Ravenna, Bologna and Piacenza.[31] Yet again and again that principle of state clashed with the social reality of the convent option's importance for elite families with too many daughters. To complicate matters, even pragmatic parents were emotionally bound to the daughters they put into convents. Roberto Bizzocchi notes that although the oligarchs who governed Florence were indeed concerned about the morality of their city's convents, they stopped short of monastic reforms so strict as to cut their enclosed daughters off completely from affectionate family ties.[32]

Undoubtedly, some nuns were left forgotten and embittered by their forced monacation, but others kept close ties to their families, acting as tutors to their marriageable kinswomen and teaching them reading and writing.[33] Few fathers were as effusively affectionate as the Venetian noble Francesco Morosini, who in 1497 bequeathed an annuity of 25 ducats to his daughter Fiusina, an observant nun at SS. Annunziata, 'whom I love as my very soul' and whom 'I have allowed no harm to befall from the time she entered that convent, in order to be a good father to her, who is my most sweet daughter and my very heart'. But his example was common among Venetians: Vito Canal left bequests to three daughters, nuns in three different convents; the widow Zanetta Contarini left 400 ducats to her three professed sisters.[34]

30. Gabriella Zarri, 'Pietà e profezia alle corti padane: le pie consigliere dei principi', in *Le sante vive: profezie di corte e devozione femminile tra '400 e '500* (Turin, 1990), pp. 54–5.

31. Ibid., p. 52.   32. Bizzocchi, *Chiesa e potere*, p. 33.

33. Sharon Strocchia, 'Learning the virtues: convent schools and female culture in Renaissance Florence', in Barbara Whitehead, ed., *Women's Education in Early Modern Europe: A History, 1500–1800* (New York, forthcoming); also Stanley Chojnacki, '"The most serious duty": motherhood, gender, and patrician culture in Renaissance Venice', in Marilyn Migiel and Juliana Schiesari, eds, *Refiguring Woman: Perspectives on Gender and the Italian Renaissance* (Ithaca, NY, 1991), p. 139.

34. ASV, Procuratori di San Marco, Commissarie de ultra, busta 221, fasc. 1, Francesco Morosini, account book, entry for 1 February 1497/98; Notarile, testamenti, busta 558, Gambaro, nos 171, 185; Giudici del Proprio, Diudicatum, Reg. 2, f. 135r.

Parental attachment to daughters in religious life spilled over
into the political arenas dominated by those same families. The
majority of the Roman women who in the early 1400s gathered
around the charismatic Santa Francesca Romana were members
of formerly prominent families which had fallen from power following an abortive coup against Pope Boniface IX in 1398. Their
association with Santa Francesca's charitable work provided an
alternative prominence to their politically disgraced families. During
political struggles between citizens and nobles in mid-sixteenth-
century Parma, the Benedictine convent of San Paolo denied entry
to the daughters of feudal families: 'no matter what means the leading feudatories might try, [the nuns] will never be willing to accept
them'. In 1533 Corpus Christi in Venice was once again embroiled
with the government, this time over the election of a new prioress.
According to the papal nuncio, the nuns on the two sides in the
dispute between them rallied the support of 'eighty patrician houses',
and it took the Council of Ten to resolve the controversy, by ordering the relatives of the dissident nuns to persuade them to submit to
the new prioress 'and to indicate in writing their obedience to the
most excellent Council of Ten'. The princely and noble families
of the northern Italian courts also put their stamp on female religiosity, notably in founding and sustaining houses of Franciscan
clarisse (clares) as convent communities for their own womenfolk.
Their power is displayed in the 'capture' of the community of Corpus
Domini in Ferrara. Founded in the early 1400s by pious middle-
class women, in the early 1430s it was taken over by a wealthy noble
widow who used her connections with the pope and the Este rulers
to reorganize it into a community of *clarisse* under the rule of her
sister, a nun in the *clarisse* motherhouse in Mantua, which had itself
been founded in 1420 by the marchioness of that city.[35]

These examples illustrate the contradictory role of convents in
the intertwining of oligarchy, state and gender. The religious charisma they radiated made them legitimating symbols for regimes
and havens for devout daughters of the elite. But the moral disorders that resulted from the use of convents as repositories for

---

35. Katherine Gill, 'Open monasteries for women in late medieval and early
modern Italy: two Roman examples', in Craig A. Monson, ed., *The Crannied Wall:
Women, Religion, and the Arts in Early Modern Europe* (Ann Arbor, MI, 1992), pp. 24–
5; Zarri, 'Monasteri femminili e città', pp. 363, 371–2; Mary Martin McLaughlin,
'Creating and recreating communities of women: the case of Corpus Domini, Ferrara',
in Judith M. Bennett, et al., eds, *Sisters and Workers in the Middle Ages* (Chicago, 1989),
pp. 272–4.

unmarriageable upper-class women provoked government regulation. Women in religion imparted moral stature to the state and evoked moral supervision by the state, contributing doubly to its institutional and ideological development. The key was the crucial importance of convents to elite families. Despite the deeply embedded convention that nuns 'died' to the secular world, women in religion exerted a multiform influence on the interconnected evolutions of government and oligarchy.[36] But not the greatest influence. The marriages of their sisters were the occasion of even more intricate interweavings of family and state.

Family and the state

In their dealings with religious women and their efforts to set parameters for orderly sexuality, governments complicated their relationship with domestic patriarchy. The authority of husbands and fathers was the mortar holding together the social order that secured regimes and elites and the main conduit between state and family. But it was also the most formidable antagonist of government regulation of private life, and was itself riven by contradictions. The state's reliance on fathers reinforced their domestic authority, but it also laid down the rules for their exercise of it. That giving-and-taking fomented tension between governmental and domestic patriarchy, most acutely in government programmes that both supported and regulated fathers' arrangements of their daughters' marriages. Those programmes pitted the state against fathers, exacerbated divisions within the elite, and added complicating new dimensions to relations between fathers, husbands, and the women who moved between them.

The most creative marriage initiative was the establishment of the Florentine Dowry Fund, the Monte delle Doti, in 1424–25. Designed to alleviate the government's fiscal problems, it was also conceived as a marriage-promoting solution to persistent demographic worries. Its creativity lay in its practicality, providing families with a government-secured investment vehicle for assembling the dowries that were indispensable for their daughters' marriages. With the Dowry Fund the state inserted itself deeply into family affairs, but its role went beyond financing marriages. The Monte delle Doti made the government the guarantor of the family honour that hinged on the transferral of the dangerous sexuality

36. Molho, 'Tamquam vere mortua', pp. 32–44.

of women from father to husband. The language of the enabling legislation stated its guiding premise: '[d]etermined to shore up the frailty of the female sex', the government undertook to ensure that 'provided with dowries, however small, women will be certain to lead virtuous and praiseworthy lives'.[37]

Only a few years earlier Venice's government had inserted itself into dowry transactions, but in the opposite way. Where the Monte delle Doti helped Florentines keep up with dowry inflation, a Venetian law of 1420 sought to arrest it, setting an official maximum of 1,600 ducats for marriage settlements. The rationale was the same: to protect families' property and honour by facilitating the marriages of as many young women as possible, in order to lessen the forced monacation of tearful daughters and relieve families of the 'shame and danger' of having unmarried adult daughters at home. The preamble made clear the government's eminent domain in patriarchal matters: since there was 'no hope' that fathers would stop competing with each other in dowry size, 'it is necessary that that corruption be corrected by our regime'.[38]

Measures to facilitate and regulate dowries put regimes at cross-purposes with their own membership and different oligarchic interests with each other, because of the conflicting claims at stake in marriage. For all families, dowries were the best protection against the threat of sexual disgrace that hovered over unmarried daughters, and the best means of repairing damaged reputations. Venice's criminal courts routinely ordered rapists and seducers of unmarried girls, deemed guilty of inflicting 'the greatest shame and perpetual dishonour' on their victims' fathers, to provide dowries so that the girls might recover their honour. For the bishop of Pistoia, dowries were the means by which girls were 'led to honour', a linkage recognized in practice by the Florentine Marco Parenti, who described one woman's dowry as 'wealth and honour, which amount to 1,400 [florins]'.[39] Private and public observers thus agreed

37. Kirshner, 'Pursuing honor while avoiding sin', p. 60; Anthony Molho, *Marriage Alliance in Late Medieval Florence* (Cambridge, MA, 1994), pp. 139–43; Julius Kirshner and Anthony Molho, 'The dowry fund and the marriage market in early quattrocento Florence', *Journal of Modern History*, 50 (1978), pp. 403–38.

38. ASV, Senato, Misti, Reg. 53 f. 70r; Stanley Chojnacki, 'Marriage legislation and patrician society in fifteenth-century Venice', in Bernard S. Bachrach and David Nicholas, eds, *Law, Custom, and the Social Fabric in Medieval Europe: Essays in Honor of Bryce Lyon* (Kalamazoo, MI, 1990), pp. 163–84.

39. Ruggiero, *Boundaries of Eros*, pp. 17–44, 89–108; Kirshner, 'Pursuing honor while avoiding sin', pp. 4–11 and *passim*; Lorenzo Fabbri, *Alleanza matrimoniale e patriziato nella Firenze del '400. Studio sulla famiglia Strozzi* (Florence, 1991), p. 73; Klapisch-Zuber, ' "The cruel mother" ', pp. 119–20; Molho, *Marriage Alliance*, pp. 139–43; idem, 'Deception and marriage strategy', pp. 207–10.

that the surest way for fathers to safeguard their families' sexual honour was by dowering their daughters. The problem was that even with government programmes, securing honourable marriages became increasingly difficult owing to a relentless rise in dowry levels. Upper-class Florentine dowries, which in 1400 ranged from 600–900 florins, increased to 1,200–1,600 in the 1460s, and around 2,000 in 1500; overall, between 1425 and 1524 the average dowry soared 83 per cent. In Venice, the median net patrician dowry (exclusive of trousseau) rose from 800 ducats in the last third of the fourteenth century, to about 1,100 in the mid-fifteenth century, and 2,000 in 1505-7.[40]

In these circumstances, fathers seized on governmental initiatives which might increase the dowries of their marriageable daughters. Thanks to the Monte delle Doti, for example, the investments of 90 and 60 florins that Francesco Tommaso made for his daughters in 1433 turned into dowries of, respectively, 548 florins in 1445 and 500 florins in 1448. Wealthier Florentines also took advantage of the Fund; 80 per cent of the 1,200 florins that Lucrezia Tornabuoni brought to no less than Piero de' Medici in 1444 came from the account her father had opened for her. The Tornabuoni had lots of company among their fellow patricians: the Adimari made investments for fifty-one of their daughters, the Rucellai for ninety-four, the Medici for 104, the Strozzi for 113.[41] Even the ledgers of the Fund served crafty Florentines: many falsely lowered their daughters' ages when opening accounts, inventing official documentation of their youthful chastity, the *sine qua non* for honourable brides. Venice's patricians also turned their government's marriage policy to private purposes. Many post-1420 marriage contracts explicitly proclaimed adherence to the 1,600-ducat ceiling, 'as the law requires', and included marriage portions of exactly that amount. For families whose membership in the patriciate was comparatively recent, or whose economic situation was shaky, meeting an officially set standard for respectable noble dowries was a ready way of demonstrating reputability.[42]

40. Molho, *Marriage Alliance*, p. 310; Stanley Chojnacki, 'From trousseau to groomgift in late medieval Venice', in Thomas F. Madden and Ellen E. Kittell, eds, *Venice: Society and Crusade: Studies in Honor of Donald E. Queller* (Urbana, IL, 1998); Venetian figures for 1468–76 (122 dowries) are in ASV, Giudici del Proprio, Diiudicatum, Regs. 1, 2, *passim*; for 1505-7 (72 dowries), ibid., Avogadori di Comun, Contratti di Nozze, Reg. 140/1, ff. 1r–66v.

41. Kirshner, 'Pursuing honor while avoiding sin', pp. 19–20; Molho, *Marriage Alliance*, p. 91.

42. Molho, 'Deception and marriage strategy', *passim*; Chojnacki, 'Social identity', pp. 354–5.

Government measures doubtless helped families, but dowry standards were a moving target because of the powerful forces pushing them upward. Not least of these were parental efforts to secure their daughters' well-being, by 'lodging' ('alogare') them with husbands who would give them, in Alessandra Strozzi's phrase, as much 'status and nobility' as possible, but also providing them with resources over and above their dowries.[43] In 1397 the Venetian noble Giovanni Morosini, who seven years earlier had given his daughter a dowry of 1,000 ducats (which in Venetian law and practice was her personal property), now bequeathed her the life income from 10,000 ducats in the state's funded debt (*prestiti*), as well as 2,000 ducats for the dowry of each of her two daughters, who of course were members of a different lineage. Fourteen years later another patrician, Nicolò Mudazzo, left his widowed daughter 3,200 ducats in the state funds, enabling her in turn to bequeath 1,450 ducats to her six married or professed sisters and her own daughter's dowry.[44] Paternal generosity, complementing that of mothers, gave such Venetian women the means of benefiting not only their fathers' but other lineages, and most especially of enriching their own daughters' dowries, further fuelling their increase. Evidence for Florence presented by Isabelle Chabot, Julius Kirshner, and Christiane Klapisch-Zuber conveys a picture of wives and widows whose propertyless dependence contrasts starkly with the social and economic resources of their counterparts in Venice. However, just as in Venice there were many patrician wives in grim circumstances, so the Florentine picture is blurred by the confident initiatives of the widow Alessandra Macinghi Strozzi, who contributed her own dowry wealth to that of her daughter, and the other widows whose wide-ranging and substantial beneficence is documented by Elaine Rosenthal.[45]

43. For 'alogare', see Molho, *Marriage Alliance*, p. 132; on concern for daughters, see Heather Gregory, 'Daughters, dowries and the family in fifteenth-century Florence', *Rinascimento*, 2nd ser., 27 (1987), pp. 233–7; Donald E. Queller and Thomas F. Madden, 'Father of the bride: fathers, daughters, and dowries in late medieval and early Renaissance Venice', *Renaissance Quarterly*, 46 (1993), pp. 705–9; Stanley Chojnacki, 'The power of love: wives and husbands in late medieval Venice', in Mary Erler and Maryanne Kowaleski, eds, *Women and Power in the Middle Ages* (Athens, GA, 1988), pp. 130, 133.

44. ASV, Notarile, Testamenti, busta 571, G. Gibellino, no. 106; busta 1255, Zane, protocollo, ff. 184v–186v, 109r–110r (24 and 26 July 1411).

45. Isabelle Chabot, '"La sposa in nero". La ritualizzazione del lutto delle vedove fiorentine (secoli XIV–XV)', *Quaderni storici*, 86 (1994), pp. 450–3; Julius Kirshner, 'Materials for a gilded cage: non-dotal assets in Florence, 1300–1500', in David I. Kertzer and Richard P. Saller, eds, *The Family in Italy from Antiquity to the Present* (New

But the most insistent pressure pushing dowries upward came not from parental generosity but the imperatives of social honour that pressed on both sides of a marriage alliance. Defending his son in a breach-of-promise suit in 1457, the Venetian noble Jacopo Gabriel declared that 'it is unthinkable that the dowry of 350 ducats which donna Orsa [Dolfin, herself a noble] promised my son Giovanni is suitable for a noble of respectable status such as my son; indeed, it would hardly be appropriate for an artisan'. He and his brother, he pointedly noted, had received dowries of 2,500 ducats from their wives.[46] Alessandra Strozzi, who had made a similarly scornful artisan reference ten years earlier, summed it up: 'whoever takes a wife demands money', and the more prominent the wife-taker, the larger his demands, and the greater the eagerness of his future wife's family to meet them, regardless of legislated limits.[47]

Not only did the dowry of Jacopo Gabriel's wife set her family and his apart from poorer nobles like Orsa Dolfin, it also violated the limit imposed in 1420. Wealthy families found the advantages of giving and getting large dowries more compelling than laws aimed at levelling the matrimonial playing field. In Venice, as many as one-half of fifteenth-century patrician dowries exceeded the legal limit; in Florence, the fathers of more than half of the richest girls of marriageable age declined to open Dowry Fund accounts for their daughters.[48] Their disregard of official norms and programmes suggests that government efforts to help hard-pressed families meet dowry standards actually ended up encouraging dowry inflation: directly, as Antonio Strozzi noted in Florence in 1450, 'because of the convenience of the Monte [delle Doti]' for well-placed families seeking to augment other dowry resources; indirectly, because they spurred wealthy families like the Gabriel and their in-laws to distance themselves from their needier fellow-patricians by disdaining

Haven, CT, 1991), pp. 184–207; Klapisch-Zuber, 'The "cruel mother"'. On Florentine widows, see Lauro Martines, 'A way of looking at women in Renaissance Florence', *Journal of Medieval and Renaissance Studies*, 4 (1974), pp. 15–28; Ann Morton Crabb, 'How typical was Alessandra Macinghi Strozzi of fifteenth-century Florentine widows?', in Louise Mirrer, ed., *Upon My Husband's Death: Widows in the Literature and Histories of Medieval Europe* (Ann Arbor, MI, 1992), pp. 47–68; Elaine Rosenthal, 'The position of women in Renaissance Florence: neither autonomy nor subjection', in Peter Denley and Caroline Elam, eds, *Florence and Italy: Renaissance Studies in Honour of Nicolai Rubinstein* (London, 1988), pp. 369–81.

46. Archivio Patriarcale di Venezia, Sezione Antica, Causarum Matrimoniorum, busta 2, fasc. 1, doc. 5 (27 July 1457).

47. Fabbri, *Alleanza matrimoniale*, pp. 66, 73.

48. Chojnacki, 'Social identity', p. 355; Molho, *Marriage Alliance*, Table 3.1, p. 87.

government restrictions and flaunting lavish settlements given and received.[49]

More than articulating social differences, the marriage initiatives of the early fifteenth century complicated gender relations by imposing a public dimension upon relations between fathers, husbands, and the women who moved between them. The crux of the issue involved what Isabelle Chabot characterizes as the 'paradox which struck at agnatic ideology', namely, that though supposedly excluded from an inheritance system whose 'material and symbolic identity was exclusively masculine, patrilineal', married women possessed a share of their family's patrimony which dowry inflation was making larger and larger.[50] This vastly complicated property relations between men and women and between families. Chabot and Klapisch-Zuber have described how Florentines responded by devising exchange practices that kept a woman's dowry and trousseau in the hands of either her husband or her father, but the example of Lena Davizzi suggests that not all women were denied possession of their dowries.[51] Recently widowed in 1422, she infuriated her helpless brothers by betaking herself and her dowry to a convent. They were doubly angry because the dowry had been more than her rightful share of the family patrimony in the first place; indeed, amassing it in order to give her 'as much ease and honour' as possible had imposed heavy hardship and obligations on them. Unremitting dowry inflation eventually increased women's property to such an alarming extent that in 1619 Francesco Acciaiuoli would warn the Grand Duke of Tuscany that lavish dowries would end up 'shifting all private wealth to women'.[52] Doubtless an exaggeration, but anchored in the reality of the conflict inherent in men's need to preserve property in the male line and their desire for honour and connections from marriage. Venetian men also made sacrifices to give their women large dowries. One wife acknowledged in 1391 that 'my father took so little account of his need to provide for his many children that he gave me a marriage portion worth more than half his worldly goods', and a man noted

49. Fabbri, *Alleanza matrimoniale*, p. 75.

50. Chabot, '"La sposa in nero"', p. 424; Thomas Kuehn, 'Some ambiguities of female inheritance ideology in the Renaissance', in his *Law, Family, and Women: Toward a Legal Anthropology of Renaissance Italy* (Chicago, 1991), pp. 238–57.

51. Fabbri, *Alleanza matrimoniale*, p. 80; Chabot, '"La sposa in nero"', pp. 449–53; Klapisch-Zuber, 'The Griselda complex: dowry and marriage gifts in the Quattrocento', in her *Women, Family, and Ritual*, pp. 224–31 and *passim*.

52. Molho, *Marriage Alliance*, pp. 303–4, n. 22.

in 1459 that his married daughter had 'received much more than all her brothers will get'. Such cases were not rare.[53]

It was the worrisome impact of women's dowries on the wealth of men that underlay government efforts to restrain them, but the state's attention only added to women's economic and social stature. One of the motives impelling Venetian legislators to limit dowries in 1420 was alarm that the fathers who gave their daughters large dowries 'gravely damaged and prejudiced their male heirs', and a 1505 law, which yielded to reality by raising the maximum from 1,600 to 3,000 ducats, invited sons to sue their fathers' estates for the equivalent of any excess over the new limit that had gone to their sisters' dowries.[54] The rulers of Pistoia echoed those of Venice and Florence in worrying that 'the price of dowries exceeds the substance and patrimony of husbands, and the fathers or brothers of the brides become poor and are stripped bare by them'.[55] Such sentiments pitted dowry-rich women against their menfolk, but the reality was more complex, because husbands and fathers had competing rather than common interests, and government intervention gave a sharper edge to their rivalry.

The Florentine government seems to have been supportive chiefly of husbands. The revised statutes of 1415 reaffirmed a husband's right to the entire dowry of his predeceased wife in the absence of children, strengthened his control over her non-dotal property during the marriage and his right to one-third of it at her death, and bluntly denied wives the right to bequeath their dowries to anyone but husband and children. They also protected the integrity of the patrilineage by forbidding a widow returning to her father's or brothers' house to bring her children with her.[56] This last measure betrays the statute-writers' sense of the opposing interests of a woman's paternal and marital relations, the conflict, emphasized by Klapisch-Zuber and Chabot, between her status as daughter and as wife. Venice's rulers tended to be more solicitous of wives'

53. ASV, Notarile, Testamenti, busta 364, Darvasio, no. 44; Cancelleria Inferiore, Notai, busta 175, Rizzo, protocollo, f. 35v.

54. Stanley Chojnacki, 'Nobility, women, and the state: marriage regulation in Venice, 1420–1535', in Trevor Dean and K.J.P. Lowe, eds, *Marriage in Italy*, 1300–1600 (Cambridge, UK, 1997).

55. Diane Owen Hughes, 'Sumptuary law and social relations in renaissance Italy', in John Bossy, ed., *Disputes and Settlements: Law and Human Relations in the West*, (Cambridge, UK, 1983), p. 95.

56. *Statuta populi et communis Florentiae, anno salutis mccccxv*, 3 vols (Freiburg [Florence], 1778–83), Vol. I, lib. 2. rubb. 129–30, pp. 223–4. Thomas Kuehn kindly made this text available to me.

natal families, levying the penalties for violations of the 1420 law on the husbands who received illegal dowries rather than the fathers who gave them, though both sides were made liable in the 1505 revision. Riches pursuing bridegrooms caused a different kind of concern. When another effort was made to stop the relentless inflation in 1535, the legislators lamented that young patricians were abandoning the time-honoured commercial and maritime traditions of their forefathers, being content instead to live off 'these excessive dowries' that their wives brought them.[57]

In the end, the state's efforts to protect the male stake in dowries foundered on the irreconcilability of fathers' and husband's interests, and the cross-purposes in its own efforts to restrain and to support dowries added a third chord to the dissonance. The overlaps and conflicts among the varied interests, public and private, rich and poor, paternal and marital, that were clustered under the umbrella of patriarchy afforded women of the elites the space and resources to pursue their own objectives, and the state's tortuous attempts to sort matters out only underscored the contradictions of male dominance. The clearest evidence comes from sumptuary legislation. A Florentine law of 1511 declared that women were spending so much on 'disorderly and sumptuous' clothing and jewels that their husbands got 'poco frutto' from their dowries, and a follow-up measure of 1516 lamented that the 1511 law was being intentionally misinterpreted 'by both men and women'. Those complaints echoed Venetian ones that women's extravagant expenditures 'on wicked and impractical' adornments 'consumed their husbands and sons' or 'ruined their husbands and fathers'.[58] The government's solution, to require husbands or fathers 'or whoever has authority over these women' to restrain them or pay a fine, reveals its own helplessness in the face of the contradictory impulses within patriarchy. Enjoining men to stop practices that 'ruined' them was unpromising in itself, but its fatuousness was accentuated by the connivance of those same men in the magnificence of their womenfolk, 'the status-bearers', in Diane Hughes's apt phrase, 'of their fathers' lineage and their husbands'.[59]

Generous dowries and trousseaux forced sisters into convents, impoverished brothers and sparked in-law competition for the property and loyalty of married women, but they also advertized the

57. Chojnacki, 'Nobility, women, and the state', forthcoming.
58. Molho, *Marriage Alliance*, p. 301, n. 15; Bistort, *Il Magistrato alle Pompe*, pp. 123, 154.
59. Hughes, 'Sumptuary law and social relations', p. 99.

wealth, status and honour of the families that gave and received them.[60] Governments may indeed have been determined to rein in expenditures on women, as Catherine Killerby Kovesi has recently insisted, but their initiatives were whipsawed by the cross-purposes of the very men who voted in the council chambers: not only between fathers and husbands but within individual men, themselves likely to be at one time or another – and often simultaneously – husbands, fathers of daughters and fathers of sons.[61] In the end, the principal effect of the state's efforts to sort out this welter of interests was to bear witness in its own decrees that the inherent rivalry of fathers and husbands gave women space and leverage in the marriage practices where public and private life merged.

Indeed, Giulia Calvi has argued that 'hundreds of women were given voice in public institutions, because the state, in its phase of centralization and expansion ... legitimated these women as its interlocutors'. Among the duties of the Florentine Magistrato dei Pupilli, created in 1393 to look after the interests of fatherless children, was that of validating widows' assumption of the family headship vested in them in their husbands' wills. The Magistrato thus officially authorized the exercise of patriarchal responsibilities by such widows. The result reverberated in family and lineage. According to Calvi, the interaction of widows and the Magistrato dei Pupilli contributed to a 'softening of the formal structure of the patrilineal system', sanctioning 'a bilineal orientation that was not only affective and informal, but, indeed, took shape on the basis of [women's] prerogatives and roles, the social and juridical importance of which [the Magistrato] explicitly and officially recognized'.[62]

The Florentine government's adaptation to the social ambiguity of well-dowered widows complicated its support for the patrilineage. At the same time that the revised statutes of 1415 reaffirmed women's lack of freedom to dispose of their dowries, they also gave them the right to reclaim the dowries when widowed, in order to facilitate their remarriage. Nor were the Florentine rulers alone in

60. Anna Esposito, 'Strategie matrimoniali e livelli di richezza', in Maria Chiabò et al., eds, *Alle origini della nuova Roma: Martino V (1417–1431), Atti del Convegno* (Rome, 1992), pp. 579–81; Christiane Klapisch-Zuber, 'Les corbeilles de la mariée', in his *La maison et le nom: stratégies et rituels dans l'Italie de la Renaissance* (Paris, 1990), pp. 215–16 and *passim*; Chojnacki, 'From trousseau to groomgift', forthcoming.

61. Katherine Kovesi Killerby, 'Practical problems in the enforcement of Italian sumptuary law, 1200–1500', in Dean and Lowe, eds, *Crime, Society and the Law*, pp. 99–120.

62. Calvi, 'Diritti e legami: madri, figli, stato in Toscana (XVI–XVIII secolo)', *Quaderni storici*, 86 (1994), pp. 487–9.

their attentiveness to widows; revised statutes in Milan in 1396 also guaranteed widows' dowries for remarriage.[63] The wealth going into dowries prompted the solicitude of Venice's rulers as well. In 1449, to alleviate the 'labore magno' that some widows had to go through to recover their dowries from their husbands' estates, a law was passed requiring notaries to deposit in the government chancery copies of all dowry receipts and wills in which husbands acknowledged their wives' dowries, thereby providing the widows with readily available documentation for reclaiming them.[64] Widows were a special category, but in Venice the government acknowledged the nuanced identities of other women as well. The dowry limitation law of 1420 explicitly exempted widows and unmarried women aged twenty-four or over, both of whom 'should retain the liberty they now possess' – evidence of official awareness of the difficulties such women had in marrying. It likewise exempted the daughters of wealthy *popolani* who married nobles; they could bring dowries of 2,000 ducats rather than 1,600 and thereby infuse new wealth into the patriciate. The attention to distinctions among women even took in physical characteristics. In 1425 the Senate waived the dowry ceiling altogether for the blind and in 1444 extended the waiver to lame and misshapen women, in order that those 'injured by nature but adorned by fortune also could marry'.[65]

Conclusion

The social interventionism of the early fifteenth-century state produced official definitions of the roles of men and women in society, fashioning a prescriptive gender structure that hardened the differences between husbands and fathers (and by silent exclusion highlighted the otherness of unmarried male adults), and gave official standing to the variations and nuances of womanhood by vocation, age, marital status and social class. Sumptuary legislation acknowledged the economic leverage of wives; dowry policies showed governmental concern with the disruptive potential of female sexuality; and efforts to regulate convents merged civic morality with the

63. Anna Caso, 'Per la storia della società milanese: i corredi nuziali nell'ultima età viscontea e nel periodo della Repubblica Ambrosiana (1433–1450), dagli atti del notaio Protaso Sansoni', *Nuova rivista storica*, 65 (1981), p. 524.

64. ASV, Maggior Consiglio, Reg. 22, Ursa, f. 176rv.

65. ASV, Senato, Misti, Reg. 53, f. 70v; Reg. 55, f. 101v; Senato, Terra, Reg. 1, f. 115v.

consequences of private marriage strategies. All those initiatives attest to the state's recognition that the social order necessary to the security of regimes required active and persistent attention to the troubling uncertainties of the ambiguous and flexible social position of women and of the manifold circumstances of men's relations with them.

That attention was part of a wide-ranging effort to regulate politics and society in a way that would secure regimes shaken by recent upheavals. The consequence was a seismic change in the boundaries between the public and the private, with the state now absorbing within its domain fundamental concerns of the domestic realm. Tracing the long-term trajectory of this process (though with a French-centred chronology different from that offered here), Roger Chartier argues that the 'construction of the modern state ... is a necessary condition for defining a private sphere as distinct from a clearly identifiable public one'. His suggestion that the state did not so much take over the private sphere as clarify its dimensions is endorsed by Elisabeth Crouzet-Pavan, who sees the effect already accomplished in Venice by the late fifteenth century.[66] Yet, continued resistance to governmental direction supports Philippe Ariès's suggestion that the ambitious reach of the early modern state exceeded its capacity to impose its will, that families withstood the governmental campaign to appropriate the public sphere.[67] In Florence, triumphant Medici partisans in 1512 revoked a dowry limit imposed the previous year, on the principle that 'marriages must be free, and everyone should be free to endow his daughters, sisters and other female relatives as he sees fit and as he likes, because one must be able to arrange his affairs in his way'; in Venice, the government's third attempt at dowry limitation, in 1535, was necessitated by the 'immoderate dowries' provided by fathers who, in spite of the previous legislation, 'had no respect' for the state's authority.[68]

Aggressive, institutionalized state intervention in the affairs of society in the late fourteenth and early fifteenth centuries, and the conflicting private responses to it, made the dimensions of the domestic realm an open, contested question, with fatherly and husbandly authority reinforced by government initiatives but also

---

66. Crouzet-Pavan, 'Sopra le acque salse', II, pp. 875–6; Roger Chartier, 'Figures of modernity: introduction', in *A History of Private Life*, Vol. 3, Roger Chartier, ed., *Passions of the Renaissance* (1986; English trans. Cambridge, MA, 1989), p. 15.
67. P. Ariès, 'Introduction', in ibid., pp. 9–10.
68. Molho, *Marriage Alliance*, p. 302; ASV, Senato, Terra, Reg. 28, f. 151r.

resistant to them when the state threatened the private interests of husbands or fathers, themselves now more clearly differentiated by state action. The divisions and conflicts within the polymorphous patriarchy of the Italian cities marked out a space where women with economic resources, social support and personal ability could manoeuvre their way through, between, or against those interests. How they did so and with what success are questions that need much research. But scholarship has already laid the groundwork for a fuller discussion of the relationship between gender and the Renaissance state, for a more comprehensive political history. Such a discussion, it is to be hoped, would explore not only how expanding government sought to shape gender roles and relations, but also the reverse: how new complications and ambiguities in the relationships between men and women, provoked by the momentous political and social developments of the fourteenth, fifteenth and sixteenth centuries, influenced the direction of governmental growth in the Renaissance.

CHAPTER FOUR

Person and Gender in the Laws

THOMAS KUEHN

When, in 1943, the legal historian Pier Leicht approached the law of persons and family in the Renaissance, he treated gender under the heading of physical factors that restricted legal capacity. Three decades later Manlio Bellomo saw the restriction of women's legal capacities as a result of their status within families as political entities, where all family members were subordinated to an overriding *ragion di famiglia*.[1] Although positing a different rationale behind this restricted status, both scholars arrived at similar conclusions regarding the lack of autonomy and self-expression that characterized the legal situation of women – conclusions that have become both pervasive and enormously influential on social historians intent on studying the actual lives and experiences of Renaissance Italian women, rather than simply the rules that applied to them. Thus, Christiane Klapisch-Zuber has observed that, in contrast to men, Renaissance scholarship has 'portrayed [the female] as confined in a straitjacket of irrefutable normative texts and never as an actor in history', and, indeed, Romeo De Maio has gone so far as to claim that the law amounted to a veritable 'prison for women'.[2]

The broadly cultural dimension of this normative situation is widely known. In just one often-cited example, Paolo da Certaldo, the fourteenth-century Florentine compiler of proverbial wisdom, warned his readers that woman 'is a very vain thing and easily moved': the source of all sorts of 'dishonours, shames, sins and

---

1. P.S. Leicht, *Storia del diritto italiano: il diritto privato*, Vol. I: *Diritto delle persone e di famiglia* (Milan, 1943), pp. 95–101; Manlio Bellomo, *La condizione giuridica della donna in Italia* (Turin, 1970), pp. 13–15, 35–41, 61–2, 69–76.

2. Christiane Klapisch-Zuber, 'The medievalist: women and the serial approach', in M. Perot, ed., *Writing Women's History* (Oxford, 1992), p. 25; Romeo De Maio, *Donna e Rinascimento* (Milan, 1987), pp. 86 and 99.

expenses' and hence dangerous when not under the control of a husband. Paolo summed up the claims of *ragion di famiglia* in distinctly gendered terms when he advised a dying man against leaving his property and children solely in the hands of his wife, '[Since she] will leave your children, take their patrimony, or treat them badly or allow them to be badly treated by others'.[3]

Some historians have reacted against this bleak picture of seclusion and lack of autonomy, and have pointed out how Renaissance women employed various forms of manipulation, subversion or expression to mitigate the rigours of their subordination to men, the patriarchal household and the patrilineage.[4] As a result, studies of gender have become more nuanced. It is no longer axiomatic that all women always shared the same interests and experiences, nor that the ideological and stereotypical notions of female weaknesses on which laws were based necessarily proved that Renaissance Italians believed there was a diversity of interests between men and women. It is now widely agreed that Italians understood the interests of both sexes in more complex terms – each as socially responsible, each often pursuing the same goals.[5] The very lineage solidarity and claims of *ragion di famiglia* that Bellomo saw as constraining women was built, in fact, on the combination of male and female, which 'suggests an important qualification to assuming the apparent autonomy of male interests'.[6] Were not fathers, husbands, brothers and sons also constrained by the legal structures of patriarchy? While the dowry, for example, signified women's exclusion from their natal patrilineage's property, the dotal system also placed limits on the men who had to raise it and, following marriage, manage it; reclaimed dowries moreover gave a certain

3. Paolo da Certaldo, *Libro di buoni costumi*, A. Schiaffini, ed., in *Mercanti scrittori: Ricordi nella Firenze tra Medioevo e Rinascimento*, V. Branca, ed. (Milan, 1986), pp. 26, 29, 90–1.

4. Klapisch-Zuber, 'Holy dolls: play and piety in Florence in the quattrocento', in her *Women, Family, and Ritual in Renaissance Italy* (Chicago, 1985), pp. 310–29; Sharon Strocchia, 'Funerals and the politics of gender in early Renaissance Florence', in M. Migiel and J. Schiesari, eds, *Refiguring Woman: Perspectives on Gender and the Italian Renaissance* (Ithaca, NY, 1991), pp. 155–68; Elaine Rosenthal, 'The position of women in Renaissance Florence: neither autonomy nor subjection', in P. Denley and C. Elam, eds, *Florence and Italy: Renaissance Studies in Honour of Nicolai Rubinstein* (London, 1989), pp. 369–81.

5. Jenny Kermode and Garthine Walker, 'Introduction', in J. Kermode and G. Walker, eds, *Women, Crime and the Courts in Early Modern England* (Chapel Hill, NC, 1994), p. 21.

6. Marilyn Strathern, 'Introduction', in *Dealing with Inequality: Analyzing Gender Relations in Melanesia and Beyond* (ed. Marilyn Strathern) (Cambridge, UK, 1987), p. 15.

power, if not authority, to widows. Patriarchy had its price, and the mechanisms of law operated quite often to make sure the price was paid, by men as well as by women. In this light, women have emerged as socially responsible persons – historical, as well as legal, agents whose rights and actions could become important, if not occasionally paramount, and whose interests were not confined in some alternative sphere with its own scale of values.[7]

Aware of such changing attitudes, some historians and anthropologists have sought to advance the discussion of Renaissance law beyond notions of gender, with their attendant sense of oppositions and limitations, to those of social personhood. While gender encompasses categorizations of persons, things and events in terms of sexual imagery, its inventive possibilities in a social context arise in the way that personal relationships are constructed through it. Avoiding any presupposition 'that takes the differentiated single sex state as a "natural" reference point', the concept of social personhood points to relationships between individuals.[8]

The social person is an agent, a conscious and intelligent actor. Western individualism takes agency in a peculiar direction, as a form of authorship: 'there is a taken for granted identity between the agent as a subject and his or her actions upon the world in so far as a person's acts and work are held to belong to that person. To take them away or control them is to dominate and diminish that person's exercise of agency.'[9] To many historians the exclusion of women from the public domain has implied diminished agency. Diane Owen Hughes, for example, urges us 'to reject an easy dichotomy between public and private, historical and natural, evenemental and cyclic: it is a means of denying agency to those whom historians have forgotten'.[10] Yet, in following her advice, we

7. Georges Augustins, 'La position des femmes dans trois types d'organisation sociale: la lignée, la parentèle et la maison', in G. Ravis-Giordani, ed., *Femmes et patrimoine dans les sociétés rurales de l'Europe méditerranéenne* (Paris, 1987), pp. 25–37; Julius Kirshner, 'Maritus lucretur dotem uxoris sue premortue in late medieval Florence', *Zeitschrift der Savigny-Stiftung für Rechtsgeschichte, Kanonistische Abteilung*, 77 (1991), pp. 111–55; idem, 'Wives' claims against insolvent husbands in late medieval Italy', in J. Kirshner and S.F. Wempel, eds, *Women of the Medieval World* (Oxford, 1985), pp. 256–303.

8. Marilyn Strathern, *The Gender of the Gift* (Berkeley, CA, 1988), pp. ix–x, 185.

9. Nicholas Thomas, 'Forms of personification and prestations', *Mankind*, 15 (1985), pp. 223–30; Strathern, 'Introduction', in *Dealing with Inequality*, p. 284.

10. Diane Owen Hughes, 'Invisible madonnas? The Italian historiographical tradition and the women of medieval Italy', in S.M. Stuard, ed., *Women in Medieval History and Historiography* (Philadelphia, 1987), p. 50; idem, 'Regulating women's fashion', in G. Duby and M. Perot, eds, *A History of Women in the West*, 5 vols, Vol. II, C. Klapisch-Zuber, ed., *Silences of the Middle Ages* (Cambridge, MA, 1992), pp. 136–58.

should also remember that agency is not at all the same as autonomy; nor should our approaching Renaissance women as persons
be taken as intending to invoke the entire range of meaning in
modern notions of individualism, which are so often coupled with
our sense of the Renaissance.[11] The fluidity between public and
private, the sharing of risks and honour by family members, kept
people in close but not intimate relations, for 'not every individual is fully a person or even a person at all, in societies which
define human beings by their place in a social chain linking past
with present'.[12] In the Renaissance both women and men had
positions in this chain and varying personhoods as a result. The
emphasis on the individual in modern Western psychology cannot
begin to encompass the wide varieties for categorizing experience
employed by others and in the past, where personhood was more
inherently social, with interactions more constrained and obligatory.[13] In such cultures, 'the boundaries of a person may be con-
ceptualized as extending far beyond the physical body'; while at
the same time, 'where personhood is a status reserved for defined
categories of people, parents or men, by implication those who
are not persons are individuals and such concepts may be said to
distinguish more clearly between these two ideas than most Western
versions.'[14]

It will not be possible here to substantiate the lives of men and
women in comparison to gendered norms, but this chapter will
survey those norms in legal sources, thereby demonstrating their
range of variability and ambiguity. It will only be possible to hint at
the further complexities that arose when these norms were applied
or manipulated in daily events and judicial cases. To remain within
the law also means that the personhood to be fleshed out will in
fact be the legal person, the *homo sui iuris*, which per force remains
abstract and flat (laid out in terms of obligations, rights, capacities)
– less dynamic and less gendered than the social personhood living

11. F.W. Kent, 'Individualism and families as patrons of culture in quattrocento
Florence', in A. Brown, ed., *Language and Images of Renaissance Italy* (Oxford, 1995),
pp. 171–92.
12. J.S. LaFontaine, 'Person and individual: some anthropological reflections', in
M. Carrithers, S. Collins and S. Lukes, eds, *The Category of the Person: Anthropology,
Philosophy, History* (Cambridge, 1985), p. 133.
13. Clifford Geertz, '"From the native's point of view": on the nature of an-
thropological understanding', in his *Local Knowledge: Further Essays in Interpretive
Anthropology* (New York, 1983), pp. 55–70.
14. Jane Fajans, 'The person in social context: the social character of Baining
"Psychology"', in G.M. White and J. Kirkpatrick, eds, *Person, Self, and Experience:
Exploring Pacific Ethnopsychologies* (Berkeley, CA, 1983), p. 370.

beings had to construct. However, social behaviour took forms and meaning from norms, and social personhood rested on the substrate of legal personhood. Neither the rules of law nor their privileged interpreters, the university-trained jurists, were blind to gender. Legal texts thus provide us with an important, if not indeed primary, point of access to understanding gender and person in the Renaissance.

Women in ius commune

During the Renaissance the meaning of legal personhood was laid out in the texts and commentaries of civil and canon law which made up the learned *ius commune*. Within this common law women possessed a limited *persona*. By an oft-quoted text of the *Digest* (D. 50.17.2), 'Women are excluded from all civil and public offices; and thus they may not be judges, nor magistrates, nor advocates; nor may they intervene on another's behalf, nor act as procurators'. Classical Roman law had restricted women in order to protect men and the agnatic transmission of property, rather than to protect women, who were seen not as inept and defenceless but rather as cunning and greedy. Roman law established separate gendered spheres, and women required guardianship when their activities took them into the male sphere. Roman law kept women from the possibility of exercising protection over men by acting as surety, while not prohibiting them from obligating themselves and being primarily responsible for their own debts.[15] In later imperial law, guardianship (*tutela*) over women came to be understood as a form of protection for them against the weaknesses inherent to their sex; and notions of female weakness then entered legal language. Thus, there was not a single consistent concept of woman in the Roman law as it passed into the medieval universities during the eleventh century.[16] Nor, for that matter, was 'maleness' clearly defined in the law. What seems most to have denoted *masculinitas* – namely, agnation and paternal legal control (*patria potestas*) – were not defining features of the legal male person, as is made clear with bastards, who, upon coming of age were termed *homo sui iuris*, even though they neither stood in a network of agnation nor were subject to *patria potestas*. Indeed, bastards, as examples of males with less

15. Suzanne Dixon, 'Infirmitas sexus: womanly weakness in Roman Law', *Tijdschrift voor Rechtsgeschiedenis*, 52 (1984), pp. 343–71.
16. Peter Goodrich, *Oedipus Lex: Psychoanalysis, History, Law* (Berkeley, CA, 1995), p. 114.

than complete personhood, present another perspective on the legal workings of gender: marked by the 'stain' of birth from parental sin, they had greatly restricted inheritance rights, or none at all, and were often excluded from public functions and rights; still, they had legal capacities, including that of themselves starting a legitimate line of agnation.[17]

Medieval jurists thus could employ a set of formulaic expressions for the lesser condition of women that linked both physical and mental inferiority: their frivolity (*lunata levitas*), inconsistency (*inconstantia*), lack of intelligence (*imbecillitas*), and weakness (*fragilitas, infirmitas*). Women were also said to be unable to keep a secret and to be naturally greedy.[18] Many present-day historians have consequently concluded that women did not have the same legal *persona* as an adult male, to whom the full range of legal rights and actions was potentially available.[19] Yet Renaissance women were not non-persons, for they did have rights and prerogatives in law, and in the life of virtually every woman who reached adulthood and had some property certain occasions could bring these legal rights into action.

In point of fact, women retained some residual public roles. The most authoritative jurist of the period, Bartolo da Sassoferrato (d. 1357), opined that a woman could act as arbitrator, be the agent (*procuratrix*) for her father or other relatives, and act as a witness for codicils, though not for the testaments to which they were attached.[20] She could also receive personal and patrimonial awards that were honorific, not utilitarian, that were devoid of real duties, and thus a form of distinction or nobility.[21] Still, many jurists like Francesco Accolti (1416–88) disagreed, claiming that the prohibition on obligating herself for others was a prohibition in the woman's person and not in the nature of the obligation. Accolti denied that women, other than those having formally recognized status (*dignitates*), could be arbitrators.[22]

17. L. Schmugge, ed., *Illegitimität im Spätmittelalter* (Munich, 1994); Hermann Winterer, *Die rechtliche Stellung der Bastarden in Italien von 800 bis 1500* (Munich, 1978).

18. Bellomo, *Condizione giuridica*, p. 46; Bartolo da Sassoferrato, D. 24.3.33, *Opera omnia*, 10 vols (Venice, 1615), Vol. 3, f. 20vb; Paolo di Castro, D. 16.1.3, *In secundam digesti veteris partem commentaria* (Venice, 1594), f. 106vb.

19. Ian Maclean, *The Renaissance Notion of Woman* (Cambridge, UK, 1980), p. 81.

20. Bartolo, D. 1.5.9, f. 22vb and D. 1.3.1, f. 15ra, *Opera omnia*, Vol. 1.

21. Bartolo, C. 10.64[62].1, *Opera omnia*, Vol. 9, f. 25ra; and C. 12.1.1, ibid., f. 46va; Angelo degli Ubaldi, *Ad decimum librum codicis*, in Baldo degli Ubaldi, *Opera omnia*, 9 vols (Venice, 1577), Vol. 8, f. 279rb–va.

22. Francesco Accolti, D. 16.1.1, *In secundam digesti veteris partem commentaria* (Venice, 1586), f. 52va.

The legal paradox regarding women is that, although *ius commune* excluded them from authoritative legal and political positions, it did not hamper them with disabilities regarding marriage, property, the capacity to dispose of it, or much else. Beyond the impediment of standing surety for another, women were free in *ius commune* to own and dispose of property by all legal means and had equal inheritance rights with men. Women had even gained the power to serve as guardian (*tutrix*) for their children after the father died – a public trust not available to them by Roman law but inserted through the influence of medieval canon law.[23]

Women and inheritance

It was not the *ius commune* but the statutes of cities – helped along by jurists supportive of patriarchy – that seem to have detracted most from the legal condition of women in the Renaissance. It was, for example, statutes giving husbands far more control over their wives' non-dotal property than was available in civil law that produced what one historian has termed a 'gilded cage' for women.[24] Where the *ius commune* could envision the mother, as partner to the head of the family (*paterfamilias*), able to manage property in both her own interests and that of her family, many statutes saw her as absorbed in her husband's or father's families, with only the men transmitting agnation and patrimony.

We will confine our investigation of statutes to two categories: those that governed inheritances, thus aiming to limit the quantities and types of resources to which women might gain title, and those that sought to impose some form of male guardianship over female attempts to use or dispose of resources. Both sorts of statutes ran contrary to *ius commune*, which contained norms of equal inheritance by sex and generous latitude regarding property. But jurists had little difficulty in invoking notions of female weakness to accommodate statutory norms to *ius commune*.[25]

The rationale behind inheritance limitations was agnation. The consistent rule to be found in communal statutes was that, as long

---

23. Gigliola Villata di Renzo, *La tutela: Indagini sulla scuola dei glossatori* (Milan, 1975), pp. 137–59.
24. Julius Kirshner, 'Materials for a gilded cage: non-dotal assets in Florence, 1300–1500', in D.I. Kertzer and R.P. Saller, eds, *The Family in Italy from Antiquity to the Present* (New Haven, CT, 1991), pp. 184–207.
25. Paolo di Castro, D. 24.3.1, *In primam infortiati partem commentaria* (Venice, 1593), f. 2va; thus Francesco Accolti, D. 29.2.5, *Commentaria in primam et secundam infortiati partem* (Venice, 1589), f. 169rb.

as there were sons, brothers or other close male agnates who could succeed, women could not claim the equal portion due them by Roman law from their father's or brother's estate but only the dowry that had been established for them at marriage. Even the share of a patrimony that could be willed to them personally was often limited in deference to the claims of male relatives. This was the essence of the bias towards agnation (*favor agnationis*) that lay at the heart of such statutes.[26] These rules would ensure that families would not be destroyed by equal partible intestate inheritance. To the jurists who approached these statutes, public utility lay in the preservation of families, which could not occur through women, 'for the woman is the beginning and end of her family'.[27] The sixteenth-century statutes of Ferrara testified that the purpose of female exclusion from inheritance was 'to preserve dignity and substance in the family, so it might not be impoverished because of women departing to other families'.[28]

Cities of all sorts, large and small, commercial centres and agricultural markets, from Lombardy to Tuscany and beyond, all adopted such rules. Thirteenth-century Volterra excluded dowered women from inheritance to father or brother, while giving them limited rights to a bequest from a child. Verona, Vicenza, Padua and Treviso all excluded dowered women from inheriting along with their sons or brothers or even more distant agnates, while Arezzo prevented women from inheriting if there were male descendants from father, grandfather or greatgrandfather, or mother, grandmother or greatgrandmother, brother or sister. In Venice a statute of 1242 established that 'daughters or granddaughters who have husbands never inherit with males but are content with their dowry'. Viterbo simply excluded dowered women in favour of father, brother, nephew or cousin, although protecting their rights to return to live with their brothers or nephews in widowhood. Cremona alone stood out in providing for the equal succession of both sexes to legacies as distant as those from uncles and aunts.[29]

26. Thomas Kuehn, *Law, Family, and Women: Toward a Legal Anthropology of Renaissance Italy* (Chicago, 1991), chapter 10.

27. Mariano Sozzini senior, X. 5.37.12, *Commentaria super secunda parte libri quinti decretalium* (Venice, 1593), f. 207ra.

28. *Statuta urbis Ferrariae nuper reformata anno domini MDLXVII* (Ferrara, 1567), Liber II, rubrica cxxxix, f. 115v.

29. Franco Niccolai, *La formazione del diritto successorio negli statuti comunali del territorio lombardo-tosco* (Milan, 1940), pp. 65–100, for most of the above. E. Fiumi, ed., *Statuti di Volterra (1210–1224)* (Florence, 1951), rubrica xiii and xv, pp. 9–10; G.M. Camerani, ed., *Statuto di Arezzo (1327)*, (Florence, 1946), Liber III, rubrica lvii, pp. 169–70; R. Cessi, ed., *Gli statuti di Jacopo Tiepolo del 1242 e le loro glosse* (Venice,

Limitations on a woman's inheriting within her family of origin were matched by statutory restrictions on her inheriting from her husband or his family – again with local variations. A Milanese statute of 1498 allowed a man to leave his wife by will up to one quarter of his estate, but Bellano in 1370 set a limit of 50 lire on such bequests and communes such as Pavia and Bergamo allowed only a lifetime usufruct. Statutes in Pisa and Florence, among others, also prohibited women from disposing of their dowries by testament to the prejudice of their own children or spouse.[30]

The personhood of both men and women was thus fitted into a scheme of relationships along which property was to be transmitted. Men were expected to own the large prestigious pieces of real property and family business capital and normally to pass this along to their sons (or brothers and so forth). As women could not, by definition, transmit agnation, they also could not pass along its most tangible real and symbolic expressions: that is, real estate, the family name and the coat of arms.

In their academic writings, jurists faced real problems in interpreting and applying such statutes. For example, in 1351 Bartolo da Sassoferrato was called on by judges in plague-battered Florence to decide that female statutory exclusion extended beyond mothers and grandmothers to all relatives, including males, on the maternal side. In another case, Baldo degli Ubaldi (1323–1400) held that a woman could not overturn a paternal will that had passed her over, since in the intestacy that would result, she would in any case have been forbidden by statute from inheriting.[31] Since women had dowry rights, widowhood rights and inheritance rights except when there were agnatic males to exclude them, it might seem that the rationale behind the statutes was agnatic. But in some instances, *masculinitas* rather than agnation seems to have been foremost, especially towards the end of the fifteenth century, when the use of fideicommissary substitutions tying patrimony to male lines of descent became more common. Was it agnation or *masculinitas* that was the more powerful factor behind Filippo Decio's (1454–1535) conclusion that a eunuch, by statute, had superior inheritance claims

1938), Liber IV, rubrica xxiiii, pp. 200–5; R. Morghen et al., eds, *Statuti della provincia romana* (Rome, 1930), *Gli statuti viterbesi del mccli–ii*, [II] Pars civilium, rubrica ii, p. 140; U. Gualazzini, ed., *Statuta et ordinamenta comunis Cremonae facta et compilata currente anno domini mcccxxxix* (Milan, 1952), rubrica lx, pp. 137–8.

30. Niccolai, pp. 170–205 and 289.

31. Kuehn, *Law, Family, and Women*, pp. 243–4.

to female relations?[32] Lorenzo Palazzi da Fano explained that the statutes looked to preserve wealth that would promote agnation and a family's standing in the community. He further noted 'if a statute speaks of the paternal estate only, I think it is made for the sake of preserving agnation. But if it speaks of maternal goods, then it is for the sake of preserving males, although they are not agnate to the mother.'[33]

There are four things to keep in mind about these statutes. First, they did not remove all connection between women and their family of origin. If there were no near agnate males to inherit, women could still claim all or a portion of a paternal or fraternal estate. To be sure, this postponement of rights made their actual inheritance all the more unlikely; but in an era of plague and other unexpected catastrophes, even the weakest claims could suddenly gain credibility. Secondly, these statutes also erected some constraints on men, who had to dower, feed and shelter women before and after marriage. They could not leave their wives or daughters a disproportionate share of the estate, and they could not change the equal division of a deceased wife's dowry among the children of both sexes. They could manage their wives' dowries with a good deal of freedom, but they were also bound by law to ensure the return of the dowry on the end of the marriage or to see that it passed to her heirs. Thirdly, and closely related, inheritance *from* men was under more constraints than inheritance from women. The normative order of civic statutes, in city after city, was based on the idea that the greater share of the patrimony, especially real property closely associated with an agnatic lineage, should pass to males through males. Property that came to and through women – largely their dowry, which was ideally to consist of cash or its equivalent – was not agnatic and instead split up equally among both sexes and both sides of the family.[34]

Finally, for all that these rules enshrining *favor agnationis* were intended to preserve families and their property, they often in fact contributed to prolonged and bitter disputes within and between

32. Filippo Decio, C. 6.22.5, *In primam et secundam codicis partem commentaria* (Venice, 1568), f. 243va.

33. Lorenzo Palazzi da Fano, *Tractatus super statuto communiter per Italiam vigente, quod extantibus masculis foeminae non succedant*, in *Tractatus universi iuris*, 29 vols (Venice, 1584), Vol. 2, f. 279ra.

34. Stanley Chojnacki, '"The most serious duty": motherhood, gender, and patrician culture in Renaissance Venice', in *Refiguring Woman*, pp. 133–54; Samuel K. Cohn, Jr, 'Le ultime volontà: famiglia, donne e peste nera nell'Italia centrale', *Studi storici*, 32 (1991), pp. 858–75.

families. This litigiousness is attributable, beyond the temperaments and interests of those involved, to the confusing normative situation, where statutory exclusions stood in contrast to *ius commune*'s rules of equality in inheritance and where rules of law and jurists could evidently disagree, so that each side might pretend to some bit of justice.[35]

A fine example is in a case opinion (*consilium*) of Francesco degli Albergotti of Arezzo (d. 1376). A Florentine died leaving only a daughter as his heir, and she in turn died young. The question was whether the estate then passed to the man's sister or to his wife, the girl's mother. The rationale behind the statute was to preserve the substance (*facultates*) of each agnatic line so that the honour of the family was preserved, and because 'perpetuating and conserving the memory of agnation' fell naturally to males, not to women, Albergotti concluded that the existence of the deceased's agnate sister did not exclude the eligibility of his wife. The fact that the statute expressly ordered that women were not to inherit houses and such showed that its concern was agnation, 'for which it is recognized to be very harmful that the ancestral home and the sites in which the shape of agnation is strongest, which usually retain the name of the agnation, see itself pass to strangers and the images of its greatest members, that is, its arms and insignia, torn away'. Angelo degli Ubaldi (1327–1400) concurred in this view.[36]

Women and legal transaction

Given that women could own property, it was also crucial that the leading citizens, as legislators and social agents in Italian cities, addressed the question of their capacity to use and dispose of it. Late imperial Roman law treated men and women as roughly equal with regard to legal capacity, except that women could not exercise the prerogatives of *patria potestas* nor exceed the limitations of the *ius commune* with regard to obligating themselves for others.[37] When the Lombards conquered Italy, however, they brought with them the practice of *mundium*, and its holder, the *mundualdus*, was a male with power over women. The original patrimonial and

35. Gian Savino Pene Vidari, 'Dote, famiglia e patrimonio fra dottrina e pratica in Piemonte', in his *La famiglia e la vita quotidiana in Europa dal '400 al '600: Fonti e problemi* (Rome, 1986), pp. 120–1.

36. Angelo degli Ubaldi, *Consilia* (Frankfurt, 1575), *cons.* 344, ff. 245ra–246va. and *cons.* 345, ff. 246va–247va.

37. Leicht, Vol. I, p. 95.

economic character of the Lombard *mundium* meant that the *mundualdus* was usually a woman's father, brother, or even her son, highlighting her kin as the more protective presence. Even if for certain acts women could choose their own *mundualdus*, making the whole matter of *mundium* seem a mere formality, nevertheless, they could not act without the consent of this male figure; as the same practice was extended to non-Lombard women, its gendered rather than kin-based nature was further accentuated.[38]

Such limitations of female contractual capacities seem a more directly gendered area of law than that restricting inheritance in agnation. These limitations were among the least uniform aspects of the different laws relating to women, if only because the laws themselves may not always have been necessary. Just as the traditional practice of family-arranged marriages continued despite the legal requirement of free consent by both parties, so too informal pressures and material incentives worked to restrain women from complete freedom in legal transactions: many women were evidently willing to shape their actions to accord with family interests, without the coercion of formal legal controls.

One area where female legal capacities remained ambiguous was that of guardianship of children. Legal doctrines almost universally viewed guardians, or *tutores*, as potential predators on the property of their wards; governments erected a number of safeguards for orphans, including special magistracies, like the Ufficiali dei Pupilli in Florence, to oversee or appoint guardians.[39] Mothers, provided that they had not remarried, were often believed to be the most reliable guardians, on the grounds that, although they could not inherit from their children by statute (possible inheritance being taken legally as a safeguard) or hold public office, they did have maternal affection.[40]

Women, who after marriage and widowhood had a foot in two different families – simultaneously guardian in one and ward of another – thus often found themselves in many areas of legal ambiguity. The responses of urban ruling bodies to the practical problems that resulted ranged along a continuum, from imposing

---

38. Camillo Giardina, 'Sul mondoaldo della donna', *Rivista di storia del diritto italiano*, 35 (1962), pp. 41–51; Maria Teresa Guerra Medici, *I diritti delle donne nella società altomedievale* (Rome, 1986), pp. 81–6.

39. Thomas Kuehn, 'Social processes and legal processes in the Renaissance: a Florentine inheritance case from 1452', *Quaderni fiorentini per la storia del pensiero giuridico moderno*, 23 (1995), pp. 365–96.

40. Maria Gigliola di Renzo Villata, 'Note per la storia della tutela nell'Italia del Rinascimento', in *La famiglia e la vita quotidiana*, pp. 59–95.

no restrictions or formal guardianship on women in legal transactions to imposing some form of male guardianship for all their formal acts.

Behind these statutes lay the problem of the liability of women and their property for debts of their fathers, husbands, sons and so forth, as well as male obligations towards wives and daughters. In both *ius commune* and statutes, female liabilities depended on the type of property in question. A dowry fell under the management of the husband; but as it was intended to protect a wife and meet her marital expenses, it could not be used to pay the husband's debts. By statute in Florence, a wife could not defend her husband's property from his creditors. In Tivoli, a wife was not held liable for spousal debts, even when her consent was clear.[41] But, when their husbands went bankrupt, wives could sue for recovery of their dowries and protect them from their husbands' creditors. Women suitably dowered were also generally held to be free of liability for obligations of their fathers, brothers or sons. Non-dotal property, most of which probably came to women in the form of inheritance and bequests, was another matter. Use or management of such property by a husband nominally required a wife's consent, but wives were also instructed to have valid legal instruments detailing such property, for otherwise it was too easy to assume it belonged to the husband. Here many cities' statutes deviated from *ius commune* and placed full control of non-dotal assets in husbands' hands, except for property bequeathed to wives by their parents or kin. Still, even as they prohibited a wife from alienating non-dotal acquests without spousal permission, statutes also affirmed her right to defend her property from her husband's creditors. Widows, on the other hand, would reacquire effective ownership of both dotal and non-dotal property.[42]

Some cities concocted no special statutes regarding female legal capacities. These included some of the larger and more active commercial centres, like Milan and Venice. In Venice, married women could do nothing against their dowry right but they could dispose of any property of their own without their husband's consent, having

41. F. Tomassetti et al., eds, *Statuti della provincia romana* (Rome, 1910), *Statuto di Tivoli del mcccv*, rubrica cxxxi and cxxxii, p. 198.

42. *Statuta populi et communis Florentiae, anno salutis mccxcxv*, 3 vols (Freiburg [Florence], 1778–83), Vol. I, Liber II, rubrica lxiv, p. 161; rubrica lxv, pp. 161–2; rubrica cxi, pp. 203–4; rubrica cxiii, p. 205; and rubrica cxv, pp. 206–7; B. Betto, ed., *Gli statuti di Treviso (sec. xiii–xiv)* 2 vols (Rome, 1986), Vol. II, pp. 383–4, rubrica v; Cremona, rubrica lxvi, pp. 141–2; Kirshner, 'Materials for a gilded cage', pp. 184–207.

the same rights through consanguinity to sell or buy property to keep it in the kin group.[43] Where civic statutes addressed questions of female capacity to alienate or obligate property, they tended to do so less to protect men from obligations arising from women's actions than more simply to safeguard a woman and her relations, male or female, from loss of property. It may be that the effective exclusion of women from ruling bodies and limitation of inheritance were sufficiently broad to reduce their sphere of activity; still, some places found it expedient to spell out those legal acts of which women could or could not avail themselves. Statutes in Tivoli specified that a husband effectively could not prevent his wife from disposing of her property by testament. Cremona legislated that a woman could not sell, give away or will her marital property without her husband's consent but that she needed no such consent for any other property.[44]

Other cities, further along the continuum, placed women under the effective, if not purely legal guardianship of their husbands. Bergamo did so by proclaiming that any property held by a married woman was her husband's, unless it could be proven to have come to her by inheritance, legacy or gift. At Volterra, a woman who consented to her husband's alienation of her property, testifying that she did so under no threat, lost any right to contest the act later. She was also allowed to transfer dotal property to him, but only up to a quarter of the dowry's value, and if she had children, she could dispose of no more than 60 soldi without her husband's consent.[45] Providing she released all her property to her creditors, Arezzo's statutes prohibited the jailing of a woman for her debts. Such legislation was clearly predicated on her ability to enter into obligations, and indeed, another statute accorded married women full ability to enter into contracts with and on behalf of their husbands, as long as they had consent of their father, adult brother or two near blood relations 'of good reputation and condition'.[46] Treviso's statutes of 1385 decreed that, although a woman could not press suit in court unless she had her husband's consent, she could still make a will, provided the act was witnessed by two of her closer blood male relatives (women were acceptable if there were

43. *Statutorum, legum, ac iurium d. Venetorum* (Venice, 1564), Liber I, rubrica xxxviiii, pp. 70–1; Liber II, rubrica xxi and xxii, p. 137.

44. Tivoli, Liber II, rubrica cxxviii, pp. 196–7; Cremona, rubrica lxxxii, p. 153.

45. C. Storchi, ed., *Lo statuto di Bergamo del 1331* (Milan, 1986), Collatio X, rubrica iii, p. 192; Volterra, rubrica xii, pp. 8–9 and 125; rubrica clii, pp. 79 and 137–8, rubrica lvii (1224), p. 134; rubrica lxiii, p. 136.

46. Arezzo, Liber III, rubrica xiiii, p. 124; and rubrica lxiiii, p. 174.

no men; it was assumed that the husband was present). Two close relatives also had to give their consent to alienation or encumbrance of any dotal or non-dotal property, regardless of whether the husband consented or not.[47]

Ferrara, in enacting similar legislation, explained that 'public utility and equity persuade that the indemnity of women should be provided for: [they] whose sex is weak [and] who also are easily enticed by the flatteries of men because of their modest sex and fearful reverence, which sex and nature induce in them'. Any obligation undertaken with or for one's husband was assumed to have been forced even if the woman later freely ratified and reconfirmed her act. Nor was a woman's oath to observe the terms of a contract considered acceptable, since the Ferrarese assumed that any such resulted from 'fear, deceit, and extorted by force and in fraud of the womanly sex.'[48]

Cities like Arezzo, Treviso, and Ferrara which adopted this intermediate position of a kin-consent restriction on women were not among the first rank of Italian cities in commerce or population. At the extreme end of the scale, however, was the vibrant commercial and banking city of Florence, which peculiarly held to and adapted the Lombard *mundualdus*. There was practically no legal act a Florentine woman could undertake without the consent of a male guardian. However, beyond the statutory presumption that it was the husband who, if present, acted as *mundualdus*, there was no restriction as to who could serve in that capacity. He could be (and often was) any male. He was available to single legal acts only; the *mundium* was not a power vested for life or any long term and it was not alienable at his discretion. A woman could seek a different *mundualdus* whenever she wished, and it only required a notary to designate one for her. Nor did the *mundualdus* bear any liabilities for the consent he gave, making him something much less than a genuine guardian for someone possessed of *imbecillitas*.[49]

Florence's statutes thus adapted the *mundualdus* into a singular, flexible legal device. Florentine women were not bound to the consent of husband or kin, who were necessarily interested parties in their dealings. Rather, it was those cities that mandated a consent function in kin that actually remained closer to the original spirit of the Lombard *mundium*: they did not have to spell out special

47. Treviso, I, rubrica vi, II, p. 309; rubrica, p. 352; rubrica, II, pp. 374–6 and 384–5.
48. Ferrara, Liber II, rubrica xc, ff. 84r–85v.
49. Kuehn, *Law, Family, and Women,* chapter 9.

penalties or responsibilities for these consenting kin because their accountability was right before them in the fate of the property. Jurists approached these statutes with full understanding of their ideological underpinnings. According to Giasone del Maino (1435–1519), such statutes were based on the assumption that not only would male relatives exert pressure on women, who 'are easily seduced by moneys or flatteries', but also that 'the closer relative to whom succession fell would be more diligent [at protecting the patrimony] than the remoter one'. Definitely not to be included among such relatives was a woman's husband. While a wife was considered to owe *reverentia* (submissiveness) to her husband, fear of his resulting influence over her lay at the heart of jurisprudential and statutory concerns.[50] Despite the widespread image of husband and wife as one flesh, or precisely because of it, the interests of her family of origin remained distinct and pertinent, with her father especially retaining a privileged position. According to Baldo, a daughter could alienate property to her father, even without consent of other relatives, 'because of the natural effect which is conceded to a father'. Such statutes were to protect her in dealing with more distant relatives 'who too often offer bad advice for girls'. More than a century later Filippo Decio repeated Baldo's assertion that the law had confidence that the father would protect the best interests of his daughter, dismissing contrary arguments that a father might deceive a daughter or use her for fraudulent purposes.[51]

If a woman had no close relatives available to perform the consent function, then jurisprudential opinion was that she was free to act. After all, the rationale of protecting others by protecting her failed when there were no others. In the event that relatives refused their consent, according to Bartolo (although others sharply disagreed), a judge could examine the reasons for their refusal and allow the woman to proceed without their consent if their reasons were insufficient.[52] To allow a woman to proceed without statutory consent rested on what jurists took that 'consent' to mean: not the cause of the transfer of ownership or other action but rather what enabled 'the person of the transferring party'. Nonetheless, it was

50. Giasone del Maino, C. 2.4.35, *In primam codicis partem commentaria* (1573), f. 96va–vb; also C. 6.38.5 and C. 6.18.1, *In secundam codicis partem commentaria* (1573), ff. 161ra–rb and 42vb; Paolo di Castro, C. 6.37.10, *In secundam codicis partem* (Lyon, 1553), f. 95ra; Francesco Accolti, D. 24.3.14,1, *Commentaria in primam et secundam infortiati partem* (Venice, 1589), f. 25vb.

51. Baldo, C. 6.20.3, *Opera omnia*, Vol. 7, ff. 49vb–50ra; Filippo Decio, C. 6.20.3, *In primam et secundam codicis partem commentaria* (Venice, 1568), f. 218va.

52. Kuehn, *Law, Family, and Women*, p. 217; Angelo, D. 1.[30].54, *Super secunda infortiati* (Monferrat, 1522), f. 10vb; Giasone del Maino, C. 6.9.7, f. 8va.

also part of the form of the legal act, so it had to have been there beforehand; it was not a simple confirmatory approval that could come later. Furthermore, not all types of legal act were seen to require consent: a woman could validly accept an inheritance (*aditio haereditatis*) without consent of kin, according to Paolo di Castro (*c.* 1360–1441), who moreover declared that a statute denying a woman the power to make a will was invalid.[53] To the argument that accepting an inheritance made one liable for outstanding debts, and that therefore a woman had to have statutory consent of relatives, different jurists responded that her obligation was not primary but a consequence of her gain, and that it would be absurd for a statute otherwise drafted in her favour to forbid a woman to accept an inheritance because of outstanding obligations.[54] At the least, Angelo degli Ubaldi had held that an estate in Ancona without any obligations incumbent upon it could be accepted without consent of relatives, for then the statute's rationale of safeguarding females from obligations surely did not hold: it was a lucrative estate and the few creditors to dispose of represented no real problem, as 'there cannot be inheritance without trouble'.[55]

In a case where a woman's will was disputed on the grounds that her husband could not consent to an act by which he gained, Angelo degli Ubaldi upheld the validity of her act. The statute was out to protect women and their relatives. To overturn the will would reverse the meaning of the statute where, in fact, the husband's consent alone was needed.[56] By such distinctions, then, were jurists able to patch together some elevation of the female legal *persona*. There were properties and rights to be moved to and through them, to their benefit or others.

Conclusions

The picture sketched out here, while obviously incomplete, provides a basis on which to venture some observations. Was law ultimately a 'prison' for women in Renaissance Italy? If so, it was hardly an effective one, and moreover it was in other ways also a prison for

---

53. Baldo, *Tractatus de statutis*, in *Tractatus universi iuris*, Vol. 2, ff. 103rb and 104ra; Bartolo, D. 29.2.5,1, *Opera omnia*, Vol. 3, f. 143rb; Paolo di Castro, D. 28.6.43, f. 98vb; on *aditio* and mainly its opposite, *repudiatio*, see Thomas Kuehn, 'Law, death, and heirs in the Renaissance: repudiation of inheritance in Florence', *Renaissance Quarterly*, 45 (1991), pp. 484–516.

54. Giasone del Maino, D. 29.2.28, *In primam infortiati partem commentaria* (1573), f. 63ra.

55. Angelo, *cons.* 317, f. 222va–vb.   56. Angelo, *cons.* 143, f. 93ra.

men, who faced obligations to their kin, spouses and progeny, and at times needed the consent of others, including females, to act. Here, as in so much else involving gender, we cannot take equality as our parameter and simply measure history in terms of specific advances or retreats in this one area.[57] Personhood was revealed and constructed in relationships, themselves expressed in rights and obligations over people and things. Women as well as men were involved in these relationships; they had personhood – standing in law – which is perhaps nowhere more apparent than in the statutory norms intended to limit it. The limitations we have examined had very different effects and resonance. Issues of inheritance, which were just about universal in northern and central Italy, generated many more legal cases and difficulties than did those involving male consent, which was not established in many cities. All of which suggests that it was the restriction of the flow of wealth to and through the 'weaker' sex that was the more important issue. Certainly, women's legal capacities would have been less of a problem if they had had little on which to exercise them, even less again if others' claims on their holdings had been powerful. Still, women did hold title to property, so they had to have access to means to acquire, alienate and use it: in Renaissance urban societies 'property was not a matter of individual claims over a material object, but an instantiation of claims between persons in relation to something charged with pecuniary and symbolic value'.[58]

According to Yan Thomas, the key to understanding gender in Roman law is that 'the unity of the domain that Roman law reserved for men and prohibited to women is not accounted for by the commonplace of *infirmitas sexus*, but the notion of a civil and virile office: action on behalf of others'. Women's *persona*, unlike that of men, could not embrace the *patria potestas*, the organizing mechanism of society in law. Women had no such transmissible power, but 'were deprived of institutional extensions of their singular personhood'.[59] Women could not transcend a narrow sphere of interest or desubjectivize their actions into abstract legal functions – hence their inability to witness a legal act like a will.

The medieval jurists and the civic statutes made more of ideologically inscribed female weakness and incapacity. We have

---

57. Yan Thomas, 'The division of the sexes in Roman Law', in *A History of Women in the West*, Vol. 1, P. Pantel, ed., *From Ancient Goddesses to Christian Saints*, (Cambridge, MA, 1992), p. 90.
58. Kirshner, 'Wives' claims', p. 302.
59. Thomas, 'The division of the sexes', pp. 98, 136–7.

seen these notions invoked to justify women's position in law, as protective of women and their interests, or protective of those who shared interests with women. At the same time, we have seen some enlargement of the sphere of authority for women – they could serve as guardians for their children, although only if there were also males acting as guardians with them. Ties of kinship, always distinguishable as 'natural' filiation from ties of *potestas*, became more prominent as reflected in incest regulations and rights accorded emancipated and illegitimate children – and women had a role in generating filiation that they could not have in transmitting authority.

Women's lack of *potestas* was explained in a fashion echoing Paolo da Certaldo by the sixteenth-century jurist, Ascanio di Clemente Amerini. *Potestas*, he claimed, had two purposes, as a reward for parents and for the good of the offspring. It was the second reason that dictated that mothers not have *potestas*. Mothers certainly loved their children no less than fathers; indeed, children were more obligated to their mothers for going through pregnancy, parturition and maternal chores. Still,

> for many things a mother is not suited as is the father for the benefit of the children because of the female sex, and the laws have more faith in the father than in the mother in providing for the children ... hence it is that in a mother are none of the effects resulting from paternal power ... except those that result also from a sort of reverence ... [and that] children are not established in the mother's power ... [nor] of her *agnatio* or family but of the family and *agnatio* of the father.[60]

The legal personhood of the *pater* rested on his supposed ability to do more for his children, including give them agnation, but not on any sense that his interests for them and hers were opposed or that she was totally incapable of managing property. Gender might give him a fuller degree of legal personhood, but that was only possible in relation to and with a mother.

Study of the law thus reinforces our growing sense of the inherent pluralism in Renaissance Italian society. Alongside the emerging styles in humanism and art, and together with the evolving forms of religious, chivalric and mercantile cultures, law offered its vision of social structure and action. And law itself was plural, as we have seen, consisting of the academic *ius commune*, statutes and

60. Ascanio Amerini, *Tractatus de patria potestate*, in *Tractatus universi iuris*, Vol. 8, part 2, f. 100ra.

jurisprudential case opinions. Applied then to the study of gender, law reveals the complexities, conceptual and actual, behind what can otherwise be easily dichotomized distinctions between male and female. It was perhaps one of the true cultural hallmarks of the Renaissance that in a variety of ways moralists, jurists, artists, and others, attempted to come to grips with such pluralism and impose, not always successfully, an adequate overall perspective.

CHAPTER FIVE

Women and Work in Renaissance Italy

SAMUEL K. COHN, JR

The recent blossoming of women's history and gender studies of the Italian Renaissance have largely skirted questions of economics and women's participation in the work force.[1] Given that Joan Kelly's 'Did Women have a Renaissance?' in part spurred this recent enthusiasm, this is enigmatic, for although she turned to sources and methods of literary history, her question was in essence about economic and social status.[2] In regard to sources, historians since Kelly have largely followed her lead by focusing on the literary representation of women and on the status and problems of elite women – Lucrezia Tornabuoni, Alessandra Strozzi, Alfonsina Orsini, and others – far removed from the everyday problems of work and industry. To be sure, sources that reflect directly on women's work are few. Personal diaries (*ricordanze*) and special tribunals such as the Florentine Onestà have provided data for two female professions: domestic servitude, both slave and free,[3] and

1. For a recent overview of the literature on late medieval Italy, see G. Piccini, 'Le donne nelle vita economica, sociale e politica dell'Italia medievale', in A. Groppi, ed., *Il lavoro della donne* (Bari, 1996), pp. 5–46.
2. Joan Kelly, 'Did women have a Renaissance?', in R. Bridenthal and C. Koonz, eds, *Becoming Visible* (Boston, 1977), pp. 139–64. See the criticisms by Judith Brown, 'A woman's place was in the home: women's work in Renaissance Tuscany', in M. Ferguson, M. Quilligan and N. Vickers, eds, *Rewriting the Renaissance: The Discourses of Sexual Difference in Early Modern Europe* (Chicago, 1986), pp. 206–24. On recent trends in Renaissance women's history, see Christiane Klapisch-Zuber's introduction to *A History of Women in the West*, Vol. II: *Silences of the Middle Ages* (Cambridge, MA, 1992).
3. See Christiane Klapisch-Zuber, *Women, Family and Ritual in Renaissance Italy* (Chicago, 1985), pp. 132–64, 165–77; 'Women servants in Florence during the fourteenth and fifteenth centuries', in B. Hanawalt, ed., *Women and Work in Preindustrial Europe* (Bloomington, IL, 1986), pp. 56–80; D. Lombardi and F. Reggiani. 'Da assistita a serva: Circuiti di reclutamento delle serve attraverso le istituzioni assistenziali (Firenze–Milano, XVII–XVIII secoli)', in S. Cavaciocchi, ed., *La donna nell'economia secc. XIII–XVIII* (Florence, 1990), pp. 301–19. On women slaves, see the excellent survey by F. Angiolini, 'Schiave', in Groppi, ed., *Il lavoro delle donne*, pp. 92–115.

prostitution.[4] As a result, these are the best-known women's professions to historians of late medieval and early modern Italy. Other
sources – literary tales (*novelle*) and a wide variety of governmental
registers – although concerned with other matters, from time to
time portray women at work in other professions, but only in passing, as though depicted in the background of a painting. From
these indirect reflections, the historian nonetheless may piece
together images of women's economic sphere.

Although fourteenth-century storytellers note far more often
men's professions than women's, women are found at work with
specialized skills. In Giovanni Boccaccio's *Decameron*, second story,
day seven, the Neapolitan Peronella, who cheats on her older poor
bricklayer husband, supplements the family income as a spinner.
She also possesses the wherewithal to sell their mutually owned
household possessions, in this case an old tub from which her lover
springs forth.[5] In story two, day eight, the lusty farm girl, Belcolore,
from the Arno village, Varlungo, whose charms her parish priest
cannot resist, knew the art of grinding (presumably flour among
other things) better than any other girl in the village (*meglio saper
macinar che alcuna altra*), implying that this occupation between
milling and baking was a female profession. She was also a spinner
and possessed the commercial freedom to take her own production
to market in Florence as well as to pawn her best Sunday dress for
spending money.[6]

Similarly, criminal records entered the work place, allowing us
an occasional glimpse of the everyday chores of women in the city
as well as in the countryside. The vicariate court records of the early
fifteenth-century territory of Florence reveal that when outside the
home, married women were most likely seduced or raped at the
village well, where they can be seen conversing with other women and
fetching water to bring home.[7] Such a cameo provides a near timeless

4. M. Mazzi, 'Il mondo della prostituzione nella Firenze tardo medievale', *Ricerche
storiche*, 14 (1984), pp. 337–63; idem, *Prostitute e lenoni nella Firenze del Quattrocento*
(Milan, 1991); John Brackett, 'The Florentine Onestà and the control of prostitution, 1403–1680', *The Sixteenth Century Journal*, 24:2 (1993), pp. 273–300.
    5. V. Branca, ed., *Tutte le opere di Giovanni Boccaccio* (Milan, 1976), Vol. 4, pp. 593–
8.
    6. Ibid., pp. 674–80. Spinning was the most common of women's professions
found in the *novellistica* tradition; see R. Greci, 'Donne e corporazioni: la fluidità di
un rapporto', in *Il lavoro delle donne*, pp. 71–91, esp. p. 78; and O. Redon, 'Images
des travailleurs dans les nouvelles Toscans des XIVe et XVe siècles', in *Artigiani e
salariati: Il mondo del lavoro nell'Italia dei secoli XII–XV* (Pistoia, 1984), pp. 395–416.
    7. Samuel Cohn, 'Sex and violence on the periphery: the territorial state in early
Renaissance Florence', in his, *Women in the Streets: Essays on Sex and Power in Renaissance Italy* (Baltimore, 1996), pp. 98–136.

impression of women and work that may have characterized their everyday lives from Biblical times (Rebecca at the well) through to the twentieth century. But such chores had little to do with sex in any biological sense. In early Renaissance cities (at least Florence in 1427, Pisa in 1429, and Verona in 1425 and 1502), such *portatori* (professional water carriers) were almost invariably men.

The criminal records afford other glimpses of women at work, which are more specific in time and place. Young and unmarried girls in village communities of early fifteenth-century Florence were often sexually violated while herding their sheep or other cattle in the long-distant march between summer and winter pastures (transhumance) – an occupation that historians have recently assumed was suitable only for 'rough and savage males'.[8] One such case regards a six-and-a-half-year-old girl who was sodomized while tending her sheep far from home on the high Apennine passes of the Romagna (Verghereto) *en route* to the southern Chianti.[9] As far as this criminal case reveals, the young girl was alone without the company or protection of parents or kin. Was such independence or neglect, like the presence of women at the well, a near timeless fact of the unwritten economic history of peasant women in Italy? Were mountain women more independent or more involved in the economy beyond the household than their counterparts in the plains, as indeed Rinaldo Comba has suggested for the Alps of thirteenth-century Piedmont?[10] Did such patterns of independence change over time and across different systems of land use?[11]

Peasant petitions for tax relief are another type of government document that sheds light on rural women at work. On 18 August 1406, the villagers of Pulicciano, six miles south of Arezzo in the Val di Chiana, described how their houses had burnt to the ground when all the men had gone off to the Saturday market in Arezzo, leaving behind their women to look after the baking of the village's bread. According to the plea, while one woman was returning to the oven with her uncooked dough, a sudden burst of wind swept hot coals through the parish.[12]

8. G. Piccini, 'Le donne nella vita economica', p. 43; and G. Cherubini, 'Lupo e mondo rurale', *Ricerche storiche,* 13 (1983), p. 205.

9. ASF, *Giudice degli Appelli: Intrinseci,* no. 102, I, 47r–v, 1429.ix.9.

10. Piccini, 'Le donne nelle vita economica', p. 44, and *Extrinseci (Giudice),* no. 102, I, 47r–v, 1429.ix.9; R. Comba, 'Produzione tessili nel piemonte tardomedievale', *Bulletino storico-bibliograpfico subalpino,* 82 (1984), p. 14.

11. On women and work in the countryside, see the essays in M. Muzzarelli, P. Galetti and B. Andreolli, eds, *Donne e lavoro nell'Italia medievale* (Turin, 1991); G. Piccini, *"Seminare, fruttare, raccogliere," Mezzadri e salariati sulle terre di Monte Oliveto Maggiore (1373–1430)* (Turin, 1980); Brown, 'A woman's place', pp. 218–20.

12. ASF, Provvisioni registri, no. 95, 159r–v.

Were women usually the bakers in Tuscan villages? Were there clear gender roles, such that men went off to market and women stayed behind? While suggestive, such cameos of village life remain problematic: from them it is difficult to examine change over time, or differences in place. Nonetheless, they give roughly the same picture of women's work that historians of pre-industrial Europe have usually assumed: work concentrated on textile production – primarily spinning – and on the provisioning of foodstuffs.[13]

To view women's roles in the work place more systematically, historians of the Italian Renaissance have focused largely on cities – in fact, largely on one city, Florence. Moreover, for occupations beyond prostitution and domestic servitude, they have concentrated on a single source – tax surveys, the fourteenth-century *estimi* and the fifteenth-century *catasti* (that is, until the appearance of textile censuses in the early seventeenth century). Even for these limited sources, however, historians have quantified only a small sliver of the information available in them – the occupational listings and the percentage of women listed as heads of households. Debtor–credit relations or how the property listings of women changed in relation to those of men over a period of time have yet to be examined. In addition, historians have only begun to analyse guild matriculation lists, testaments and other notarial contracts to assess women's work and economic status beyond questions of women's control over their dowries and their freedom to initiate contracts without a male protector (*mundualdus*).[14]

Despite the recent scholarly concentration on tax records for the study of women's occupations, such data are fraught with dangers for accurately gauging women's work beyond the family.[15] First, other sources make it clear that men and women alike often practised a variety of skills or trades; yet notaries and tax officials rarely

13. David Herlihy, *Opera Muliebria: Women and Work in Medieval Europe* (New York, 1990), p. 1; P. Goldberg, *Women, Work, and Life Cycle in a Medieval Economy: Women in York and Yorkshire c. 1300–1520* (Oxford, 1992), p. 86; C. Bynum, *Holy Feast and Holy Fast: The Religious Significance of Food to Medieval Women* (Berkeley, CA, 1987), pp. 189–94; Piccini, 'Le donne nella vita economica', p. 39; and Greci, 'Donne e corporazioni', p. 78.

14. On the matriculation of women into the guild of doctors and spicemakers, see Katherine Park, *Doctors and Medicine in Early Renaissance Florence* (Princeton, NJ, 1985); on the *mundualdus*, see Thomas Kuehn, '"Cum consensu mundualdi": legal guardianship of women in *quattrocento* Florence', *Viator*, 13 (1982), pp. 309–33. An excellent essay on women and guilds, Greci's 'Donne e corporazioni', relies largely on guild statutes and not matriculation lists, as does Herlihy's, *Opera Muliebria.*

15. See the remarks of Brown, 'A woman's place'; and Piccini, 'Le donne nella vita economica', p. 18.

identified their subjects with more than a single occupation. More damaging, tax officials rarely listed the occupations of more than 40 per cent of household heads, whether male or female, and with few exceptions, ignored the occupations of other household members.[16] For viewing women in the work force, such conventions meant that women were more under-represented than men, since fewer women were recognized as heads of households (rarely over one-third and often as little as 10 per cent). Further, most women became heads of families only with the death of their husbands. In Florence, 90 per cent of women household heads in 1427 were widows, in 1480, the figure had climbed to 96 per cent, and in Verona in 1502, 99 per cent of women household heads were widows. Thus, the vast majority of women headed a household only in old age, in many cases probably after they had ceased to participate in the work place beyond the home. While in 1427 the average age of male household heads in Florence was forty-six, that of women was fifty-nine. In Pisa, women heads of households were even slightly older, 61.5 years, as were Pisan men, who were 52.7 years.[17]

Finally, tax records conceal another avenue important to women's power, independence and their value to the urban economy – the world of the nunnery. Not only did women lead sequestered lives in convents, praying for the dead, they supplemented the incomes of their religious houses through highly skilled labour, by running convent schools for lay girls and *scriptoriae* for the copying of manuscripts. In addition, nuns made and sold silk purses and ribbons and practised other crafts within the textile industry for commercial gain.[18]

With these caveats in mind, this chapter will begin with an analysis of the occupational structure of Renaissance Florence from the perspective of tax records before venturing into other sources, questions and places, both in Italy and across the Alps. As problematic as tax surveys may be, they make clear that women practised a wide range of occupations, including heavy tasks once believed to have been performed only by men. As the comparative study of

16. F. Franceschi, *Oltre il 'Tumulto'. I fiorentini dell'Arte della Lana fra Tre e Quattrocento* (Florence, 1993), p. 97.

17. I have calculated these figures and others below concerning occupations in Florence, Pisa and Verona based on the *catasto* computerized files compiled in the 1970s by David Herlihy and Christiane Klapisch-Zuber. They are now available in ASCII format from the Data and Program Library, The University of Wisconsin (Madison), and on the internet.

18. See Sharon Strocchia, 'Learning the virtues: convent schools and female culture in Renaissance Florence', in Barbara Whitehead, ed., *Women's Education in Early Modern Europe: A History, 1500–1800* (New York, forthcoming). For textile workers in the Humiliati, see Greci, 'Donne e corporazioni', p. 84.

women's work over place and time illustrates, women's roles in the occupational structure of pre-industrial Europe were not simply a matter of the biological differences between the sexes, but instead turned on the economic and cultural differences of gender. Even in Florence, one of the worst places to be born a woman in Renaissance Italy, as far as the law was concerned,[19] the tax officials identified Florentine city women in 1427 as active in a wide variety of occupations, even those requiring heavy labour in the wool industry, as skinners (*scardassiere*), carders, shearers and stretchers.

Whether for medieval Paris, late medieval York or Renaissance Florence, historians have explained changes in women's occupations and their participation in the work force by pointing to the competition for jobs between men and women. Historians, however, have reached less agreement about the chronology and geography of these changes as well as about the precise causes that underlay the often dramatic changes that the tax registers suggest about women's work.

From the appearance of women's occupations in the tax registers of Paris and Florence, David Herlihy has shown that women's work beyond the home began to decline in urban centres at the end of the thirteenth century.[20] With populations reaching their pre-industrial ceilings and urban economies in decline, men pushed women out of the work place, especially in the skilled trades and professions. Yet after the Black Death (1348–50), such a demographic argument ceases to make sense. Although a handful of women in the medical profession may have benefited temporarily from the drastic labour shortages created by the plague,[21] the surviving tax registers of Florence suggest that the rapid decline of women's professions occurred after the plague, against a backdrop of labour scarcities.[22] Thus, historians such as Gabriella Piccini and Roberto Greci, along with Herlihy in his later work, have recently stressed political causes: the 'monopolization' of work by guilds

19. See Cohn, *Women in the Streets*, pp. 1–15; Julius Kirshner, 'Materials for a gilded cage: non-dotal assets in Florence (1300–1500)', in R. Saller and D. Kertzer, eds, *The Family in Italy from Antiquity to the Present* (New Haven, 1991), pp. 184–207; and Isabelle Chabot, 'Risorse e diritti patrimoniali', in A. Groppi, ed., *Il lavoro della donna* (Bari, 1996), pp. 47–70.
20. Herlihy, *Opera muliebria*; and his 'Women's work in the towns of traditional Europe', in Cavaciocchi, *La donna nell'economia*, pp. 103–30.
21. Park, *Doctors and Medicine*, p. 71.
22. Isabelle Chabot, 'La reconnaissance du travail des femmes dans la Florence du bas Moyen Age: contexte, idéologique et réalité', in Cavaciocchi, *La donna nell'economia*, pp. 563–76; Brown, 'A woman's place'; and J. Brown and J. Goodman, 'Women and industry in Florence', *Journal of Economic History*, 40 (1980), pp. 73–80.

and, in particular, the emergence of guilds into the political realm with the mid-thirteenth-century rise of the Popolo.[23]

But the chronologies of Italian city-states fit no better with this explanation than with an argument about the competition between men and women for a decreasing pool of jobs. Again, to consider Florence: Franco Franceschi has shown that the shift away from hiring Florentine women as weavers in favour of long-distance male migrants from the low countries and Germany occurred at the end of the fourteenth and during the early fifteenth centuries,[24] that is, after the fall of the government of the minor guilds (*Arti Minori*) in 1382 and during the decline of the guilds as a political force in Florentine history.[25]

Finally, labour shortages, economic decline or expansion, or the strength of guilds in individual cities fail to explain women's participation in the work force when Italy is compared with countries across the Alps. In this respect, P.J.P. Goldberg has argued that late-medieval York was the mirror opposite of Florence. While according to Goldberg, women's work outside the home steadily deteriorated in Mediterranean areas after the Black Death, new jobs opened for women in York and moved beyond traditional female tasks, such as spinning and laundering.[26]

To explain the ebb and flow of women's work in late medieval York, Goldberg has created a demographic-economic model with three distinct chronological periods. In the first, demographic collapse after 1348 stimulated economic expansion, which in turn heightened the demand for female labour beyond the home. As a result, women could become more selective about marriage, postponing or avoiding it altogether.[27] A second period, 1420 to 1450, brought more vigorous economic expansion to York, which led to further strides in women's independence and work beyond the home, while rates of nuptiality sank to their low-point. In the late fifteenth century a third period of economic decline engendered a struggle for scarce jobs, in which men forced women out of job markets and, as a consequence, women began to marry earlier and more often.[28]

23. Greci, 'Donne e corporazioni'; and Piccini, 'Le donne nella vita economica', p. 17.

24. Franceschi, *Oltre il 'Tumulto'*, p. 132; and Samuel Cohn, *The Laboring Classes in Renaissance Florence* (New York, 1980), pp. 91–114.

25. John Najemy, *Corporatism and Consensus in Florentine Electoral Politics, 1280–1400* (Chapel Hill, NC, 1982).

26. Goldberg, *Women, Work, and Life Cycle*, p. 86.

27. Ibid., pp. 325–7.   28. Ibid., p. 337.

In an ambitious last chapter, Goldberg attempts to temper what might appear to be a mechanistic relation between women's participation in the work force, rates of nuptiality and changes in economic fortune. Here, the variable 'culture' suddenly enters his equations, and despite his earlier caveats about geographic variability,[29] the evidence from York suddenly stands, not only for all of Britain, but for a northern European model of nuptiality and women's work, while early fifteenth-century Florence is generalized as 'the Mediterranean model'.

According to Goldberg, the 'Mediterranean' values of honour and shame caused Florentine men to shield their women from the sexual risks of the work place, and as a consequence, teenage girls refrained from entering the work place and instead married much older, established men.[30] Thus Goldberg concludes: 'The labour shortages created by the plague could, therefore, only be met by males . . . women did not engage in paid employment, nor was service well developed as an institution. . . . Hence, the fall in the proportion of female-headed urban households, the steady rise in MHS [mean household size] and increase in especially large, multi-generational households.'[31]

Unlike York or northern Europe writ-large, these patterns of nuptiality and work-force participation would not change, Goldberg argues, until the seventeenth century, when, as Brown and Goodman have shown, female labour dominated textile production,[32] and when a 'European Marriage Pattern' finally began to shape Florentine and Mediterranean demography.

How well do Goldberg's generalizations match the Florentine or Italian world with respect to women's work during the Renaissance? Did fifteenth-century Florentine women 'not engage in paid labour'? Did domestic servitude languish? Did women's economic clout or independence as household heads decline steadily over the century? Was Florence part of a near-seamless Mediterranean world as far as women's work was concerned, without significant variations even within Italy itself?

First, as stark as the economic realities for women may have been in early Renaissance Florence in comparison to those of medieval Paris or late-medieval Cologne,[33] the tax records reveal that

29. Ibid., p. 19.   30. Ibid., p. 342.   31. Ibid., pp. 343–4.
32. Brown and Goodman, 'Women and industry in Florence'.
33. See Herlihy, *Opera Muliebria*, p. 162; and M. Wensky, 'Women's guilds in Cologne in the later Middle Ages', *Journal of European Economic History*, 11 (1982), pp. 631–50.

Florentine women were never totally dependent on their fathers or husbands, but earned livelihoods as traders and artisans. In 1427, the tax officials identified 237 women household heads, or 13 per cent of all such women, as having a profession. Nor were all these professions and trades located at the bottom of the occupational ladder. Indeed, unlike York and other places, where women's occupations have been studied, women in Florence, at least those who were heads of households, were not concentrated in provisioning or in textiles. Only 5 per cent of women identified by occupation, for example, were providers of food. As a proportion of listed occupations, food-providing played a no more important role for women than it did for men, who were in the food-providing trades in even slightly larger proportion (6.4 per cent) than were women.[34] Moreover, the women identified by these tasks were not all at the bottom of the occupational ladder, as street vendors and greengrocers (*ortolane* or *treccone*), but also held positions regulated and protected by guilds, as bakers, vintners, oil merchants and cheese dealers.

Similarly, while in Florence more than a quarter of the female heads of households with professions (27.43 per cent) were involved in textiles, a larger proportion of men engaged in these occupations than women.[35] Again, women were not clustered exclusively at the very bottom of the textile crafts as spinners. Indeed, there were three times as many women listed as weavers than spinners. Moreover, women carried out tasks throughout textile production, from the heavy primary tasks (as we have seen) to the highly skilled jobs of finishing, sewing, embroidering and dyeing.

Women can be found throughout the occupational hierarchy of early Renaissance Florence. In 1427, 15 per cent of the female heads of households with known occupations were engaged in the activities of the respectable minor guilds: as carpenters, goldsmiths, butchers, grain dealers, painters, cobblers, and simply as masters. We even find a woman blacksmith, a vintner, a baker, an oil merchant, a grocer, a stationer, a slipper-maker, a linen manufacturer and a dealer in brass. More strikingly, women appear in major-guild professions, that is occupations at the top of the Florentine occupational hierarchy, as merchants in the wool and silk industries, bankers or money-changers; there is a furrier, and even an international merchant. Could these women have been matriculated

34. Among men, 5.42 per cent bore occupations in the provisioning trades, a negligible difference of less than one per cent.
35. Almost one-third of the male household heads listed by occupation (29.5 per cent) were in textile production.

members of the major guilds? Or were they simply associated with the professions of their dead husbands or fathers, from whom they took their occupational identities?[36]

Evidence from last wills and testaments also supports the argument that women were not completely cut off from the world of property, merchandise and trade. As Diane Hughes has remarked for late-medieval Genoa, 'aristocratic women came of age at widowhood'.[37] In Florence, such a rite of passage for women appears to have been general across class lines. Despite the manifold difficulties in conflicting systems of kinship support,[38] as widows Florentines could exercise considerable control over property. Not only could they control and bequeath their dowries, they also gave money and landed property from other sources of wealth – from their own inheritances and from earned income. While Florentine inheritance customs and changes in dowry law certainly impinged on Florentine women's property rights, they nonetheless continued to bequeath landed property in their wills through the fifteenth century. Although Florentine women may have had less leverage over property than women in Renaissance Venice or Tivoli,[39] their wills show a greater range of choice over the distribution of their property than that practised by Florentine men, who, because of the dictates of patrilineal succession, used their wills more often to channel the bulk of their possessions down the male line. In at least one case in the samples of Florentine wills I examined, a fifteenth-century widow even bequeathed to her youngest brother that most prized of possessions, usually protected against any alienation and earmarked for the occupation and control by male heirs – the urban *palazzo*.[40]

Although men certainly dominated the world of capital and business, Florentine women had not completely disappeared as 'donne d'affari' after the thirteenth century, as at least one historian has recently alleged.[41] Their last wills show that they remained in

36. Herlihy and Klapisch-Zuber distinguished between those women identified with their own professions from those identified with the profession of their husbands or fathers.

37. Diane Hughes, 'Domestic ideals and social behavior: evidence from medieval Genoa', in C. Rosenberg, ed., *The Family in History* (Philadelphia, 1975), pp. 115–43, esp. p. 142.

38. See Klapisch-Zuber, *Women, Family and Ritual*, pp. 117–33.

39. Stanley Chojnacki, 'Patrician women in early Renaissance Venice', *Studies in the Renaissance*, 21 (1974), pp. 176–203; and idem, 'Kinship ties and young patricians in fifteenth-century Venice', *Renaissance Quarterly*, 38:2 (1985), pp. 240–70; and Chabot, 'Risorse e diritti patrimoniali', pp. 54, 63–4.

40. ASF, Dipl., Osp. S.M. Nuova, 1411.v.27.

41. Chabot, 'Risorse e diritti patrimoniali', p. 60.

control of commercial capital throughout the fifteenth century. Frequently, they were the donors and beneficiaries of credits and debts. Although women constituted less than one-third of Florentine testators, they distributed over 13 per cent of such commercial obligations, transferred in wills. Moreover, they donated rental properties, merchandise, shops, shares in the Florentine public debt (*monte*), as well as shares in business and banks (traffico) to their heirs and friends.[42] Even more remarkable, the testaments give evidence that women in Renaissance Florence on occasion kept account books (which, according to the *paterfamilias* Giannozzo degli Alberti, were 'like sacred and religious objects', never to be allowed in the sight of wives or other female kin).[43] In the plague year 1374, a widow (who did not even bear a family name) gave all the possessions itemized in her own business accounts to one of her two sons.[44]

Did the Tuscan economy, in contrast to York, become progressively less favourable to women's participation in the work place over the late fourteenth and fifteenth centuries? Whereas in the region of York women were poised to take advantage of these opportunities created by the plague, according to Goldberg, in Florence male peasants from the surrounding countryside (*contado*) filled the vacuum in city jobs left by the plague's devastation. His evidence rests on the small differences in the sex ratios between the city of Florence and its *contado* (117.6 versus 108.9), calculated by Herlihy and Klapisch-Zuber for 1427.[45] Goldberg claims that the higher ratio of men in the city is evidence that male peasants had migrated to take advantage of the new job opportunities in the city.

Such a leap from these small discrepancies in sex ratios, however, is hazardous. Causes other than migration, such as infanticide and abandonment may have contributed to these differences. Peasants from the *contado* of Florence also left their homesteads for places other than the city of Florence.[46] Indeed, late fourteenth- and early fifteenth-century tax records allow the historian to do more than speculate about Florentine rural migration on the basis of skewed sex ratios. From 1371 to 1414, these records reported the

42. See for instance, ASF, *Notarile antecosimiano*, A195, 219r–v; and ASF, Dipl., Osp. S.M. Nuova, 1374.xii.17.
43. Leon Battista Alberti, *The Family in Renaissance Florence*, trans. R. Watkins (Columbia, SC, 1969), p. 209.
44. ASF, *Notarile antecosimiano*, A205, 59r.
45. Goldberg, *Women, Work, and Life Cycle*, p. 343.
46. Cohn, 'Insurrezioni contadine e demografia: il mito della povertà nelle montagne toscane (1348–1460)', *Studi Storici*, 36:4 (1995), pp. 1023–49.

movements of Florentine peasants to and from villages as well as into the city of Florence. Emigration to urban centres and into Florence, in particular, was hardly constant over time.[47] While peasants may have rushed into the city immediately after the plague of 1348,[48] rural migration to Florence declined steadily over the last decades of the fourteenth and early fifteenth centuries.[49] Secondly, the city's immigrants were not predominately rural men but rather unattached women, either young girls or widows, who came to work as domestic servants (*fante*) in the households of the Florentine patriciate. Such trends are corroborated on the receiving end, where Franco Franceschi has found that during the late fourteenth and early fifteenth centuries, the majority of those apprentices in the wool industry who came from the countryside were young girls between the ages of seven and twelve.[50] The males who did emigrate to Florence came from further afield, from Flanders and Germany.[51] But they came not in the immediate aftermath of plague, but in the fifteenth century, when, contrary to Goldberg's claims, women's participation in the work force and economic clout were increasing and not declining.

To argue for the progressive decline in Mediterranean women's independence during the Renaissance, Goldberg turns to the percentage of households headed by women in the Florentine subject city of Prato. Yet this evidence does not chart the steady decline that Goldberg claims. Instead, the proportion of household heads in Prato who were women increased from 16.7 per cent in 1371 to 19.2 per cent in 1427 and then declined in 1470 to 10.3 per cent, thus reflecting more closely the three-part chronology of women's work and independence that Goldberg claims was distinctive of northern Europe than a chronology of steady Mediterranean decline. Moreover, in Florence, the data suggest an even more pronounced three-period chronology than in Prato. Already by 1427, the proportion of Florentine households headed by women came to 18.43 per cent and in 1458 increased to 21.52 per cent, surpassing York's peak of just over 19 per cent. Then, in keeping with the

47. Samuel Cohn, 'Insurrezioni contadine'; and idem, 'Inventing Braudel's mountains: the Florentine Alps after the Black Death', in S. Cohn and S. Epstein, eds, *Portraits of Medieval and Renaissance Living: Essays in Memory of David Herlihy* (Ann Arbor, MI, 1996), pp. 383–416.

48. Niccolò Rodolico, *La democrazia fiorentina nel sul tramonto, 1378–82*, (Bologna, 1904) pp. 1–45; C. de la Roncière, *Prix et salaires à Florence au XIVe siècle (1280–1380)* (Rome, 1982), pp. 661–70; and Cohn, 'Insurrezioni contadine'.

49. Cohn, 'Insurrezioni contadine', pp. 1032–4, 1048.

50. Franceschi, *Oltre il 'Tumulto'*, p. 130.

51. Ibid., p. 121; and Cohn, *The Laboring Classes*, chapter 4.

trends traced for late-medieval York, the proportion of women-headed households in Florence sank sharply to 6.74 per cent with the economic slump of the 1470s and 1480s.

For the most part, widows, rather than single women, headed households, but even this percentage changed over time and, again, does not suggest a steady decline in Florentine women's economic independence. While 90 per cent of these female heads were widows in 1427, the proportion shrank to 75 per cent in 1458. In the following decades, however, the trend turned in the opposite direction (96 per cent). Of course, it might be assumed that female households were among the poorest in Renaissance Florence and thus might represent economic destitution more than feminine independence. On this score, the *catasto* data reveal some unexpected surprises. In terms of taxable assets, male-headed households were 1.6 times more wealthy than those headed by women in 1427 (829.33 versus 521.31 florins). But by 1458, women's taxable assets had grown: female households had become even wealthier than those headed by men (606 versus 610 florins). Once again, however, by 1480 a third economic phase had set in, and with it, the wealth of women-headed households had declined both absolutely and relative to men's (434 versus 307 florins).[52] Correspondingly, in the 10 per cent sample collected by Herlihy and Klapisch-Zuber for the *catasto* of 1480, not a single woman was identified by an occupation of her own.

Although in some respects the *catasti* shed unexpected light on previously unknown aspects of women's economic lives, they also mask a great deal, such as the importance of domestic servants in fifteenth-century Florence. As Herlihy and Klapisch-Zuber were careful to point out, the low visibility of female domestics in the *catasto* does not indicate that women were absent from these occupations, as Goldberg has assumed. The *catasto* did not tax servants as a part of their employers' urban households but as members of their native households, which most often were located in Florence's rural hinterland.[53] Yet evidence from personal diaries suggests that the absolute number, as well as the proportion, of women domestics expanded in the households of urban Florence during the first half of the fifteenth century – just as they did in York. At the same time,

---

52. On the *catasto* of 1480, see note 55.
53. David Herlihy and Christiane Klapisch-Zuber, *Les Toscans et leurs familles. Une étude du catasto florentin de 1427* (Paris, 1978), trans. as *The Tuscans and their families* (New Haven, CT, 1985), p. 60; and David Herlihy, 'The population of Verona in the first century of Venetian rule', in J. Hale, ed., *Renaissance Venice* (London, 1973), pp. 101–2.

female servants' salaries increased along with improvements in their living arrangements. Moreover, by the last decades of the fifteenth century, women increasingly lost out to men in acquiring positions as domestics, and the wages of female domestics and wet nurses declined.[54] Once again, the chronology of this sector of women's 'paid' work resembles the three-period chronology drawn for York.

Can we then say that Goldberg's model applies to the 'Mediterranean' as well as northern European societies? Was there a consistent relationship between nuptiality and women's participation in the work force – that is, did increases in female celibacy and higher ages at marriage for women give rise to increases in women's independence and participation in the paid work force? Again, I have my doubts.

First, women's ages at first marriage in Florence increased steadily from the *catasti* of 1427 to 1458, along with increases in the proportion of women as heads of households and increases in their wealth, both absolutely and relative to men. But this pattern did not continue through the fifteenth or into the sixteenth century. For Florence, as for northern Italy more generally, women's ages at marriage increased and the age gap separating husbands and wives narrowed. Yet, against this demographic backdrop, matters did not proceed apace in economic terms for Florentine women, as would be expected from the pattern found by Goldberg for York. Instead, by 1480 the wealth of Florentine women had declined both absolutely and relative to men,[55] along with the decline in their proportion as heads of households and as the bearers of occupations.

In addition to experiencing these changes in nuptiality, which moved Florence towards 'the European marriage pattern', Florence continued in this direction along another parameter. The proportion of women who remained celibate grew from the end of the fifteenth to the mid-seventeenth century, as nubile girls entered nunneries throughout northern Italy.[56] Yet the reasons for

54. By the sixteenth century, the demand for slaves had also shifted in favour of males; see Angiolini, 'Schiave', p. 95ff.

55. Anthony Molho has calculated that Florentine property values declined by 3.1 per cent between 1427 and 1480 (*Marriage Alliance in Late Medieval Florence* (Cambridge, MA, 1994), pp. 363–4), but the drop would be greater once prices are adjusted for inflation and the widening gap between the values of florins and lire.

56. Richard Trexler, 'Le célibat à la fin du Moyen Age: les religieuses de Florence', *Annales: ESC*, 27 (1972), pp. 1329–50; Molho, *Marriage Alliance*, pp. 218 and 300–4; idem, '"Tamquam vere mortua": Le professioni religiose femminili nella Firenze del tardo medioevo', *Società e storia*, 43 (1989), pp. 1–44; Cohn, *Women in the Streets*, pp. 76–97; and Judith Brown, 'Monache a Firenze all'inizio dell'età moderna: un'analisi demografica', *Quaderni Storici*, 29 (1994), pp. 117–52.

this increase in female celibacy, especially for the wealthy, were tied directly to what Goldberg and others have seen as the underpinning of the late medieval 'Mediterranean model' of nuptiality – the emphasis on honour and its cornerstone, the dowry. As class divisions hardened through the sixteenth century, Tuscan fathers as well as those from other Italian city-states used the dowry to preserve class distinctions. As dowry prices rose in economies which were in stagnation or even decline, fathers could not afford to marry all their daughters off and thus, class, honour and dowry in early modern Italy were the stimuli, not bulwarks, for increases in the proportion of women never marrying in Italian urban households.

Moreover, changes in average household size in the city of Florence do not correspond with the theory that women's economic independence and participation in the work force declined, as Goldberg's model would predict. Instead, family size continued to increase steadily from the plague-stricken years of the late fourteenth and early fifteenth centuries through the early modern period, that is, across times when women's participation in the work force beyond the home increased and decreased. In short, the connection between household size and women's participation in the labour force, or with their economic power and independence, is not so simply linked for Florence as it appears to have been for York.

Was economic expansion, then, the key for understanding differences in the economic independence of women and their participation in the work force whether in the 'Mediterranean' or north of the Alps? Here, a comparison between Verona and Florence is instructive. While the Florentine population grew only modestly during the fifteenth century and its economy showed signs of decline by the 1470s, Verona's population increased from that of a middle-size town of 15,000 in 1425 to 42,000 in 1502 – rivaling Florence itself.[57] According to Herlihy, Veronese demographic growth followed from its economy, reflecting a shift in trade and industry during the fifteenth century away from the old economic centres of central Italy to the more dynamic economies of northern Italy and southern Germany.[58]

Yet against this backdrop of economic expansion, women's participation in the work force of Verona, as best the tax records

---

57. David Herlihy, 'Mapping households in medieval Italy', *Catholic Historical Review*, 58 (1972), pp. 1–21; and idem, 'The population of Verona', p. 101.
58. Herlihy, 'The population of Verona', pp. 112, 114–16.

reveal, do not differ markedly from those in Florence in 1427; nor do they show progress in tandem with Verona's economic expansion. Instead, the tax rolls suggest the opposite. At Verona, the proportion of women who were heads of households declined from 16.73 per cent to 9.44 per cent; their average taxable assets edged downward from 11.01 to 10.74 lire; and they were no better represented in the professions of the expanding economy of Verona than in the stagnating economy of Florence. In 1425 about the same percentage of women in Verona as in Florence were identified with a profession (13.8 per cent); nor had this figure increased significantly by the end of the century (16 per cent). Moreover, while women's professions in Florence fanned across a wide spectrum of the work force, crossing guild barriers and entering even into the major guilds, women's professions in Verona, for both the *estimi* of 1425 and 1502, clustered around the less prestigious and menial tasks usually associated with women's work in pre-industrial Europe. According to the *estimi* of 1425, 78 per cent of the women identified by occupation in Verona were either weavers or spinners. By 1502, they had become active in a slightly wider number of occupations. Their ranks included a porter, a carpenter, a baker, an ironmonger, a barrel-maker, a money changer and a swordmaker. But the vast majority (69 per cent) were weavers, servants and manual labourers, reflecting a much less variegated female work force than that of Florence in 1427.

Nor, when measured by other means, do women appear to have been significantly better off or more independent in the more progressive economy of Verona than in Florence. Veronese women were less often the heads of households than their Florentine counterparts, and when they were, they were less often independent, single women than in Florence. Further, Veronese women controlled a smaller proportion of taxable wealth compared to male-headed households than did Florentine women.[59] Yet, Verona's demographic profile – women's ages at marriage and household structure[60] – more closely resembled a northern pattern than 'Mediterranean' Florence. Here, no simple model linked rates of celibacy, ages at marriage and household size with the economic independence of women across time or space.

Even in cities as regionally and culturally close as Florence and Pisa, comparisons offer little support for the 'Mediterranean'

59. Veronese women owned two-thirds the wealth of their menfolk.
60. Herlihy, 'The population of Verona', pp. 104–5.

variant of the demographic-economic model of women's economic status and independence. Little appears to distinguish women's economic or demographic profiles in Pisa from those of Florence, according to the *catasti* of 1427–29. Marriage patterns in Pisa fit well within the Tuscan model of nuptiality in which teenage girls married middle-aged men; the age difference in both towns was twelve years.[61] Just as was the case in Florence, few Pisan households were headed by women (15.6 per cent), and most of those were headed by widows (93 per cent). The proportion of female-headed households and the proportion of widows in that role were slightly lower in Pisa than in Florence (89 per cent versus 93 per cent). Yet, in other important ways women in Pisa differed radically from those in Florence. Women in Pisa were identified much less frequently as participants in the work force than in Florence. While in 1427 over 13 per cent of women heads of households carried their own occupational identity in Florence, only 4 per cent were so identified in maritime Pisa. Moreover, in contrast to Florence, the occupations of Pisan women were much more concentrated on the lower rungs of the occupational ladder, as servants, religious tertiaries and bearers of less skilled jobs in the textile industry (combers and washers of raw wool). Only one woman appeared with a trade that carried guild status (an innkeeper), and none bore a major-guild profession.

From these differences in occupational identity should we then conclude that women in Pisa possessed less status, independence and economic power than their counterparts in Florence? Other data bring into question the possibilities of making such sweeping conclusions from the occupational listings found in tax surveys, even in meticulously executed ones such as the remarkable *catasto* of 1427. Unlike late-medieval Florence, Pisa allowed women to redact notarial contracts of all sorts freely, without first gaining the contractual approval of a male protector (*mundualdus*). In Pisa, women could also represent themselves in criminal and civil courts.

Last wills and testaments draw further differences in women's independence and power between Pisa and Florence, where, to the detriment of women, Lombard law was revived in Florence at the expense of Roman precedents. First, greater proportions of women in Pisa had the daring or power to draw up last wills. While fewer than one-third of women in late medieval Florence (29 per cent) redacted wills, women in Pisa exercised this final judgement over

---

61. Herlihy and Klapisch-Zuber, *Les Toscans et leurs familles*, pp. 399–400.

their goods and last pious hopes in numbers equal to men (49 per cent versus 51 per cent). Further, in Florence three-fourths of women testators were widows, and under 10 per cent allocated their last properties while married. By contrast, in the maritime city of Pisa nearly 40 per cent were married at the time of writing their wills.

Moreover, in Florence 40 per cent of the testaments of married women were simple transactions that nominated husbands as the universal heirs. This is not surprising, since it is obvious from some cases that these husbands were hovering over their wives as their appointed *mundualdi*.[62] The testaments of married Florentine women generally handed over their few remaining non-dotal properties to their husbands and made few pious or non-pious choices. By contrast, only one will out of 134 redacted by married women in Pisa conveyed to a husband the bulk of her property, and that will (actually a codicil) was redacted by a non-native Pisan.[63]

For Pisa, the customary practice for a married woman was instead to leave her husband a mere 15 lire, which after the Black Death certainly did not constitute a sizeable gift, even by artisan standards. As a result, married Pisan women had far greater freedom over their itemized bequests to pious institutions as well as to friends and kin. They elected as their universal heirs nieces, nephews or even men and women who bore no apparent relation to them.

Part of the reason why women in Pisa could exercise a broader range of choice in their wills stemmed from the testamentary conditions husbands had imposed on their soon-to-be widows. Typically, a Florentine husband would write a will granting his widow the usufruct over his properties provided that she remain chaste, not remarry, and not ask for the return of her dowry. Further, these arrangements were often even more restrictive among the Florentine merchant class, where the usufruct of the husband's property earmarked for the support of his wife was confined to a small portion of his estate – her linen, jewelry and other personal items found in her bedroom. Such arrangements were absolutely unheard of in the numerous wills and codicils analysed for Pisa.[64] Here, the dowry was inviolate no matter what the widow did and was accompanied with the rights of usufruct over all the husband's property provided that she did not remarry.

62. See for instance, ASF, Dipl., S.M. Novella, 1309.iii.6; *Notarile antecosimiano.* G 167, 53r, 1328.xi.24; and Florence, Archivio di San Lorenzo, no. 1012, 1374.vii.25.
63. ASPi, Ospedale di S. Chiara, no. 2078, 80r, 1311.i.6.
64. Based on a sample of 715 wills and codicils.

Can we then speculate that women in maritime cities possessed greater economic independence and control over property than in inland manufacturing cities during the Renaissance? Indeed, evidence of will-writing in late medieval Ragusa[65] and early Renaissance Venice might suggest that such a pattern existed.[66] But the remarkable testamentary practices of Tivoli, an inland city where women initiated three-quarters of wills,[67] runs against such a simple correlation, as does evidence from seafaring Genoa. For Genoa, Hughes finds that the mentalities and structures of the male lineage restricted the economic independence of patrician women in ways comparable to those found in Florence. On the other hand, Genoese artisan women exercised greater control over their lives and property at least until the fourteenth century. But, as in Florence and most other Tuscan and Umbrian cities, broad changes in dowry and property laws led to a deterioration in the property rights of Genoese artisan women by the fifteenth century.[68]

In conclusion, despite the current state of research on women's economic independence and especially the participation of women in the work force, comparative studies show that 'Mediterranean' society even within the Italian peninsula was more variegated and complex than has recently been assumed or was earlier allowed by Joan Kelly's question, 'Did Women have a Renaissance?' With regard to control over property, for example, Florence was perhaps the worst place in Tuscany or even in central Italy to have been born a woman. Yet, not even in Florence were women excluded from the paid work force, nor were they barred, as widows, from exercising considerable control and choice over the allocation of moveable as well as landed property.

Moreover, the trajectory of women's participation in the work force and their control of wealth as heads of household do not plot a steady deterioration in their rights from the Black Death to the seventeenth century. Instead, tax records, along with other sources, at least for Florence, show more a three- or even four-part chronology whose broad outlines resemble late-medieval York and what Goldberg has generalized as a distinctive northern European model. After the Black Death of 1348, with the loosening of guild regulations,

65. S. Stuard, *A State of Deference: Ragusa/Dubrovnik in the Medieval Centuries* (Philadelphia, 1992), chapter 4.
66. See Chojnacki's numerous articles on Renaissance Venice.
67. Isabelle Chabot, 'Risorse e diritti patrimoniali', p. 63; and S. Carocci, *Tivoli nel basso Medioevo: società cittadina ed economia agraria* (Rome, 1988), p. 226.
68. Greci, 'Donne e corporazioni', p. 87.

the lowering of barriers for matriculation, and the rush of immigrants from the countryside into urban jobs, labour conditions improved for Florentine men and women alike. But by the early fifteenth century, entry into the Florentine professions appears to have been restricted more vigorously to women as well as to certain male 'outsiders'. By the middle of the fifteenth century these labour patterns changed again, showing greater percentages of women as household heads and as members of the paid labour force, especially as domestic servants. Finally, by the end of the century, the patterns changed a fourth time: women's positions in the work force and their independence as measured by their proportions as household heads deteriorated significantly once more.

The limited comparative studies sketched in this chapter suggest that these shifts were not tied to broad changes in nuptiality or to shifts in the economy. Women's fate in the expanding economy of Verona, for example, did not vary significantly from that of women in the stagnating economy of late fifteenth-century Florence. At the same time, women's independence and power over property in Pisa contrasted markedly with that of Florence, although both appeared to have been wedged into the same Tuscan patterns of nuptiality.

In posing these micro-cycles for women and work and their differing histories in individual Italian city-states, I do not wish to condemn the sweeping and ambitious models that link broad economic and demographic forces with changes in women's work and economic independence. Such models, like those developed by Wrigley and Schofield for modern Britain[69] or by Goldberg for medieval York, need to be built across the Italian peninsula. To do so, however, will first require the same painstaking archival research across Italian cities and their territories that historians have done over the past two decades for Britain.

69. A. Wrigley and R. Schofield, *The Population History of England, 1541–1871: A Reconstruction* (London, 1981).

PART THREE

The Social Body

CHAPTER SIX

Medicine and Magic: The Healing Arts

KATHARINE PARK

After several years of marriage, the Pratese merchant Francesco Datini and his wife Margherita had failed to conceive a child, to their growing consternation. Their friends and relatives were eager to help. Among various tactful and not so tactful suggestions, they recommended to Francesco and Margherita the services of various sorts of healers. In 1393, for example, Margherita received a letter from her sister in Florence:

> Many women here are with child, and among them the wife of Messer Tommaso Soderini and many others. I went to enquire and found out the remedy they have used: a poultice, which they put on their bellies. So I went to the woman and besought her to make me one. She says she will do so gladly, but it must be in winter. . . . She has never put it on any woman who did not conceive, but she says it stinks so much, that there have been husbands who have thrown it away. So discover from Francesco if he would have you wear it.[1]

Two years later, the physician Naddino di Aldobrandino, a family friend, wrote to Francesco to suggest that Margherita's problem was connected to 'pains she had every month before her purgations'. He noted that he had recently cured a patient of a similar condition. 'I will send you everything I did', he wrote, 'and if it appears to your current doctors [*medici*] that it is appropriate to your wife's case, you can do it, otherwise not.'[2] Shortly afterward, Margherita's

---

1. ASPr, Datini CP, 1103 (7 September 1393). Translated in Iris Origo, *The Merchant of Prato: Francesco di Marco Datini* (London, 1957), p. 160.
2. ASP, Datini CP 1102/busta (11 February 1394/95). For the sake of convenience, I have used the term 'doctor' here and throughout to translate the Latin or Italian *medicus* or *medico*, despite the etymological problem: *medici* was a general term used to refer to well-established and/or officially recognized healers, including physicians, surgeons and empirics, of whom only the first would have qualified as *doctores*, licensed to teach through their university degrees.

sister offered (through her husband Niccolò) yet another recom-
mendation: a belt with an inscribed incantation. As Niccolò wrote
to Francesco,

> she says it is to be girded on by a boy who is still a virgin, saying first
> three Our Fathers and Hail Marys in honour of God and the Holy
> Trinity and St Catherine; and the letters written on the belt are to
> be placed on the belly, on the naked flesh. . . . But I, Niccolò, think
> it would be better, in order to obtain what she wishes, if [Margherita]
> fed three beggars on three Fridays, and did not hearken to women's
> chatter.[3]

Thus over the course of two years, the relatives of this wealthy,
literate and socially prominent woman recommended to her four
markedly different kinds of healing. The physician Naddino di
Aldobrandino belonged to the highest social and intellectual level
of the contemporary hierarchy of healers; educated at the university in a demanding course of Latin study that emphasized skill in
theoretical disputation as well as familiarity with a wide range of
ancient, Arabic and contemporary texts, he could boast among his
clients bishops, cardinals, and eventually the pope himself. The
Florentine woman with the poultice occupied a much lower place
in that hierarchy and was probably what official documents usually
called an 'empiric': someone who had learned the craft of healing
orally, often from a relative, or by personal experience.[4] In contrast
to the prescriptions of empirics and learned physicians, who typically used naturalistic remedies, made of animal, vegetable or
mineral ingredients, the belt sent by Margherita's sister was magical,
working through oral prayers and a written incantation; the fact
that it required the services of a virgin boy, who had not yet begun
to expend his generative force and was therefore at the height of
his own fertility, is further evidence of its non-naturalistic character.
Finally, Margherita's brother-in-law recommended traditional acts
of Christian piety, as an alternative to magical charms.

Three things are worth noting here. First, no one suggested to
Margherita that these different levels of practice and types of
healing – learned, empirical, magical and religious – were incom-
patible, let alone mutually exclusive. Furthermore, all were considered appropriate to a woman of her station, able to consult any

---

3. ASP, Datini CP 1103 (23 April 1395). Origo, *Merchant of Prato*, p. 161.
4. On physicians and empirics, see Katharine Park, *Doctors and Medicine in Early
Renaissance Florence* (Princeton, NJ, 1985), chapter 2; the empirics that appear in
documents of this sort should not be confused with the ancient medical sect of
Empirics.

practitioners she wished. Secondly, these separate types of healing were nonetheless to some extent gendered. Women's total exclusion from university study in this period meant that only men could take medical degrees and earn the learned credentials of Latinate physicians like Naddino and his colleagues. Similarly, Margherita's brother-in-law considered acts of piety (feeding three beggars on three Fridays) as, if not a specifically male practice, then at least sanctioned by the predominantly male authority structure of the Church and opposed to the 'women's chatter' represented by his wife's magical charm. In contrast to these two male-identified forms of healing, Francesco and Margherita's correspondence reveals two female-identified ones, both recommended by Margherita's sister: the fertility belt and the foul-smelling poultice, prepared by a woman referred to Francesca through a network of female acquaintances. Finally, as Naddino's own intervention testifies, although women healers were frequently consulted by both men and women on matters concerning sex, reproduction and fertility, they did not by any means have a monopoly on the medical care of women in this or in any other area, including obstetrics and gynaecology; Naddino himself appears in Florentine tax records as a 'birth doctor' (*medico da parto*).[5] Women consulted male healers for conditions ranging from infertility to diarrhoea to fractures, while men went, though less frequently, to women healers as well.

In general, there is little evidence that the practices of Renaissance healers were strictly segregated according to either the class or the gender of the patient or practitioner.[6] Rather, the pluralistic map of healers and their clients was more fluid and complex, at least in larger towns and cities. But even if medical practice was not gendered in the simple and monolithic sense of women treating only women and men treating only men – just as it was not 'classed,' in the sense of elites treating only elites and the folk treating only the folk – nonetheless gender, like class, dramatically shaped the kinds of healing offered by, and available to, both men and women, as it shaped the careers, working conditions, and social and economic prospects of the healers themselves.

In approaching this topic, I have defined healing broadly, to include all kinds of assistance offered to men and women who

5. ASF, Prestanze 1322, fol. 22r.

6. For a more recent and modulated view, see (on gender) Monica Green's article, 'Women's medical practice and health care in medieval Europe', *Signs*, 14 (1989), pp. 434–73; and (on class) Carlo M. Cipolla, *Public Health and the Medical Profession in the Renaissance* (Cambridge, 1976), pp. 80–5; Park, *Doctors and Medicine*, chapter 3.

thought of themselves as ill, by men and women whose special skill in this area was acknowledged and sought out by their contemporaries. This definition excludes midwifery – pregnancy and uncomplicated childbirth, unlike infertility, were not considered illnesses that required medical treatment – as well as the domestic nursing by mothers, daughters, sisters, female servants and slaves, that constituted the vast bulk of the care of the sick in this period. I have also had to omit any discussion of contemporary religious healing by 'living saints' such as Fra Domenico da Pescia or Santa Francesca Romana. Even with these exclusions, however, the practitioners and healing practices I will discuss spanned cultural domains that many historians have attempted to differentiate, under the separate rubrics of 'medicine', 'magic' or 'religion' – boundaries that in the Renaissance often did not correspond to modern ones, and in many cases are hardly to be discerned at all.[7]

Throughout this study, my treatment has been shaped by the extraordinary unevenness of the available documentation. The archives of the principal Italian cities and their universities contain mountains of unpublished information about learned male physicians and surgeons, whose works also survive by the hundreds in libraries, though relatively few have made it into modern editions or English translation. Many male empirics were also officially licensed, and they appear in tax and political documents, as well as in the records of their guilds – material surveyed in a number of important local studies.[8] The situation was very different for more casual male practitioners, rural practitioners, and virtually all women healers: female, usually of the lower orders, and for the most part illiterate, the last group laboured under a triple disability when it came to leaving written evidence of their ideas and their work. Indeed, except for fugitive glimpses like those in the correspondence of Francesco Datini or in the often hostile treatises of learned physicians, the main information about their practice relates to

7. See also Richard Kieckhefer, 'The specific rationality of medieval magic', *American Historical Review*, 99 (1994), pp. 813–36.

8. Irma Naso, *Medici e strutture sanitarie nella società tardo-medievale: il Piemonte dei secoli XIV e XV* (Milan, 1982); on Bologna, Gianna Pomata, *La promessa di guarigione: Malati e curatori in Antico Regime* (Rome/Bari, 1994); Richard Palmer, 'Physicians and surgeons in sixteenth-century Venice', *Medical History*, 23 (1979), pp. 451–60; Guido Ruggiero, 'The status of physicians and surgeons in Renaissance Venice', *Journal of the History of Medicine*, 36 (1981), pp. 168–84. One of the very few historians to have looked at conditions in the countryside is D. Pesciatini, 'Maestri, medici, cerusici nelle communità rurali pisane nel XVII secolo', in Paolo Rossi et al., eds, *Scienze, credenze occulte, livelli di cultura* (Florence, 1982), pp. 121–45. For other older but still useful local studies, see Park, *Doctors and Medicine*, p. 11 n. 22.

women accused of witchcraft. Not only were such women by definition atypical, but the representation of their activities contained in the records of trials and inquests often reveals more about the theories and assumptions of medical, legal and theological authorities than about the women themselves. Trial documents are also our main source for patient attitudes, expectations and experiences concerning illness and healing, the study of which is still in its infancy.[9] Historians can also use diaries and letter collections, like those of Francesco and Margherita Datini, to track the attitudes, choices and experiences of elite patients, but the world of the poor and illiterate still remains largely out of reach.

Gender and healing

Where historians of medicine have traditionally described a social, economic and epistemological hierarchy of healers, ranging from (often female) empirics or cunning people on the bottom to (exclusively male) physicians on the top, patients like Margherita and Francesco saw a broad spectrum of functionally differentiated practices and practitioners, arranged in what is sometimes called a hierarchy of resort. In the pluralistic and loosely regulated world of Renaissance medical practice, urban patients, particularly well-to-do urban patients, had a wealth of choices as to whom to consult for a given condition, and many exercised those choices to the full. If home nursing – together with the advice of friends and relatives – were inadequate, they might look to a local empiric, barber or apothecary, or, if they had the resources, a learned physician or surgeon. Even the urban poor often had some access to such services, through municipal poor doctors and local hospitals.[10] If professional help failed or was unaffordable or unavailable – usually the case in rural areas – they might look to magical or supernatural healing, through a cunning person or sorcerer, a faith healer, or a

9. For a model discussion of such sources, see Pomata, *Promessa di guarigione*, chapter 5; also, Monica Green, 'Documenting medieval women's medical practice', in Luis Garcìa-Ballester, Roger French, Jon Arrizabalaga and Andrew Cunningham, eds, *Practical Medicine from Salerno to the Black Death* (Cambridge, UK, 1994), pp. 322–52.

10. Vivian Nutton, 'Continuity or rediscovery? The city physician in classical antiquity and medieval Italy', in Andrew W. Russell, ed., *The Town and State Physician in Europe from the Middle Ages to the Enlightenment* (Wolfenbüttel, 1981), pp. 9–46; Park, *Doctors and Medicine*, pp. 89–94, 101–6; idem, 'Healing the poor: hospitals and medical assistance in Renaissance Florence', in Jonathan Barry and Colin Jones, eds, *Medicine and Charity before the Welfare State* (London, 1991), pp. 26–45.

priest, or they might engage in a serious regime of charity and prayer, buttressed by ritual appeals to God and the saints.

Both male and female healers operated within this framework of patient options. In the organization of their working lives, urban healers fell into two main groups. The first consisted of licensed practitioners, who were matriculated in the municipal guilds that regulated and theoretically monopolized urban medical practice.[11] For the most part full-time workers, these men – and exceptionally women – received fees from private patients and salaries from the hospitals, monasteries, confraternities and other institutions that employed them. Guild records often divided these officially licensed healers into three main groups, depending on training and type of practice: physicians (*fisici*), who had university degrees and treated mainly internal illnesses; surgeons (*cerusici*), who were mostly trained by formal apprenticeship and cared for patients with wounds, fractures, skin conditions and other external illnesses; and empirics (*empirici*). The last treated a range of illnesses, but most specialized in a single condition or a small set of conditions, usually surgical, such as cataracts, wounds, fractures and dislocations, hernias or bladder stones. Besides these licensed practitioners were also the apothecaries (*speziali*), who sold medicines and provided medical advice, and barbers (*barbieri*), who bled patients, pulled their teeth, and supplied other sorts of minor medical care; members of these last two groups were not identified as doctors (*medici* or *mediche*), nor did they use the usual professional honorific of *Maestro/Maestra* (in Latin, *Magister/Magistra*).[12]

The officially licensed urban doctors were overwhelmingly male, although in the absence of more local studies, it is impossible to give statistics for more than a few cities. The most complete information published to date comes from the cusp between the Middle

11. For the guilds' role in shaping urban medical practice, see Park, *Doctors and Medicine*, chapter 1, esp. pp. 15–42, and the literature cited there.

12. On physicians and surgeons, see Nancy G. Siraisi, *Medieval and Early Renaissance Medicine: An Introduction to Knowledge and Practice* (Chicago, 1990), chapters 2, 5 and 6. On empirics and barbers, see Tiziana Pesenti Marangon, '"Professores chirurgie", "medici ciroici" e "barbitonsores" a Padova nell'età di Leonardo Buffi da Bertipaglia (+ dopo il 1448)', *Quaderni per la storia dell'Università di Padova*, 11 (1978), pp. 1–38; Park, 'Stones, bones, and hernias: surgical specialists in fourteenth- and fifteenth-century Italy', in Jon Arrizabalaga, ed., *Medicine from the Black Death to the French Disease* (London, 1998); Gianna Pomata, 'Barbieri e comari', in Giancarlo Susini et al., *Medicina, erbe e Magia* (Milan, 1981), pp. 161–83. On apothecaries, see Richard Palmer, 'Pharmacy in the republic of Venice in the sixteenth century', in A. Wear, R.K. French and I.M. Lonie, eds, *The Medical Renaissance of the Sixteenth Century* (Cambridge, UK, 1985), pp. 100–17.

Ages and the Renaissance, and from the Kingdom of Naples, where 3,670 medical licences issued between 1273 and 1409 include thirty-four conferred on twenty-four women – a rate of slightly under one per cent.[13] All these women were empirics (*ydiote* or *perite*, according to the documents), specializing in the treatment of particular surgical conditions. Often, the licences limited their practice not only to those conditions, but also to female patients. In the words of the 1345 licence granted to Raimonda da Taverna, for example,

> the aforesaid Raimonda . . . has been examined by our surgeons as an empiric [*ydiota*] and has been found competent to cure the aforesaid illnesses ['cancers' (*cancri*), wounds and fistulas]. Although it is unsuitable for women to associate with men, lest they compromise their feminine modesty and fear the blame of forbidden transgression, [nonetheless] they have a legal right to practise medicine, given that women are more fitted to treat sick women, especially in conditions that involve their modesty.[14]

As this document specifies, women had the right to practise medicine in the Kingdom of Naples, but the licensing authorities hedged this right with numerous restrictions. In the first place, they limited women to the less lucrative and less prestigious work of surgical specialists, which required no book learning or broad training. (Men, in contrast, received licences to practise as physicians and general surgeons as well as empirical surgeons.) In the second place, the authorities were inclined, ostensibly for moral reasons, to restrict women's practice to female patients and to conditions where attendance by a male doctor would violate their modesty, requiring him to examine or touch parts of their bodies that were normally clothed, especially their breasts or genitals. Of the twenty-four women mentioned above, only six received licences that did not restrict them to female patients and conditions. (There were no corresponding restrictions on male practice.) It is of course impossible to determine how many female practitioners obeyed such restrictions, but the evidence of the licences shows that political and medical authorities viewed female practitioners as largely auxiliary to male ones, limited by their lack of formal education to the humblest sector of official medical practice and suitable to treat only those illnesses of female patients that modesty would forbid their male colleagues.

13. Raffaele Calvanico, *Fonti per la storia della medicina e della chirurgia per il regno di Napoli nel periodo angioino (a. 1273–1410)* (Naples, 1962). Both men and women could receive multiple licences: see Green, 'Women's medical practice', p. 48 n. 25.
14. Calvanico, *Fonti*, no. 3643, p. 277.

Officially recognized women practitioners were equally rare in the few northern Italian cities for which some information has been collected. The almost 350 doctors who matriculated in the Florentine Guild of Doctors, Apothecaries and Grocers between 1345 and 1444 included only five women, corresponding to between one and two per cent of the total, although the guild listed an additional five as apothecaries. Of these five women doctors (*mediche*), two were doctors' daughters – one of them a Jew.[15] In Venice, Ladislao Münster found documents relating to seven female practitioners from the early fourteenth century; these included a physician with the honorific title of *Magistra*, a surgeon's widow who was fined for malpractice, and an empiric who specialized in eye problems and gout.[16] As Münster has shown, although women were not officially licensed in Venice, as in Florence or Naples, the state permitted them to practise by special dispensation (*per grazia*).[17]

Thus there was some regional variation in patterns of licensing. In northern Italy, unlike Naples, we find women officially recognized as physicians, as well as surgeons and empirics, albeit with a distinct preponderance in the latter two categories, and there is little evidence that they were expected to treat primarily or exclusively women patients. (An exception to this rule were the *mediche di casa*, or 'house doctors', who lived and worked in the women's wards of large urban hospitals like Florence's Santa Maria Nuova.)[18] In Naples, women practised under apparently greater restrictions, being limited exclusively to certain types of empirical surgery and, often, to female patients. On the other hand, southern Italy seems to have had a stronger tradition of autonomous licensed female practice than the north, where virtually all of the women whose family ties can be identified were the daughters, wives or widows of licensed and guilded male doctors. Indeed, the relative independence of southern Italian women practitioners – also reflected in the

15. Park, *Doctors and Medicine*, pp. 71–2, which lists four women; I have since found a fifth, Monna Iacopa, wife of Iacopo, daughter of Giusto (ASF, AMS, 9, fol. 16v). Statistics based on matriculations lists in ASF, AMS, 7, 8, and 9.

16. Ladislao Münster, 'Notizie di alcune "medichesse" veneziane della prima età del Trecento', in *Scritti in onore del Professore Adalberto Pazzini* (Saluzzo, 1954), pp. 180–7. In 1324, the government kept thirty-one male doctors on the public payroll to treat the general population: B. Cecchetti, *Per la storia della medicina in Venezia: spigolature d'archivio* (Venice, 1888), p. 22.

17. Münster, 'Notizie'; Green, 'Documenting medieval women's medical practice', pp. 342–3.

18. Park, 'Healing the poor', p. 32; Katharine Park and John Henderson, '"The first hospital among Christians": the Ospedale di Santa Maria Nuova in early sixteenth-century Florence', *Medical History*, 35 (1991), p. 186. These women did not matriculate as doctors in the guild.

textual tradition associated with the Salernitan Trotula – may have been fostered in part by heightened southern Italian concerns about the modesty of female patients at the hands of male doctors.[19]

The relative paucity in northern Italy of licensed female practitioners and the prominence of their family connections reflect more general findings concerning women's employment in this period: whatever their occupations, women rarely received formal training in the work place and tended, as a result, to be segregated into lower-status and marginal positions. Because their employment was often bound up with and limited by family relationships and responsibilities, women usually worked intermittently, or in more than one job, and they often entered the official work force only on the death of a father or husband, to whom their shop or practice had originally belonged.[20]

If, however, we turn to unlicensed and unguilded practitioners – that cloud of casual and unofficial healers that served as the first line of defence for villagers and for city-dwellers of humble means – we find a very different situation. Here, women like Margherita's poultice doctor figured much more prominently, and both men and women exhibited the 'female' pattern of employment described above. Many combined disparate activities: shoemaker and cataract surgeon (both jobs required a sure hand with a needle), priest and hernia doctor, homemaker and herbalist,[21] and they lent or sold

19. On the tradition of Trotula and the *mulieres Salernitane*, see John Benton, 'Trotula, women's problems, and the professionalization of medicine in the Middle Ages', *Bulletin of the History of Medicine*, 59 (1985), pp. 30–53; Monica Green, *Women and Literate Medicine in Medieval Europe: Trota and the 'Trotula'* (Cambridge, UK, forthcoming). For references to female modesty from fourteenth- and fifteenth-century northern Italian physicians, if not licensing authorities, see Antonio Falcucci, *Sermones medicinales*, 7.3.43, 4 vols (Venice, 1490–91), fol. 87v; Helen Rodnite Lemay, 'Antonius Guainerius and medieval gynecology', in Julius Kirshner and Suzanne F. Wemple, eds, *Women of the Medieval World: Essays in honour of John H. Mundy* (Oxford, 1985), pp. 321–3. Nevertheless, male physicians were apparently free not only to direct the actions of midwives or *mediche*, but also to palpate, examine or even operate on female patients themselves; see the examples in Antonio Benivieni, *De abditis nonnullis ac mirandis morborum et sanationum causis*, 28, 31, ed. and trans. Giorgio Weber (Florence, 1994), pp. 89, 91.

20. Maryanne Kowaleski and Judith Bennett, 'Crafts, gilds, and women in the Middle Ages: fifty years after Marian K. Dale', in Bennett, et al., eds, *Sisters and Workers in the Middle Ages* (Chicago, 1989), pp. 11–38; Judith C. Brown, 'A woman's place was in the home: women's work in Renaissance Tuscany', in Margaret W. Ferguson, Maureen Quilligan and Nancy J. Vickers, eds, *Rewriting the Renaissance: The Discourses of Sexual Difference in Early Modern Europe* (Chicago, 1986), pp. 206–24; and Green, 'Documenting medieval women's medical practice', pp. 331–2.

21. Examples respectively in ASF, Catasto 78, fol. 242r; Benivieni, *De abditis*, ed. Weber, 73, pp. 132–3; and Claudio Bondi, *Strix: Medichesse, streghe e fattucchiere nell'Italia del Rinascimento* (Rome, 1989), pp. 5–22.

their services to friends, neighbours, and clients who knew them personally or who were referred to them by word of mouth.

Because such practitioners were unlicensed, male as well as female, it is impossible to compile statistics for either their absolute or their relative numbers, and the paucity of documentation about their practice makes it hard to collect specific information concerning their activities. In particular, it is hard to judge how many men and women of this sort employed purely naturalistic remedies, since most of those who ended up in the legal records generally did so not because they violated the (apparently largely ineffectual) laws protecting the monopoly of healing by guilded doctors, but because they were engaging in what local religious authorities considered theologically dubious activities, involving incantations and charms. Certainly, some of these men and women developed powerful reputations for their skills in identifying plants and their healing properties – skills recognized even by contemporary learned physicians. Michele Savonarola carefully copied into his mid-fifteenth-century work on medical practice the vernacular names by which Ferrarese women referred to particular herbs,[22] while Antonio Guaineri recorded the recipes used by local women against miscarriages and suffocation of the uterus in his mid-fifteenth-century *Treatise on Wombs.*[23] It is worth noting, however, that Guaineri also warned against the malice and incompetence of midwives, enchanters and other female healers, and he strongly recommended that his colleagues 'establish a difference between [themselves] and vulgar practitioners'.[24]

But the distinction between naturalistic and magical healing was blurry, even in the eyes of learned physicians: Guaineri refused to rule out the efficacy of charms and incantations, and he recorded apparently magical remedies for epilepsy and some women's disorders, though hedged with caveats and reservations.[25] This blurring is even more apparent in vernacular medicine, where simple herbal remedies were often administered, or recorded, in conjunction with charms. The promiscuous character of this type of healing appears clearly in a vernacular collection of recipes and formulas

22. Albano Biondi, 'La signora delle erbe e la magia della vegetazione', in Susini et al., eds, in *Medicina, erbe e magia*, pp. 186–8.
23. Lemay, 'Antonius Guainerius', pp. 326–31.   24. Cited in ibid., p. 327.
25. Danielle Jacquart, 'De la science à la magie: le cas d'Antonio Guainerio, médecin italien du XVe siècle', in Y. David-Peyre et al., eds, *La possession* (Nantes, 1988), esp. pp. 147–50; H.R. Lemay, 'Women and the literature of obstetrics and gynecology', in Joel T. Rosenthal, ed., *Medieval Women and the Sources of Medieval History* (Athens, GA, 1990), pp. 195, 197–8.

compiled in 1364 by Ruberto di Guido Bernardi, an otherwise unknown Florentine layman, who listed naturalistic remedies and incantations side by side. Bernardi's remedies for worms, for example, include several that are purely herbal (garlic mashed with tepid vinegar, a plaster made of leeks and peach-tree leaves, an infusion of cabbage seeds), together with an obvious incantation: 'If someone has worms', he noted, 'write these words and he will not perish. On his forehead write *ono*, on his chest write *manovello*, on his hands *manasti*, on his knee write *gobo*, on his foot write *vermi*.'[26]

Although we do not know for what purposes Bernardi copied such charms and recipes, it is clear that others used such techniques as part of their healing practices. In 1375, for example, the judicial authorities of Reggio Emilia condemned Gabrina di Gianozzo degli Albeti to have her tongue amputated. Her crime was an eclectic practice which involved prescriptions that ranged from administering camomile tea (for bad temper, in abusive husbands) to sleeping beside a sword used to perform a murder (for impotence).[27] Elena, called la Draga, prosecuted by Venetian authorities for witchcraft in 1591, treated backaches with an ointment made of chestnut oil and catarrh with honey and sage. But she also had frequent recourse to magic. To cure an illness caused by witchcraft, for example, she said,

I go and take five sprigs of rue and five of ambrosia and five of incense and five of *erba stella*, and five cloves of garlic, and while preparing it I say five *pater nosters* and five *ave marias* in honour of the five wounds of [our lord] Jesus Christ. And I also take soot from Christmas Eve, and I crush all these things between two pieces of marble, and then I put on that five penniesworth of bay: and the child should be anointed with that poultice in a cross starting with the arm right down the body, saying:

'In the name of Christ and the glorious virgin Mary and of the Most Holy Trinity that the Lord should be the one to heal you from this illness.'[28]

26. [Ruberto di Guido Bernardi], *Una curiosa raccolta di segreti e di pratiche superstiziose fatta da un popolano fiorentino del secolo XIV*, ed. Giovanni Giannini (Città di Castello, 1898), pp. 31, 132 (quotations). See David Gentilcore, *From Bishop to Witch: The System of the Sacred in Early Modern Terra d'Otranto* (Manchester, 1992), chapter 5.

27. Bondì, *Strix*, pp. 14–15. Gabrina's downfall was obviously caused by her involvement in the latter practices rather than in the former. On the use of herbs by men and (especially) women accused of witchcraft, see Biondi, 'Signora delle erbe'.

28. Cited in Ruth Martin, *Witchcraft and the Inquisition in Venice, 1550–1650* (Oxford, 1989), p. 142.

Most regions had a wealth of healers like Gabrina and la Draga, who certainly outnumbered officially licensed practitioners, at least in rural areas and poorer urban neighbourhoods.[29] When Francesco da Lignamine made an episcopal visit to the countryside surrounding Ferrara in 1447 and 1448, for example, he found more than twenty cunning men and women practising what he described in his report as 'enchanting wounds', 'enchanting blood and wounds' or 'making precantations and incantations'; prominent among them was the priest of Tresigallo, who 'made written charms [*brevia*] for fevers'.[30] With the exception of one Giuliana, denounced as having cast a spell on another woman, none of these practitioners were examined or prosecuted, probably because they were seen as intending to heal rather than harm and because they avoided the more extreme remedies and rituals like those prescribed by Gabrina in Reggio.

It is difficult to estimate the relative numbers of men and women active in this type of healing, but certainly both sexes were well represented. The list of such practitioners compiled by the archpriest of Guagnano on the occasion of the archbishop's 1565 visitation of Brindisi seems to have been typical in its mix of men and women and in the specialization it reveals:

> Andrea Cappuccella; Antonio Agliano, alias Pipici enchants [*incantat*] the pains of animals; Clementia Memma enchants the bewitched; Don Giuseppe Memmo enchants the diseases of animals; Pompilio Candido enchants the chill fevers of men; Sister Avenia enchants the pains of joints; Sister Rosata enchants headaches; the above are from Guagnano; Don Gabriele Passante enchants chill fevers.[31]

This list included three women (two of them nuns) and five men (two of them priests). The presence of nuns was somewhat unusual, but the relatively high proportion of women and priests also appears in other contemporary documents.

Although both male and female 'enchanters' used many of the same techniques and methods, their practices seem nonetheless to reflect certain gender-related patterns. For one thing, clients consulted women particularly (though not exclusively) for problems

29. On the importance of this kind of practice around the Venetian Arsenal, for example, see Robert C. Davis, *Shipbuilders of the Venetian Arsenal: Workers and Workplace in the Preindustrial City* (Baltimore, 1991), pp. 109–15.

30. Albano Biondi, 'Streghe ed eretici nei domini estensi all'epoca dell'Ariosto', in Paolo Rossi et al., eds, *Il Rinascimento nelle corti padane: società e culture* (Bari, 1977), p. 168.

31. Cited in Gentilcore, *From Bishop to Witch*, p. 130.

concerning reproduction and sexuality: male impotence, female infertility or, conversely, the need for a contraceptive.[32] (A related aspect of many women's practices – though this moves beyond the realm of healing proper – involved the preparation of love potions meant to keep unfaithful husbands and lovers at home.) In this connection, as Luisa Accati has noted, it is striking how many of the remedies prescribed by women involved the female genitals and female excretions or secretions, most commonly milk and menstrual blood.[33] Thus, Gabrina da Reggio recommended to one woman, whose husband had left her for a concubine, that she take some of her own pubic hairs and some nail parings from her husband, place them into the heart of a black hen, insert the heart in her vagina, and then, having taken nine steps bearing a lighted holy candle, remove the heart, chop it up, and give it to him to eat.[34] When a similar remedy did not work for another woman, Gabrina tried stronger magic, instructing her to throw salt on a fire and, having recited a charm, touch first her vulva and then his mouth, 'and she would [thus] kiss her husband with the lips of her privates [*labiis pudibondis*]'.[35] Even the physician Antonio Guaineri recommended treating excessive menstruation with a remedy that included menstrual blood, though he warned his colleagues to hide this fact from their female patients.[36]

I will discuss the meanings implicit in this use of the female body shortly. Here, however, it is enough to contrast it with the forms of magical healing practised by men, which much less often involved the material male body. When the male genitals figured at all, they usually did so in the abstract form of pictorial representations, accompanied by written charms called *brevi*, worn on the body. For example, Pietro da Arezzo was denounced in 1496 for paying a priest to say mass on Friday ('il giorno di Venere') and for having in his possession 'a certain *breve* on which were written certain characters, with in the middle the image of the virile member'.[37] In general, probably because of their higher level of literacy, the magical

32. For an example of the latter, see Bondì, *Strix*, p. 37.

33. Luisa Accati, 'The spirit of fornication: virtue of the soul and virtue of the body in Friuli, 1600–1800' (1979), trans. Margaret A. Gallucci, in Edward Muir and Guido Ruggiero, eds, *Sex and Gender in Historical Perspective* (Baltimore, 1990), esp. pp. 116–21; also Guido Ruggiero, *Binding Passions: Tales of Magic, Marriage, and Power at the End of the Renaissance* (New York, 1993).

34. Bondì, *Strix*, p. 12.   35. Ibid., p. 17; also see Biondi, 'Streghe', p. 172.

36. Cited in Lemay, 'Antonius Guainerius', p. 324.

37. Biondi, 'Streghe', p. 173.

and informal medical practice of priests often emphasized the written word, in the form of charms, books (like Bernardi's) that could be mined for specific incantations, or techniques that involved writing names on, for example, leaves to be eaten or beans to be thrown into a fire.[38] The bookish nature of the magic practised by men learned in the Latin language reached its apogee in *On Life*, the erudite treatise on magical astrological healing composed in the later fifteenth century by the Florentine Marsilio Ficino. Son of a Medici family physician and himself a philosopher with some medical training, Ficino used both medieval medical theory and Hellenistic magical lore to compile an influential set of recommendations for the practice of a refined form of magical healing; this mobilized beneficent planetary influences using music and expensive natural substances, such as incense, precious metals and incised gems.[39]

If, on a less exalted level, there was a great deal of overlap between the magical healing practised by women and that practised by (especially) laymen, there is nonetheless one respect in which the impact of gender was unambiguous: the significantly greater frequency with which women were prosecuted for witchcraft by civil and ecclesiastical authorities. This preponderance is visible as early as the beginning of the fourteenth century – of the nine people examined for witchcraft in Piedmont between 1300 and 1337, for example, eight were women – but it was not without exception: the eight sorcery cases prosecuted in fourteenth-century Florence involved five men and only four women, perhaps as a result of local political, and therefore masculine, concerns.[40] The general tendency to single out women increased markedly over the course of the fifteenth and, especially, the sixteenth centuries, as legal and theological authorities came increasingly to suspect that female practices previously accepted as at worst misguided and ineffective were in fact demonic, if not part of a wide-ranging satanic conspiracy. The outlines of this process are already visible in the years around 1400, when the Dominican friar Filippo of Siena could describe all women enchanters as 'cursed demoniacs [*maladette pessime diaboliche*]'

38. Biondi, 'Streghe', pp. 173–5; note also the prevalence of books and written texts in the cases of male sorcerers described in Gene Brucker, 'Sorcery in early Renaissance Florence', *Studies in the Renaissance*, 10 (1963), pp. 7–24.

39. Marsilio Ficino, *Three Books on Life*, ed. and trans. Carol V. Kaske and John R. Clark (Binghamton, NY, 1989). On Ficino's magical medicine, see D.P. Walker, *Spiritual and Demonic Magic from Ficino to Campanella* (London, 1958), pp. 3–53 and 75–84.

40. Naso, *Medici e strutture sanitarie*, p. 133 n. 39; Brucker, 'Sorcery'.

and 'doctors of the devil', who 'believe that what God does not want to do, all the devils in hell can'.[41]

The reasons behind this Europe-wide 'feminization' of sorcery (in the perception of the prosecutors, if not in actual practice) are complicated and as yet poorly understood. Rooted in a longstanding tradition of misogyny, particularly pronounced among Dominican writers, it seems to have fed on the complicated dynamics of village life and the particular responsibility of women to care for infants, children and puerperal women, whose health was particularly vulnerable.[42] But it also reflects more general attempts to limit the activities of women as healers. These attempts formed part of a longer and more gradual process whereby doctors (primarily male) formally accredited by municipal guilds and universities acted to exclude their socially and politically more marginal competitors (including many women). Already clearly visible in the thirteenth century, this process had its roots in the gradual institutionalization and professionalization of medical practice that accompanied the growth of late medieval cities.[43] Women were not the only ones targeted. The *Regimen of Health*, an influential medical poem produced at Salerno sometime after 1250, inveighed against a miscellaneous list of what it identified as false doctors (*medicastri*): 'The illiterate, the empiric, the Jew, the monk, the actor, the barber, the old woman – each pretends to be a doctor. ... While they seek profit, the power of medicine suffers.'[44]

Physicians and surgeons continued to criticize the practice of all these groups, but by the late fourteenth and fifteenth century, women (particularly old women, or *vetule*) had come to stand metonymically for the range of empirical and informal practitioners castigated in the rhetoric of officially licensed doctors. This rhetoric identified old women with ignorance, superstition and malice; these qualities were the obverse of those claimed by the emergent

41. Cited in Giuseppe Bonomo, *Caccia alle streghe: le credenza nelle streghe dal secolo XIII al XIX con particolare riferimento all'Italia* (Palermo, 1959), p. 139 and chapter 7. Bonomo documents the gradual growth of the conviction among theologians and legal theorists that much popular magical activity was demonic.

42. Helen Rodnite Lemay, 'Introduction', in her *Women's Secrets: A Translation of Pseudo-Albertus Magnus's De secretis mulierum with Commentaries* (Albany, NY, 1992), esp. pp. 49–58; Martin, *Witchcraft and the Inquisition*, pp. 226–38; and Lyndal Roper, *Oedipus and the Devil: Witchcraft, Sexuality, and Religion in Early Modern Europe* (London, 1994), esp. chapter 9.

43. Katharine Park, 'Medicine and society in medieval Europe, 500–1500', in Andrew Wear, ed., *Medicine in Society* (Cambridge, 1991), pp. 75–9.

44. *Flos medicinae* 3472–6, in Salvatore de Renzi, ed., *Collectio salernitana* 5 vols (Naples, 1852–59), Vol. V, p. 103.

profession in its quest for privileges and recognition, which thus both drew on and shaped a stereotype that helps to explain the large and growing preponderance of women implicated in the witch trials of the fifteenth through to the seventeenth century.[45] In its most extreme form – as expressed, say, in the *Malleus maleficarum*, or *Hammer of Witches* (1486), of the German Dominican inquisitors Heinrich Kramer and Jakob Sprenger – this stereotype portrayed all women, but especially old women, as physically and psychologically venomous, their bodies sinks of toxic residues that could be controlled only by monthly evacuation.[46] The post-menopausal lacked even that mechanism, unable to release their internal toxins except through the eyes, in the form of a poisonous gaze known as 'fascination'.[47]

But virulently misogynistic works such as the *Malleus* should not be taken as expressing the only, or even the dominant view of female corporeality in the Renaissance period, especially in Italy, where the prosecution of witches was neither as frequent nor as extreme as in Germany and other parts of northern Europe. Contemporary physiological ideas were complicated and multivalent, and even the learned often disagreed on matters as basic as the nature of menstruation or whether women, like men, contributed seed in the process of conception.[48] In fact, contemporary constructions of the body tended to emphasize the physical similarities between men and women far more than their differences – and in some respects far more than we do today. One of the most

45. Jole Agrimi and Chiara Crisciani, 'Savoir médical et anthropologie religieuse: les représentations et les fonctions de la *vetula* (XIIIe–XVe siècle)', *Annales ESC*, 48 (1993), pp. 1281–308; ibid., 'Medici e "vetulae" dal Duecento al Quattrocento: problemi di una ricerca', in Paolo Rossi et al., eds, *Cultura popolare e cultura dotta nel Seicento* (Milan, 1983), pp. 144–59.

46. See Lemay, 'Introduction', in her *Women's Secrets*, pp. 48–58. On the internal workings of the female body according to Renaissance medical theory and natural philosophy, see Ian Maclean, *The Renaissance Notion of Woman: A Study in the Fortunes of Scholasticism and Medical Science in European Intellectual Life* (Cambridge, UK, 1980), chapter 4.

47. On fascination and its folk analogue *malocchio*, see Agrimi and Crisciani, 'Savoir médical', pp. 1297–303; Danielle Jacquart and Claude Thomasset, *Sexuality and Medicine in the Middle Ages* (1985), trans. Matthew Adamson (Princeton, NJ, 1988), pp. 71–8; and Gentilcore, *Bishop to Witch*, pp. 147–8. On the noxious qualities of menstrual blood, see Ottavia Niccoli, '"Menstruum quasi monstruum": monstrous births and menstrual taboo in the sixteenth century', trans. Mary M. Gallucci, in Muir and Ruggiero, eds, *Sex and Gender in Historical Perspective*, pp. 1–25.

48. Maclean, *Renaissance Notion*, pp. 35–7; Jacquart and Thomasset, *Sexuality and Medicine*, pp. 61–78. The authoritative treatment of this topic is Joan Cadden, *Meanings of Sex Difference in the Middle Ages: Medicine, Science, and Culture* (Cambridge, UK, 1993).

extreme manifestations of this tendency was the (predominantly Aristotelian) strand of thought that described women exclusively as defective males, their colder and moister bodies unable fully to digest the food they ate, or even to push their genitals to the outside of their bodies.

It is certainly possible to find statements of this idea among both professional anatomists and natural philosophers, particularly those with a strong neo-Aristotelian bent, but it did not dominate the minds of lay patients or shape the therapeutics of most medical practitioners. Rather, as Gianna Pomata has argued, the general physiology that informed much medical practice, both popular and learned, focused on ideas of evacuation. Male or female, the body was imagined less as a congeries of organs than as a system of flowing humours or liquids, which might be internally or externally obstructed, so that they rotted ('became corrupted', in contemporary terminology) and produced disease.[49] Healing thus became a matter of evacuating superfluous or corrupt humours, through menstruation, urination, excretion, bleeding, vomiting, sweating, salivation and the like. This might happen spontaneously, as part of the healing power of nature, or might be provoked by medical practitioners, using medication or external and surgical means such as cupping, scarification, cautery, and plasters.

This more gender-neutral view of health and disease appears clearly in *Certain Hidden and Wonderful Causes of Illness and Healing*, a collection of case studies compiled in the later fifteenth century by the Florentine physician Antonio Benivieni and published posthumously in 1507. In this work, Benivieni repeatedly undercut the notion of specifically male or female diseases; his one apparent case of 'suffocation of the uterus' turned out to be demonic possession.[50] Instead, he universalized even this quintessentially female complaint. Describing a girl from Arezzo who suffered from seizures, for example, he attributed these to vapours ascending to her brain, presumably from her uterus; 'the issue afforded plain proof', he noted, 'as when her monthly courses began she was freed from the disorder'. Yet he immediately extended this model to the male body: 'For as the advent of puberty often ends this disease in boys

49. Pomata, *Promessa di guarigione*, pp. 261–75; ibid., 'Uomini mestruanti. Somiglianza e differenza fra i sessi in Europa in età moderna', *Quaderni storici*, 79 (1992), pp. 51–103.

50. Benivieni, *De abditis* 8, trans. Charles Singer (Springfield, IL, 1954), pp. 34–7. On suffocation of the uterus in the European medical tradition, Ilza Veith, *Hysteria: The History of a Disease* (Chicago, 1965); and more recently, the essays in Sander L. Gilman, et al., eds, *Hysteria Beyond Freud* (Berkeley, CA, 1993).

so do the menses for girls'.[51] In general, Benivieni presented a remarkably consistent view of the male and female bodies and their illnesses. He emphasized the harmful effects of occlusion of both the male and female genitals, and he described many cases, among men as well as women, in which rotting humours inside the body produced worms in various organs by spontaneous generation.

But the most striking example of Benivieni's tendency to ascribe a similar physiology and analogous disease processes to both men and women is his account of the case of a 'menstruating man', which is worth transcribing in some detail:

> I knew a man of robust health and in his thirty-sixth year who complained frequently to me of a flux of blood which gave him serious trouble monthly. When I asked him from what part of the body it came, he said he did not know. I was astonished at this and told him to uncover the part whence the blood flowed. He took off his clothes and showed me his right flank where the lowest part of the liver is situated. I scrutinized the place very carefully to see if there was any orifice or scar there, but the whole had the even appearance of smooth soft flesh and I could see no sign of an opening or scar. I suspected the man of deceit. . . . He returned two days later with a finger covering the place to check the flow. When this was removed blood poured out as from a pierced vein, nor did it cease until a *libra* had issued. . . . I therefore treated him with a mere monthly bloodletting from the vein of the liver.[52]

The point here, as Pomata has emphasized, is not only that both men and women needed to purge themselves regularly, according to early modern medical opinion, but also that, in this respect, the female body was the paradigm and the model, rather than the male.[53]

This is not to downplay the pervasive misogyny of Renaissance medical learning, nor the extensive defects attributed to the female body and psyche in both lay and learned thought. But physicians, unlike most natural philosophers and theologians, tended to interpret this inferiority as moral and behavioural rather than purely corporeal. Thus the reason women needed to menstruate, while most men did not, was in large part their self-indulgent and sedentary lifestyle, which left their bodies cool and unable to concoct their own internal humours. As Benivieni himself complained, 'as is the nature of women, especially of noble birth, once cured they

51. Benivieni, *De abditis* 97, trans. Singer, p. 183.   52. Ibid., 4, pp. 27–9.
53. Pomata, 'Uomini mestruanti', p. 91.

observe none of the precautions advised for the protection and establishment of their health, but live as they please . . .'.[54]

But what of specifically magical practices and the implicit intellectual structures that underpinned them? Here one finds a less universalizing view – one that attributed peculiar powers to the female body. Working from seventeenth-century rural Friulian sources, Luisa Accati has described a set of ideas that located the magical power of women in their genitals and in the substances that issued from these: milk, menstrual blood, female pubic hair, the placenta and the caul. Accati argues that 'the prevalence of women in witchcraft was linked to the female body'; thus all women possessed the ability to heal and harm, while men had to work through external tools or special learning, since 'no part of the male body had magical powers'.[55] Accati has certainly overstated her case: male semen was also used in witchcraft (especially against impotence), and enchanters attributed special powers to virgin and pre-pubescent boys as well as girls, as the instructions for Margherita Datini's fertility belt show.[56] But the prominence of the female body and its products in contemporary witchcraft may offer yet another explanation for the special interest of civil and ecclesiastical authorities in female witches. At least in the eyes of those authorities, the acknowledged efficacy of women's magic came from harnessing demonic forces, and if women mobilized those forces using their own bodies, then those bodies might have to be destroyed.

Conclusion

The constellation of types of healing that I have described – magical, medical and religious – remained roughly constant throughout the Renaissance period. On the whole, men and women of the Italian cities and countryside had access to similar kinds of healing in the early seventeenth century than they had in the early fourteenth. There were important changes, to be sure, notably in medical organization and institutions for the delivery of health

54. Benivieni, *De abditis* 99, trans. Singer, p. 187; Lemay, 'Antonius Guainerius', pp. 334–5.
55. Accati, 'Spirit of fornication', pp. 110, 116; and ibid., 'The larceny of desire: the Madonna in seventeenth-century Catholic Europe', in Jim Obelkevitch, Lyndal Roper and Raphael Samuel, eds, *Disciplines of Faith: Studies in Religion, Politics, and Patriarchy* (London, 1987), pp. 73–86.
56. For an enchanter's use of semen, see Marcello Craveri, *Sante e streghe: Biografie e documenti dal XIV al XVII secolo*, 2nd edn (Milan, 1981), p. 172.

care: these three hundred years saw the appearance of large urban hospitals and other institutions offering professional medical care to the sick poor and training to physicians and surgeons, as well as the emergence of a wide-ranging and coercive regime of plague control and public health.[57] But these developments reveal more about the roots of the modern European and North American medical order than they do about the experience of contemporary patients: the hospitals were inadequate to meet the needs of the poor in most cities, and neither of these developments would have had much impact on the healing available to the majority of the population in non-epidemic years.

Perhaps of greater impact, and associated with the Counter-Reformation, was the buttressing of religious and medical authority against the claims of magical healers. In the years after 1570, Italy saw a dramatic increase in inquisitional activity, most of it directed not against heresy – relatively few Italian regions experienced any widespread diffusion of Protestantism or other forms of evangelical belief – but against 'superstition'. This last included many types of what ecclesiastical authorities considered ignorant or misguided religious observance and practice, much of it related to magical healing. In effect, the Church was attempting to consolidate its monopoly on the control of supernatural forces in this and other areas, just as the official medical profession, led by university-educated physicians, was trying increasingly to monopolize the functions of naturalistic treatment.[58] This process was made both more urgent and more difficult by the lack of clear boundaries between the practices of the three realms, which, as I have already argued, borrowed from each other's characteristic rituals and used many of the same means. Ecclesiastical and medical authority buttressed one another in their attempts to eliminate competition from magical and informal healers: in his influential *Medico-Legal Questions*, the early seventeenth-century papal physician Paolo Zacchia declared recourse to unlicensed healers a sin.[59]

This process was not focused in the first instance on gender; there is little evidence, as has sometimes been argued, that men

57. Ann Gayton Carmichael, *Plague and the Poor in Renaissance Florence* (Cambridge, UK, 1986); and the many studies of Carlo M. Cipolla, including *Public Health* and *Fighting the Plague in Seventeenth-Century Italy* (Madison, WI, 1981).

58. Mary R. O'Neil, '*Sacerdote ovvero strione*: Ecclesiastical and superstitious remedies in sixteenth-century Italy', in Steven L. Kaplan, ed., *Understanding Popular Culture: Europe from the Middle Ages to the Nineteenth Century* (Berlin, 1984), pp. 53–83; Gentilcore, *Bishop to Witch*, esp. pp. 138–44; Pomata, *Promessa di guarigione, passim.*

59. Pomata, *Promessa di guarigione*, pp. 250, 277 n. 9.

were trying to edge women out of the healing arts simply because they were women. But it inevitably had a strong gender dimension, precisely because most women healers were unlicensed, while priests, Church-accredited exorcists and most licensed doctors were male. The implicit competition appears clearly in the testimony given by Gasparino da Carpo on the occasion of an enquiry into the healing activities of one Hippolita da Figarolo, which took place in Modena in 1600. Suspecting that his wife had fallen ill on account of witchcraft, Gasparino called on a local friar to heal her by ecclesiastically approved measures, blessing her and signing her with the cross. 'Having learned that my wife had come to have herself signed by Fra Benedetto', according to Gasparino, 'Hippolita arrived at our house and said these or similar words to my wife: "Why have you not allowed me to heal? Did you not think I could heal you without going to the friar of San Domenico?"'[60] Squeezed, on the one hand, by ambitious doctors and, on the other, by suspicious priests and inquisitors, healers like Hippolita practised under increasing pressure. Conversely, the ability of both Church and medical profession to provide acceptable alternatives to magical healing may in turn account for the relative infrequency of witch trials in Italy, compared to areas like England or Germany. But this did not mean that informal female healers definitively lost their powers and their clienteles. Into the modern era, men and women continued to consult them when professional or ecclesiastical healing was unappealing or unavailable, or when, as in the case of Margarita and Francesco Datini, professional and ecclesiastical healers had failed to provide relief.

60. Cited in O'Neil, '*Sacerdote*', p. 70.

CHAPTER SEVEN

Gender and Sexual Culture in Renaissance Italy

MICHAEL ROCKE

In February 1496, friar Girolamo Savonarola, campaigning to reform the morals of Florentine society, fulminated against the sexual debauchery that, in his view, had 'ruined the world, . . . corrupted men in lust, led women into indecency, and boys into sodomy and filth, and made them become like prostitutes'. His condemnation of erotic licence stemmed not merely from its immorality, but also from his conviction that the indulgence of sexual pleasures produced a dangerous confusion of gender boundaries: 'Young lads have been made into women. But that's not all: fathers are like daughters, brothers like sisters. There is no distinction between the sexes or anything else anymore.'[1]

Savonarola's comment reveals some central assumptions of the culture of sex and gender in Renaissance Italy. Sexual behaviour was in fact a basic component of the complex of cultural and social signifiers that distinguished individuals, beyond their belonging to one biological sex or the other, as gendered beings, as masculine or feminine. His insistence on the transformative capacity of sex to make men into women, and presumably vice versa, indicates an awareness that gender identity was not a natural or fixed quality but was constructed and malleable, and as such it needed to be adequately shaped, reinforced and defended. The friar's remarks also betrayed deep anxiety about establishing and enforcing borders, not only between licit and illicit sexual comportment, but also between related virile and feminine conventions and ideals, for it was in part around such confines that society was properly ordered.

In recent years, historians have dedicated growing attention to sexual practices, beliefs and attitudes, and to how unauthorized sex

1. Girolamo Savonarola, *Prediche sopra Amos e Zaccaria*, P. Ghiglieri, ed., 3 vols (Rome, 1971–72), Vol. I, pp. 194, 200 (23 February 1496).

was regulated in various regions of late medieval and early modern Italy. Although much remains to be learned about the peninsula's distinctive sexual cultures and about local systems of policing sex, these studies have already deepened our understanding of Italian society and have thrown new light on relationships between sexuality, gender ideology, and masculine and feminine identities. Here I would like to chart some of these connections, beginning with the ideological conventions that shaped and constrained men's and women's sexual comportment in different ways; then examining how gender differences were configured in certain religious and legal prescriptions regarding sex; and finally exploring perspectives on gender that have emerged from unauthorized or illicit sexual behaviours.

Norms and ideals

In this strongly patriarchal and patrilineal society, the control of women's sexual conduct and reproductive functions was accorded especially high importance. Centuries-old philosophical, medical, legal and religious discourses on sexual difference continued to sustain the notion that women were inferior in all ways to men and subject to their dominion. Medieval understanding of female biology contributed to beliefs that women were passive and receptive in their sexual nature yet possessed a powerful yearning for semen and a more ravenous sexual appetite than that of men – a view reinforced by the Judeo-Christian myth of Eve the temptress, responsible for original sin and the fall from grace. Both religious doctrine and lay society upheld chastity as the supreme virtue of women, whether as young unwed virgins, wives or widows. The purity and modesty of the *donna onesta* was regularly contrasted with the shamelessness and incontinence of the 'indecent' woman, embodied especially in the figure of the prostitute.

The defence of female virginity before marriage and chastity thereafter also played an essential role in the pervasive culture of honour, a woman's sexual behaviour largely defining both her own standing and reputation and those of her family and of the males responsible for 'governing' her. Such concerns loomed especially large for wealthy and propertied families, for whom the guarantee of paternity determined the transmission of patrimonies and the competition for public honour carried momentous political stakes. This obsession was aptly stated by the Florentine patrician and humanist Matteo Palmieri in his *Vita Civile*:

Wives must exercise the greatest and most extraordinary guard not only against uniting with another man, but even to avoid all suspicion of such filthy wickedness. This error is the supreme disgrace to decency, it effaces honour, destroys union, renders paternity uncertain, heaps infamy on families and within them brings dissension and hatred and dissolves every relationship; she no longer deserves to be called a married woman but rather a corrupt wench, worthy only of public humiliation.[2]

It was in part to safeguard both their daughters' virginity and the family's honour that parents rushed their girls into marriage as soon as possible after sexual maturity, usually between the ages of fifteen and eighteen. For the same reason, unmarriageable patrician girls were quickly made nuns and secluded within a convent. To preserve their chastity, women of middle- and upper-class families tended to be isolated in their homes and their contacts with men were carefully controlled. Women at lower social levels, who generally lacked this powerful familial protection, had greater exposure to males and more freedom in their daily lives; for them, the conventions regarding virginity and chastity were probably somewhat less rigid.

Despite religious proscriptions against all extra-marital sex, standards and expectations with regard to male sexual behaviour were generally more flexible than those applied to women. No social ideal compelled men to remain virgins before marriage or demanded fidelity of them afterward. They were supposed to obey laws against rape, adultery, and other illicit acts, but lax enforcement and light penalties for many offences helped dull their dissuasive force. While men were to respect the virtue of women of honourable families, they had a large pool of slaves and servants, poor or immodest women, and prostitutes with whom they could acceptably indulge their desires. This sexual liberty was reinforced by the late age at which men normally married – from their late twenties to early thirties – and by substantial rates of men who never married. Denied economic autonomy under their fathers' patriarchal rule, and forbidden significant civic roles, young men lived in a state of prolonged and powerless adolescence. These footloose bachelors were the main protagonists of the violence and sexual debauchery characteristic of Renaissance Italy. City fathers, themselves once young, viewed their profligacy with some sympathy and indulgence; it also provided an excuse for barring them from

2. Matteo Palmieri, *Vita Civile*, F. Battaglia, ed. (Bologna, 1944), p. 133.

the serious business of governing, since 'they say youths should not discuss public affairs, but pursue their sexual needs'.[3]

Masculine identity did not, however, lie only in the double standard that allowed men the sexual freedoms denied to women, but also in conventions that identified manliness solely with a dominant role in sex. In this regard, males' sexual and gendered norms were as rigid as those imposing chastity on females. Potency figured among the constitutive features of masculinity, such that a man's failure to achieve erection was grounds for annulment of his marriage or divorce.[4] The association of virility with dominance was one source of the religious ban against couples engaging in intercourse with the woman on top, an 'unnatural' position considered emblematic of woman's usurpation – or man's abdication – of males' superior status.[5] Similar notions pervaded same-sex relations, in which adult men were expected to take an exclusively 'active' role in sex with adolescents, behaviour that corresponded fully with masculine ideals, while a mature man's assumption of the receptive role was abhorred as a dangerous transgression of gender norms.

Conjugal relations and religious precepts

The Church, the most authoritative source of moral teachings on sexual behaviour, established guidelines and norms which in principle were equally applicable to men and women. For all, sex was licit only within marriage, with the conscious aim of procreation, in prescribed times and conditions, and in a single position, with the couple facing and the man above. All intercourse outside marriage, as well as conjugal sex for mere pleasure, in forbidden positions, or in a manner that might impede generation, was condemned and prohibited. Although some late medieval theologians began to modify these tenets somewhat, sanctioning sensual pleasure as a

3. Donato Giannotti, *Opere politiche e letterarie di Donato Giannotti*, F. Polidori, ed., 2 vols (Florence, 1850), Vol. I, p. 230. On late male marriage and sexual behaviour, see David Herlihy, 'Vieillir à Florence au Quattrocento', *Annales, ESC*, 24 (1969), pp. 1346–9; Guido Ruggiero, *The Boundaries of Eros: Sex Crime and Sexuality in Renaissance Venice* (New York, 1985), esp. pp. 159–62; Michael Rocke, *Forbidden Friendships: Homosexuality and Male Culture in Renaissance Florence* (New York, 1996), pp. 113–32.

4. James A. Brundage, *Law, Sex, and Christian Society in Medieval Europe* (Chicago, 1987), p. 512; Vern Bullough, 'On being a male in the Middle Ages', in *Medieval Masculinities: Regarding Men in the Middle Ages*, C.A. Lees, ed. (Minneapolis, MN, 1994), pp. 41–2.

5. Natalie Davis, 'Women on top', in her *Society and Culture in Early Modern France: Eight Essays* (Stanford, CA, 1975), pp. 124–51.

reproductive aid and even permitting unconventional positions, the Church's sexual orthodoxy remained restricted.[6] How closely couples observed these prescriptions is another matter and is difficult to ascertain. That moralists continued to vehemently denounce practices such as anal intercourse that could serve contraceptive aims, and the rapid decline in wives' fertility that has been observed in fifteenth-century Tuscany would suggest that many spouses disregarded the sexual guidance of their preachers and confessors.[7]

However its teachings on sexual conduct were received, the Church played an important and perhaps more effective role in forming and transmitting notions of gender. While all were supposed to bear equal liability for their carnal acts, preachers presented sexual doctrines to the faithful in ways that carried considerably different messages for men and women. The sermons of Bernardino of Siena to the Sienese and Florentines in the 1420s offer some pertinent illustrations.[8] Bernardino's preaching on conjugal life fitted well with his culture's growing emphasis on marriage as a form of companionship between spouses who were to treat each other with mutual love and respect.[9] Regarding sex, he maintained that spouses shared responsibility for preventing each other from sinning, stressed that fidelity was a duty of wives and husbands, and reproached both for sexual failings. His teachings were embedded in a framework of values, consistent with Church doctrine and patrician ideals, that endorsed sexual moderation for both sexes, sustained the notion that women's frailty of reason made them more inclined than men to sin, and upheld wives' subjection to their husbands' authority. Within these traditions, however, the emphases and omissions of his remarks, or the shifts depending

6. Nicholas Davidson, 'Theology, nature and the law: sexual sin and sexual crime in Italy from the fourteenth to the seventeenth century', in *Crime, Society and the Law in Renaissance Italy*, T. Dean and K.J.P. Lowe, eds (Cambridge, UK, 1994), pp. 77–85.

7. David Herlihy and Christiane Klapisch-Zuber, *Les Toscans et leurs familles: une étude du catasto florentin de 1427* (Paris, 1978), pp. 441–2; Christiane Klapisch-Zuber, 'Famille, religion et sexualité à Florence au Moyen Age', *Revue de l'histoire des religions*, 209 (1992), pp. 381–92; Maria Serena Mazzi, *Prostitute e lenoni nella Firenze del Quattrocento* (Milan, 1991), pp. 55–9, 61–86.

8. *Prediche volgari sul campo di Siena 1427*, Carlo Delcorno, ed., 2 vols (Milan, 1989), Vol. I, pp. 538–621 (hereafter, *Siena 1427*); *Le prediche volgari*, C. Cannarozzi, ed., 2 vols (Pistoia, 1934), Vol. I, pp. 380–404 (hereafter, *Florence 1424*); *Le prediche volgari*, C. Cannarozzi, ed., 3 vols (Florence, 1940), Vol. II, pp. 173–90 (hereafter, *Florence 1425*).

9. For example, *Siena 1427*, I, pp. 556, 568–9; *Florence 1424*, I, p. 412; *Florence 1425*, II, p. 177. On increasingly positive evaluations of marriage, see Herlihy and Klapisch-Zuber, *Les Toscans*, pp. 586–8.

on the audience addressed, show some ways in which gendered assumptions framed his teachings and how ideal genders were shaped.

This can be seen most clearly in Bernardino's sermons about a basic tenet of Church doctrine, that is, the equality of spouses' rights and duties with regard to the 'marriage debt': while carefully observing the proper times, position, devout spirit and procreative aim of sex, husbands and wives possessed an identical right to intercourse, which their spouse was obliged, under penalty of mortal sin, to 'render' to them. Bernardino reiterated that this injunction applied indistinctly to both partners, but in developing this egalitarian theme he employed examples and lessons that revealed and reinforced assumptions about gender difference. He normally directed his remarks on rendering the debt to wives, rather than to husbands, as if he assumed that males more commonly importuned their spouses for sex, thus implicitly fortifying notions of man's 'active' nature and pressing desire and of woman's 'passivity' and, ideally, her modesty.[10] Sexual continence and shame were considered women's crowning virtues, and when he discussed marital sex Bernardino reminded wives to remain as chaste as possible, never allowing their spouses to see them naked, to look at their 'shameful parts', or to touch them indecently. On the few occasions he acknowledged wives' prerogative to request intercourse, he in effect disempowered them by insisting on their modesty. So as to reduce a wife's temptation to commit adultery, it was better, he claimed, that the husband anticipate her request and render his carnal obligation voluntarily, rather than for her to voice her longings. While a wife was bound to respond only if asked expressly for sex and was exonerated if her husband's signals were unclear, he was obliged to react to the 'smallest sign' of his wife's yearning to protect her from the indelicacy of having to express her desire.[11]

Although Bernardino stressed women's virtue and modesty in carnal relations, he paradoxically also placed on them a greater burden of sexual knowledge and responsibility. He began one discussion on conjugal sex by warning that ignorance of sin exculpated neither partner, but proceeded to address only the wives, mothers and nubile girls in the congregation. Girls about to marry 'had to know how to do it', and sinned if they neglected to learn; mothers who failed to impart the facts of life to their daughters committed

10. *Florence 1424*, I, pp. 381–404; *Siena 1427*, I, pp. 573–603.
11. *Siena 1427*, pp. 594, 617–18; *Florence 1425*, II, p. 179; *Florence 1424*, I, p. 393.

a serious mortal sin.[12] Rarely, if ever, did he encourage fathers to give their sons lessons in sex education.

Accordingly, Bernardino often instructed wives about the times and conditions when they could and should legitimately refuse their husbands' requests, thereby giving them some control over the frequency and character of intercourse. Although he warned both partners about the evils of unrestrained passion and specific sins, he tended to represent husbands as more inclined to 'disorderly affections' and excessive lust, which it was wives' duty to curb and correct. He insisted that, while wives were bound to obey their husbands, this never meant yielding to sinful requests. They were to refuse especially when their spouses wanted, as he implied they often did, to engage in acts *contra naturam* that impeded procreation. He also warned the wife to decline if her husband had imbibed too much wine, was crazed with lust, or desired sex so frequently that it might devitalize his seed, make him lose his senses, or cause illness or death.[13] Repeating an ancient taboo, revived vigorously in the Renaissance, he admonished women to rebuff husbands' requests for coitus during their menstrual period, which according to both popular and learned belief risked generating deformed or leprous children.[14] But in Italy, he conceded, a wife had better conceal her menstruous state and quietly render the debt, because otherwise her husband would demand anal intercourse. Bernardino also instructed wives, not husbands, to assess their mates' age and their physical and spiritual condition when considering whether or how often to consent to intercourse. He more often mentioned husbands' threats to satisfy their desires elsewhere as binding wives to render the debt, a tacit acknowledgment of men's greater opportunities to pursue extra-marital relations. It was only wives, however, whom he urged to grant consent selectively, in order to wean their husbands gradually from sex and convince them to embrace abstinence – for the Church, the 'perfect state'.[15]

12. *Siena 1427*, pp. 577–83.
13. *Florence 1424*, I, pp. 388–9, 395–8; *Siena 1427*, I, pp. 588–91, 593, 600, 602–3.
14. *Florence 1424*, I, pp. 387–8; *Siena 1427*, I, pp. 591–2. On menstruation beliefs, see Joan Cadden, *Meanings of Sex Differences in the Middle Ages: Medicine, Science, and Culture* (Cambridge, UK, 1993), pp. 173–6, 268; Ottavia Niccoli, '"Menstruum quasi monstruum": monstrous births and menstrual taboo in the sixteenth century', in E. Muir and G. Ruggiero, eds, *Sex & Gender in Historical Perspective* (Baltimore, 1990), pp. 1–25.
15. *Siena 1427*, I, pp. 592, 594–7, 600–1.

The law and the courts

Distinctions in the treatment of men and women also character-ized the regulation of illicit sex, both in law and in court practice. Italian governments between 1400 and 1600 took a forceful role in legislating and policing sexual behaviour. Although legal norms, judiciary systems and enforcement of sex laws varied widely, mak-ing generalization difficult, these distinctions commonly reflected male assumptions about the sexes' different natures and the need to enforce conventional gender roles and ideals. Laws and courts were influenced by beliefs that women's desires were more raven-ous than men's, that women were more prone to sin, and that therefore their sexual behaviour had to be regulated more strictly. 'The laws presume that all women are usually bad', according to one commentator, 'because they are so full of mischief and vices that are difficult to describe'; a Belluno law of 1428 decreed that no woman over the age of twenty should be presumed to be a virgin, unless her virtue could be convincingly proved.[16]

Frequently, the social status, life-cycle stage or reputed virtue of the woman involved in illicit sex helped determine distinctions in guilt or penalties. This was especially true of rape and fornication, in which women were usually considered victims and absolved, but also of adultery or sodomy, in which women were often held crimi-nally liable. Generally, the higher the woman's status was the greater the penalty levied on her seducer or lover, but finer distinctions were also drawn. The Florentine statutes of 1415 set a fine of 500 lire for men who had intercourse, whether consensual or forced, with a virgin, a respectable widow or a married woman, and allowed harsher punishment depending on the 'condition and quality of the person'. For the violation of women 'of lesser condition', the fine fell to 100 lire, while sex with a consenting servant or a prostitute carried no penalty at all.[17] Venetian authorities levied progressively milder penalties on rapists according to whether their victims were pre-pubescent girls, wives, widows or, at the bottom of the scale, sexually mature nubile women; the severest penalties were reserved for those who raped women of high status.[18]

16. Brundage, *Law*, p. 492; quote from Giovanni Nevizzani, *Silva nuptialis* . . . (Lyon, 1524), fol. 21va (cited in ibid., pp. 548–9).
17. *Statuta populi et communis florentiae publica auctoritate collecta castigata et praeposita anno salutis MCCCCVI*, 3 vols (Fribourg, 1778–83), Vol. III, rubric 112, p. 318.
18. Ruggiero, *Boundaries of Eros*, pp. 96–108.

The treatment of adultery revealed the sharpest gender discrepancies and bore the most onerous consequences for women. Despite the gender-blind injunction against extra-marital sex, in practical terms adultery was a crime of wives. Husbands' infidelity, unless with a married woman, was considered of little significance, while that of wives was deemed a most serious offence that dishonoured their spouses and undermined the conjugal bond. Courts commonly punished an adulteress more severely than her partner, and her penalty usually included the forfeiture to her husband or children of her dowry – a key commodity in the definition of a woman's honour and often her sole means of subsistence in widowhood. Sometimes adulterous husbands were also legally subject to punishment: in Venice this might mean prison or exile plus the loss of their wife's dowry. But from 1480 to 1550 not a single Venetian husband was convicted for infidelity, unlike scores of wives prosecuted from the 1360s on.[19] This gender disparity concorded fully with religious precepts. According to Bernardino, in addition to her dowry an adulteress's husband had the right to expel her from his house, yet he forbade the wife of a philandering man to abandon him under any circumstances. He once stressed the differently gendered implications of infidelity by asserting that a husband's adultery was a greater sin, since as a man he was more rational and should therefore be more devoted, but a wife's unfaithfulness resulted in her 'perpetual shame', for she had 'no other virtue to lose' than her sexual honour.[20]

Women's shame also influenced the courts' tendency to punish them with public humiliation. Floggings and mutilations were common penalties for men too, but it appears that women convicted of sex crimes were more frequently exposed to public derision. While male adulterers were usually fined, jailed or exiled, adulteresses (besides losing their dowry) were often whipped along the streets, in various states of undress and sometimes wearing a defamatory mitre on their heads; occasionally their heads were shaved. In Pescia in 1419 an adulteress, half-naked and wearing a 'crown of shame', was placed on a donkey and whipped through the countryside.[21] In Florence between 1490 and 1515, more than half of the women

19. Ibid., pp. 45–69; Giovanni Scarabello, 'Devianza sessuale ed interventi di giustizia a Venezia nella prima metà del XVI secolo', in *Tiziano e Venezia*, exhibition catalogue (Vicenza, 1980), p. 79; Brundage, *Law*, pp. 517–21.

20. *Siena 1427*, I, p. 557; *Florence 1424*, I, p. 413; *Florence 1425*, II, p. 178.

21. Samuel Cohn, Jr, *Women in the Streets: Sex and Power in Renaissance Italy* (Baltimore, 1996), p. 114; see also Brundage, *Law*, p. 520; Ruggiero, *Boundaries of Eros*, pp. 54–5.

convicted of sodomy with men were sentenced to a flogging or the pillory, while only a third of their partners received similar penalties; most of the men, unlike the women, were allowed to avoid the shaming by paying an alternate fine. Since women's honour and reputation were more contingent than men's on community opinion, authorities tended to punish them in precisely that public fashion that would be most defaming.

Unauthorized sexual behaviour and gendered identities

Social conventions, religious precepts and the policing of sex all played important roles in constructing and transmitting notions of gender ideals and of distinctions between the sexes, but so did sexual behaviour itself. The forms of sexual compartment that are best documented, however, are those that were illicit or occured outside marriage, and it is consequently this realm of unauthorized sex that has proven most fruitful for historians seeking to throw new light on gender relations and identities in Renaissance Italy.

A key figure here was the prostitute, central to the sexual culture and gender system of Renaissance Italy both for the services she provided and for the symbolic functions she performed. Christian society had long considered prostitution a distasteful but necessary evil, a 'lesser sin' that was grudgingly tolerated to prevent greater transgressions: 'Do you see that in cities prostitutes are tolerated? This is a great evil, but if it were to be removed a great good would be eliminated, because there would be more adultery, more sodomy, which would be much worse.'[22] In a sexual regime that prescribed female chastity but tacitly condoned male fornication, the prostitute played the dual role of furnishing an outlet for incontinent bachelors and philandering husbands, while also diverting their desires from adolescent males and women of 'good' families, whose virtue and honour were thus safeguarded. Prostitutes and their clients were usually exempt from laws against fornication and adultery, though authorities limited the locations and visibility of their debauchery to protect the morality of upright citizens and defend the purity of civic and sacred buildings. During the Renaissance, the notion of the public utility of prostitution underwent a

22. Giordano da Pisa, *Quaresimale fiorentino 1305–1306*, Carlo Delcorno, ed. (Florence, 1974), p. 210.

significant evolution, however. From the mid-1300s, governments began to abandon earlier exclusionary policies that relegated prostitutes and brothels outside the city walls and forced the women to wear identifying signs or apparel. Instead, the state became the official sponsor of urban sexual commerce, establishing municipal brothels or designated residential areas where whores could lawfully ply their trade. Dress codes and other norms intended to distinguish prostitutes were relaxed or abandoned. Some cities created magistracies to administer the bordellos or defend whores from assault and other offences, such as the 'Officers of Decency' in Florence in 1403 and the 'Protectors of the Prostitutes' in Lucca in 1534.[23]

By around 1500, however, this attitude of tolerance was beginning to change again, in Italy as elsewhere. The complexity of the marriage market and the steady escalation in dowries made it increasingly difficult for girls to marry. Convents thrived as patrician families discarded growing numbers of unwed daughters into nunneries, while humbler women slid into situations of solitude and poverty that made them easy recruits to the ranks of occasional and professional whores. The spread of prostitutes from brothel areas into 'honest' neighbourhoods, together with the new phenomenon of prosperous courtesans who imitated the fashions and demeanour of patrician women, heightened concerns both about the bad example these unruly females posed to chaste women and about the blurring of social and moral distinctions between the *donna onesta* and the lusty *meretrice*. The sixteenth century consequently saw a return to a more negative assessment of the ancient sexual trade. Brothels remained open, but authorities revived or tightened policies on residence or dress to stigmatize prostitutes – laws that only a few wealthy courtesans could evade by buying licences or exploiting the protection of powerful clients.[24] Influenced also by

23. Richard C. Trexler, 'Florentine prostitution in the fifteenth century: patrons and clients', in idem, *The Women of Renaissance Florence* (Binghamton, NY, 1993), pp. 31–65; Mazzi, *Prostitute*; John Brackett, 'The Florentine Onestà and the control of prostitution, 1403–1680', *Sixteenth-Century Journal*, 24 (1993), pp. 273–300; Elisabeth Pavan, 'Police des moeurs, société et politique à Venise à la fin du Moyen Age', *Revue historique*, 264 (1980), pp. 241–88; Romano Canosa and Isabella Colonnello, *Storia della prostituzione in Italia dal Quattrocento alla fine del Settecento* (Rome, 1989).

24. Trexler, 'Florentine prostitution', pp. 60–5; Mazzi, *Prostitute*, pp. 225–31, 403–7. On rising dowry values, see Anthony Molho, *Marriage Alliance in Late Medieval Florence* (Cambridge, MA, 1994), pp. 298–310. On the growth of monasteries and convent populations, see Richard C. Trexler, 'Celibacy in the Renaissance: the nuns of Florence', in idem, *The Women of Renaissance Florence*, pp. 10–19; Judith C. Brown, 'Monache a Firenze all'inizio dell'età moderna: un'analisi demografica', *Quaderni storici*, 29 (1994), pp. 117–52. On courtesans, see Brackett, 'Onestà', pp. 293–5; *Il gioco dell'amore: le cortigiane di Venezia dal Trecento al Settecento*, exh. cat. (Milan, 1990).

religious reform movements, institutions proliferated to convert prostitutes and to prevent poor or precarious females from slipping into the profession.[25]

Prostitutes, whether professionals in brothels, courtesans catering to upper-class clients, or women who occasionally sold themselves, undoubtedly played an important role in men's sexual education and experience and thus in the formation of masculine identity. This was precisely one of the criticisms levelled by Catholic reformers after the Council of Trent against the evil influence prostitution had in shaping men's sexual habits and attitudes towards women.[26] In their heyday the brothels were also central institutions of male sociability, especially for young bachelors. They provided a public forum where camaraderie and erotic licence mingled with outbreaks of violence, where men tested and displayed their virility in brawls and sexual conquests. It was in the brothel, an anecdote by the Florentine humanist Poliziano suggests, that youths who were once sodomites' 'passive' boyfriends could redeem their reputations by proving their manliness with compliant whores.[27]

Unauthorized sex involving males and females encompassed far more than men's commerce with prostitutes, however. Legal records suggest that fornication, rape and adultery were typical features of the sexual culture, such activities hardly being discouraged by the light penalties usually levied on (male) offenders. But even the serious crimes of sex with nuns and (by the later 1400s) heterosexual sodomy were also commonplace occurrences on the rosters of carnal offences.[28]

Evidence on unauthorized sex tends to confirm that, for women especially, the relationship between sexual behaviour and gender was subtly but significantly shaped by their social status. This illicit realm involved men from the entire social spectrum, but the women who were implicated were – except for nuns – mainly from the class of artisans, peasants, poor labourers and shopkeepers. Women of higher status were rarely embroiled in sexual scandals or crimes, and if they were, their families had the means to conceal the disgrace,

25. Sherill Cohen, *The Evolution of Women's Asylums since 1500: From Refuges for Ex-Prostitutes to Shelters for Battered Women* (New York, 1992); Lucia Ferrante, 'Honor regained: women in the Casa del Soccorso di San Paolo in sixteenth-century Bologna', in Muir and Ruggiero, eds, *Sex & Gender*, pp. 46–72.

26. Brackett, 'Onestà', p. 293; Guido Ruggiero, 'Marriage, love, sex, and Renaissance civic morality', in J.G. Turner, ed., *Sexuality and Gender in Early Modern Europe: Institutions, Texts, Images* (Cambridge, UK, 1993), pp. 25–6.

27. Angelo Poliziano, *Detti piacevoli*, T. Zanato, ed. (Rome, 1983), p. 78, number 211.

28. Rocke, *Forbidden Friendships*, pp. 215–16; Canosa and Colonnello, *Storia*, pp. 67–71; Ruggiero, *Boundaries of Eros*, pp. 70–84, 118–20.

to discipline the fallen or defiant woman privately, or to ensure that their assailants or lovers were severely punished. On the whole, the protective net thrown up by patrician males around their families' females effectively minimized women's perilous liaisons with men outside their kin group. Conscious of their family's status and indoctrinated from childhood that its honour depended on their chastity, genteel women probably tended to assimilate the values and gender ideology of their class, scrupulously avoiding behaviour that could defame them as much as their fathers, husbands and kinsmen.[29] The morality of humbler women was perhaps no less principled, but their circumstances of hardship and work, or their lack of networks of male kin, exposed them to the flattery of dishonest or fickle seducers, to sexual molestation by employers and social superiors, and to assaults by individuals or gangs. Court records are littered with such stories: plebeian girls and women attacked while alone on country roads or in the fields, servants and apprentices exploited sexually by their masters, isolated widows and their daughters powerless to defend their homes and virtue against assailants. Moreover, whether forced or consensual, most sexual relations between socially dominant men and their servants, slaves and other disadvantaged women simply evaded any judiciary control. The abandoned offspring of such unions swelled the overflowing foundling homes of Renaissance Italian cities.[30]

Because the imperatives of status, property and paternity that so heavily constrained patrician women's sexual behaviour carried less force among the less wealthy, working women appear to have had their own sense of proper sexual conduct and illicit activity, implying different customs and norms from those that prevailed among the dominant classes. For both rural and urban young people of the lower classes, for instance, premarital intercourse was evidently accepted and widespread, as long as relations were initiated with an intent to marry, or at least to create a stable bond. Such romances generally came to court as fornication only when the man failed to maintain his promise of marriage and abandoned his lover, often pregnant or with a young child. The loss of virginity impaired a woman's future chances of marrying, and the tribunals to which

29. For unchaste women from 'good' families, see ibid., pp. 36–9, 55–64; and Mazzi, *Prostitute*, pp. 88–96.

30. Christiane Klapisch-Zuber, 'Women servants in Florence during the fourteenth and fifteenth centuries', in B.A. Hanawalt, ed., *Women and Work in Preindustrial Europe* (Bloomington, IN, 1986), pp. 69–70; Philip Gavitt, *Charity and Children in Renaissance Florence: The Ospedale degli Innocenti, 1410–1536* (Ann Arbor, MI, 1990), p. 207.

these deflowered victims of desertion or rape turned for redress usually sought to redeem their honour and restore their marriage prospects by forcing their seducers or violators to give them a dowry or, alternatively, to marry them. Prosecution of fornication often became embroiled in ambiguities about what constituted a valid marriage, since, according to the pre-Tridentine Church, this required no other formalities than the partners' mutual consent. For this same reason, long-term informal unions and clandestine marriages remained unexceptional outside the upper classes well into the sixteenth century, and even women's extra-marital relations were not uncommon.[31] Facilitated by the contacts that they forged with men through neighbourly ties, work and sociable occasions, these plebeian romances were sometimes the fruit of an intolerable marriage, the evasion from a violent or overbearing husband, and may have been aided by neighbours and relatives. Such affairs typically attracted judicial attention only when they exceeded bounds of discretion or when a wife actually fled with her lover, signalling the open rupture of her conjugal union.[32]

Studies of illicit sex have also begun to illuminate in sharp relief the problem of men's sexual abuse of children, both female and male. In Florence from 1495 to 1515, over one-third of the forty-nine documented victims of convicted rapists were girls between the ages of six and twelve, and at least half were aged fourteen or under; numerous others were seduced without force or were sodomized. One man condemned in 1488 regularly picked up children begging in the market, sodomized them in his home, and then offered them to others to ravish; some of his cronies, conducted before one ten-year-old victim, were reportedly repelled by her tender age and refused to touch her, but others had no such scruples.[33] In a typical year, an average of four boys aged twelve or under would also come before the courts as victims of sodomizers, often having suffered severe anal injury. In Venice, too, pre-pubescent children

31. Brundage, *Law*, pp. 514–18; Ruggiero, *Boundaries of Eros*, pp. 16–44, 89–108; Sandra Cavallo and Simona Cerruti, 'Female honor and the social control of reproduction in Piedmont between 1600 and 1800', in Muir and Ruggiero, eds, *Sex & Gender*, pp. 73–109; Gene Brucker, *Giovanni and Lusanna: Love and Marriage in Renaissance Florence* (Berkeley, CA, 1986); Daniela Lombardi, 'Intervention by church and state in marriage disputes in sixteenth- and seventeenth-century Florence', in Dean and Lowe, eds, *Crime, Society and the Law in Renaissance Italy*, pp. 142–56. In Florence, unlike Venice, men condemned for fornication or rape were rarely given the option of marrying their victims, though they commonly had to provide a dowry for the unmarried ones.

32. Ruggiero, *Boundaries of Eros*, pp. 45–69; Mazzi, *Prostitute*, pp. 103–8.

33. ASF, OGBR 79, fols 9v–10r (8 March 1488).

were common victims of sexual abuse. A Venetian law of 1500, which prohibited pimps from prostituting girls under the age of twelve, revealed that it was regular practice to offer clients girls as young as seven to nine years of age to be sodomized. The abuse of children merits further attention, for this was evidently not merely a problem of individual aberration. The frequent subjugation of impotent juveniles probably reflects a psychosexual immaturity and aggressiveness, and an insecurity about masculine identity that had deep social, cultural and familial roots.[34]

Another prominent, if less explored, aspect of male behaviour were assaults by gangs against women or younger boys. In Florence between 1495 and 1515, nineteen out of forty-nine documented female rape victims were attacked by at least two men, and typically by three to six or more; in 1499, thirteen men abducted a married woman from her home and violated her. Many more men took part in collective ravishings (89) than in single assaults (30), and among the perpetrators, patrician youths figured prominently (34 of 89). Groups of men also brutally sodomized women, such as Costanza, a thirty-year-old servant sodomized and raped by fourteen youths in 1497, or Francesca, a married woman who in 1501 was anally raped by thirty assailants. Gangs attacked adolescent males as well, part of a broader context in which the sexual 'possession' of boys by groups of men, whether by force or not, was both common and deeply implicated in the fashioning of manly and social identities. The gangs that terrorized women and boys offered strength in numbers to overpower their victims and guarantee the success of their sordid ventures, but their members also gave one another psychological incentive and support, an incitement to prove their virility before their comrades as, one after the other, they humiliated their help-less prey.[35]

Beside reinforcing an impression of the aggressive and preda-tory character of masculine behaviour and identity, evidence about illicit sex can also provide glimpses of individuals who implicitly evaded or openly challenged not only the law but also prevailing gender conventions. A few mature men, as will be seen, defied mas-culine norms by taking the proscribed receptive role in same-sex

34. Rocke, *Forbidden Friendships*, pp. 162–3; Scarabello, 'Devianza', p. 80; Patricia Labalme, 'Sodomy and Venetian justice in the Renaissance', *Legal History Review*, 52 (1984), pp. 236–7; Ruggiero, *Boundaries of Eros*, pp. 95, 121–5, 149–54.
35. Rocke, *Forbidden Friendships*, pp. 163, 182–9; Ruggiero, 'Marriage', pp. 17–18; Mazzi, *Prostitute*, pp. 110–12. Cases cited: ASF, OGBR 113, 78v (6 March 1499); ASF, UN 31, 65r–66v, 119v (21 February–5 April 1497); ibid. 34, 56r (26 August 1501).

relations. Women, by contrast, were not always passive victims but instead often assumed an assertive role in seeking to fulfil their sexual desires and in shaping their own affective experiences and sense of identity. Some enterprizing nubile girls apparently engaged calculatingly in pre-marital sex, to circumvent parental objections over their choice of a spouse. In extra-marital affairs wives are commonly found taking the initiative, perhaps to relieve the monotony of a loveless union or escape the brutality of a cruel husband.[36] Especially striking examples of women resisting gender and social conventions to pursue erotic pleasure and male companionship come from what is, at first glance, a most unlikely source – the nunnery. Many of the women who swelled Italy's bulging convents were deposited there, willingly or not, by genteel families unable to place them in suitable marriages; not all were prepared or willing to submit to a regime of chastity or to renounce the world. Not only were nuns often implicated in sexual scandals involving laymen or priests, but some managed to conduct quite rich sexual lives, apparently shielded by a web of complicity within and perhaps outside the convent.[37] Other women confuted the submissive role assigned them in gender ideology by withstanding assailants or by denouncing abusive husbands. A distinct sense of determination and proud identity emerges from the protest that a young Florentine patrician wife, Agnoletta de' Ricci, made to her husband Ardingo, whom she publicly accused in 1497 of having repeatedly sodomized her: 'I told him that in no way did I want him to treat me like an animal, but like a woman of perfect character.'[38] Such examples serve as reminders that, though the dominant ideology of gender and sexual behaviour was powerfully constraining, it was also contestable – and contested – terrain.

Same-sex relations and masculine identity

Same-sex relations between males, classified as sodomy, provide an especially revealing perspective on the construction of masculine identity. Ranked among the most nefarious of carnal acts in both

36. Elizabeth S. Cohen, 'No longer virgins: self-presentation by young women in late Renaissance Rome', in M. Migiel and J. Schiesari, eds, *Refiguring Woman: Perspectives on Gender and the Italian Renaissance* (Ithaca, NY, 1991), pp. 172–4; Ruggiero, *Boundaries of Eros*, pp. 16–69; Mazzi, *Prostitute*, pp. 87, 103–16; Scarabello, 'Devianza', p. 78.
37. Ruggiero, *Boundaries of Eros*, pp. 78–84; Scarabello, 'Devianza', pp. 78–9.
38. ASF, UN 31, 44v (3 January 1497).

Church doctrine and legal rhetoric, sodomy – mainly but not only sex between males – was one of the most frequently prosecuted and heavily penalized crimes in Italy between 1400 and 1600. Reputedly common across the peninsula, sodomy so alarmed the governments of Venice, Florence and Lucca that they created special judiciary commissions to prosecute it (in 1418, 1432 and 1448 respectively). Penalties and patterns of control varied, but in Florence the Office of the Night, as the magistracy there was known, unearthed an exceptionally thriving sodomitical milieu. Between 1432 and 1502 as many as 17,000 males were incriminated and some 3,000 convicted for homosexual relations. Indeed, sodomy was so common and its policing in the later fifteenth century so effective that, by the time they reached the age of forty, probably two of every three Florentine men had been officially implicated.[39]

Whether this 'vice' was as pervasive elsewhere remains to be seen; nonetheless, the evidence suggests that throughout Italy same-sex relations shared similar forms, contexts and ascribed cultural meanings. Generally, homosexual behaviour had little to do with current notions of sexual orientation or identity, but was organized instead around notions of gender and life stages. For most males, same-sex sodomy was a sporadic or temporary transgression that did not preclude relations with females or imply anything about long-term inclinations.[40]

Some contemporaries saw connections between homoeroticism and the quality of relations between men and women. Bernardino of Siena singled out sodomites for their loathing and paltry esteem of women, while the Sienese *novelliere*, Pietro Fortini, attributed the homoerotic bent of both Florentine and Lucchese men to their universal misogyny, asserting that their 'vices are such [referring to sodomy] that they cannot bear to look at women, who they say are their enemies'. Acting in part on the belief that making public women accessible would help curtail sodomy, the governments of both Florence and Lucca promoted municipalized prostitution. This sexual equation was given a different twist by Savonarola: Florentine parents, he said, so feared the disgrace of unwed pregnant daughters that they encouraged their sons to engage instead in what they deemed the 'lesser evil' of sex with men.[41]

39. Rocke, *Forbidden Friendships*; Ruggiero, *Boundaries of Eros*, pp. 109–45; Labalme, 'Sodomy'; Pavan, 'Police', pp. 266–88; Canossa and Colonnello, *Storia*, pp. 57–73.

40. Rocke, *Forbidden Friendships*, pp. 87–132.

41. Bernardino of Siena, *Florence 1425*, II, p. 276; *Siena 1427*, I, p. 560; ibid., II, pp. 1158, 1160, 1166; *Novelle di Pietro Fortini*, T. Rughi, ed. (Milan, 1923), p. 64; Girolamo Savonarola, *Prediche sopra i Salmi*, V. Romano, ed., 2 vols (Rome, 1969), Vol. I, p. 164.

Notions of gender also shaped sex between males in more direct ways, while homosexual behaviour in turn had important implications for masculine identities – implications that were relevant for all males, whether they engaged in sodomy or not. Same-sex relations in Italy corresponded to a hierarchical pattern, very ancient in Mediterranean cultures and long-lasting throughout Europe, in which adult males took the so-called active, usually anally insertive role with 'passive' teenage boys or adolescents to the age of about eighteen or twenty. In Florence, the best-documented example, nine out of ten active partners were aged nineteen and above; mainly in their twenties and thirties, their mean age was twenty-seven. Of those who took the passive role, nine out of ten were between the ages of thirteen and twenty, with a mean age of sixteen. Reciprocal or age-reversed relations were rare, and limited to adolescence, while it was rarer still for mature males to have sex together. Indeed, the assumption of the receptive sexual role by adult men constituted a widely respected taboo.[42]

Sex between males thus always embodied oppositions – older and younger, active and passive, penetrator and penetrated. These were far from neutral distinctions, for contrasting values related to gender adhered to them, values such as dominance and submission, honour and shame, and, not least, masculine and feminine. These differences were neatly expressed in fourteenth-century Florentine laws, which blandly designated the active partner either as *pollutus* (morally corrupt) or as someone who committed sodomy with another, but contemptuously branded the passive as one who had dirtied or disgraced himself, or who 'willingly suffered the said crime to be inflicted upon him'.[43]

The gendered meaning of sexual roles, central to conceptions of same-sex behaviour, emerged most vividly from denunciations accusing men and boys of sodomy. Informers commonly referred to the passive partner, and only to him, with derogatory feminine expressions and metaphors. People derided sodomized boys with the epithets *bardassa*, derived from an Arabic word for slave and designating a debauched boy who offered himself to men, usually for payment; *puttana* (whore); *cagna* or *cagna in gestra* (bitch or bitch in heat), all evoking the commonplace of voracious female

42. Rocke, *Forbidden Friendships*, pp. 94–7, 113–19. Passive partners in Venice appear somewhat younger than in Florence, though this may only reflect poorer reporting of age there; Ruggiero, *Boundaries of Eros*, pp. 118, 121–5; Pavan, 'Police', p. 284.

43. R. Caggese, ed., *Statuti della repubblica fiorentina*, 2 vols (Florence, 1910–21), Vol. II, p. 218; ASF, PR 52, 128rv (13 April 1365).

lust. Most often, however, informers referred to them simply as women, stating that a man kept or used a boy 'as a woman', or even 'as his wife'. What turned these boys symbolically into women was not any effeminate appearance or manner, but rather their assumption of the subordinate position in sex, which was construed in this culture as feminine. In contrast, accusers virtually never represented the 'active' partner in feminine terms, calling him at most a 'sodomite' or 'bugger'. Neither term bore overt gendered connotations other than indicating the dominant role in sex. Indeed, while passive partners were hardly ever described with these terms, both were regularly used to indicate men who sodomized women.[44] Late medieval and early modern Italians evidently found it difficult to conceive of same-sex relations – whether between males or females – outside the traditional gender dichotomy of masculine and feminine roles.[45]

These representations suggest that the sodomite, though castigated as a criminal and a sinner, was perceived as conforming to the behaviours and values defined in this culture as masculine. As long as he observed proper conventions, a man's sexual relations with boys did not compromise his status as a 'normal' and virile male. Indeed, the act of dominating another male, even if a boy, might well have reinforced it. Since sodomizing someone did not constitute deviation from 'manly' norms, and the 'womanly' role was in effect limited to very young males, this permitted all mature men to engage in same-sex activity – as very many did – without endangering their masculine identity or being relegated to a distinctive category of deviants.

What was an aberration was, of course, the passive sexual role. But as this was normally restricted to the phase of physical and social immaturity, it marked only a temporary detour from a boy's progress towards manhood. In Florence, virtually all adolescent passives whose later same-sex activity is documented converted with success to a solely dominant role with teenage boys. This helps explain why passive minors usually received much lighter penalties than their companions, or, as in Florence, no punishment whatsoever, no matter how promiscuous they were. If penalties were levied, they often involved corporal punishments of the sort usually applied to women.[46]

44. Rocke, *Forbidden Friendships*, pp. 105–10.

45. Judith C. Brown, *Immodest Acts: The Life of a Lesbian Nun in Renaissance Italy* (New York, 1986).

46. Rocke, *Forbidden Friendships*, pp. 51–2, 61, 99–101, 214–15; Ruggiero, *Boundaries of Eros*, pp. 121–4.

This also accounts for the paramount significance attributed to the transition to sexual adulthood, with its expectations of adherence to virile conventions. For Florentine boys up to the age of eighteen or twenty the passive role was considered more or less consonant with their status, but afterward most men carefully avoided the shame of being penetrated 'like a woman'. This was a crucial experiential and symbolic passage, and the border between passive and active, boyhood and maturity, feminine and masculine, was anxiously patrolled by both community and state. With a combination of embarrassment and derision, informers castigated the rare youth or older man who still 'let themselves be sodomized', emphasizing their dishonour and disgrace. The authorities often reinforced these concerns about proper masculine roles by punishing over-aged passives with exemplary penalties of public floggings, exorbitant fines or exile. So powerful was the aversion to older men's sexual receptivity, in particular, that when Salvi Panuzzi, a sixty-three-year-old citizen long notorious for sodomizing boys, publicly admitted in 1496 that he himself had been sodomized by several youths, the Night Officers condemned him to death by burning, one of only three known capital sentences they levied in their seventy-year activity. Yet while they abhorred his acts, they also feared that his execution, by rendering public his womanish 'evil ways, . . . might bring shame on the entire city' and make a mockery of Florentine manhood. They therefore commuted his sentence, upon payment of a huge fine, to life imprisonment hidden away in *la pazzeria*, the prison ward for the insane.[47]

The exemplary punishments imposed on adult men for taking the 'unmanly' sexual role emphasize that individual erotic behaviour and collective gender norms and identity formed part of a seamless whole. Informers expressed concern that the passivity of older men, a disgrace to themselves, would also implicate and malign the honour – that is, the virility – of the entire male community. By defusing the potential shame of Panuzzi's execution, and by secluding this violator of manhood among the dangerously insane, the Night Officers affirmed both the public nature of gender and the Commune's role to defend the conventions that helped fashion masculine identity. Such worries were hardly limited to Florence. In 1516, Venetian lawmakers, their offended sense of masculine propriety fairly bursting from their words, resolved to stamp out 'an absurd and unheard-of thing [that] has recently become known, which can in no way be tolerated, that several most

47. Rocke, *Forbidden Friendships*, pp. 101–5.

wicked men of 30, 40, 50, 60 years and more have given themselves like prostitutes and public whores to be passives in such a dreadful excess'. This revelation scandalized local commentators, in part because it evoked a deep anxiety that the hierarchy of age and gender on which masculine identity was constructed risked being subverted. One nobleman was appalled that 'Fathers and Senators', men who were 'mature, full of wisdom, with white beards' – the very symbols of patriarchy – would shamelessly allow youths to penetrate them, and he branded this 'truly a wicked and abhorrent thing, never before heard of in our times, especially among old men'. Equally menacing to their manly sense of self and civic image was the news that informed foreigners were now gleefully ridiculing the virility of all Venetians.[48] Similar concerns about defending Florentine manhood led the government of Duke Cosimo I, in a law of 1542, to single out the adult man who dared allow himself to be sodomized by ordering his public execution by burning, 'for his own punishment and as an example to others', as 'a wicked and infamous man'.[49]

Perhaps more effectively than any other contemporary erotic behaviour, the same-sex practices described here, with their age-, role- and gender-bound conventions, underline the distance that separates the culture of sex and gender in Renaissance Italy from that which prevails in the modern Western world. Little trace, if any, can be found then of the categories that today largely define sexual experience and personae; it was not, in other words, the biological sex of one's partners in erotic pleasures that significantly distinguished and classified individuals, but rather the extent to which their sexual behaviour conformed to culturally determined gender roles. In different but related ways, the norms and ideology of gender forcefully shaped and constrained the experience of sex for both women and men. And sexual activity, in turn, played important roles in fashioning gendered identities and in reinforcing – or sometimes challenging – traditional gender conventions. As historians and other scholars continue to explore the complex and still relatively uncharted universe of sexual comportments, attitudes and controls throughout the rural and urban communities of the Italian peninsula, their studies promise to further enrich our understanding of the culturally specific modes of the construction of sex and gender in late medieval and early modern Italy.

48. Labalme, 'Sodomy', pp. 243 n. 73, 251 n. 160; Scarabello, 'Devianza', p. 82.
49. L. Cantini, ed., *Legislazione toscana raccolta e illustrata*, 32 vols (Florence, 1800–8), Vol. I, pp. 211–13.

PART FOUR

The Renaissance of the Spirit

CHAPTER EIGHT

Spiritual Kinship and Domestic Devotions*

DANIEL BORNSTEIN

A tension between the religious ideal of celibacy and the social imperative of reproduction has marked Christianity from the very start. In his first letter to the Corinthians (1 Cor. 7:1–9), Paul expressed his wish that everyone might be like him and remain single, only reluctantly conceding that since it was better to marry than to burn with passion, those who could not follow him in celibacy should marry and form families. But this tension assumed particular force and urgency in the late fourteenth century, when recurrent epidemics of bubonic plague threatened entire populations with extinction and imperilled the survival of families as never before. Faced with this new social reality, conservative theologians and traditional moralists struggled to address and balance two antithetical impulses. On the one hand, shocked and dismayed at the devastation wrought by the plagues, wars and famines of the calamitous fourteenth century, many abandoned the world, renounced family and fortune, and took refuge in monastic institutions, where they sought the comfort of a spiritual kinship that could take the place of their brutally truncated biological families. On the other, the desperate longing to fill both a personal void and the general societal need to replenish the massive population losses led many others to marry, cling to their families and bear numerous children.

This practical and theoretical obsession with families, both literal and figurative, marked the religious culture of early Renaissance

* Research for this chapter was supported by a Faculty Development Leave and Women's Studies Faculty Fellowship from Texas A&M University, a National Endowment for the Humanities Fellowship at the Newberry Library, a grant-in-aid from the American Philosophical Society, and a grant from the Gladys Krieble Delmas Foundation. I am grateful to all these institutions for their generous support, and to Jane Burrows for her helpful comments on the text.

Italy. Preachers and authors of devotional handbooks joined humanist theorists of marriage and the family (such as Leon Battista Alberti and Francesco Barbaro) in promoting marriage and fertility and defining a sexual ethic appropriate to an era of demographic catastrophe.[1] At the same time, however, confessors and spiritual guides sought to assert clerical control over sexual ethics and to sanctify the household by encouraging domestic devotions. And even while mendicant and monastic ideals penetrated the household and shaped domestic duties, family affections suffused convent piety, giving force and meaning to an alternative family – with all of the tensions that such competing emotional claims could entail.

One would expect that men and women felt those tensions very differently, since the cultural expectations and social and religious roles of men and women differed. In this chapter, I shall examine a group of Dominican authors who addressed themselves to cloistered nuns, female tertiaries and patrician housewives, and forcefully defined women's roles in the household and in the Church. These authors were prominent figures in their order and in the Catholic Church: Raymond of Capua was master general of the Dominican order from 1380 to his death in 1399; Giovanni Dominici served Raymond as vicar general for the reformed Dominican houses in Italy and ended his career as an archbishop, cardinal and papal legate; Tommaso d'Antonio of Siena helped Giovanni make Venice the seed-bed of Dominican reform and secured papal approval for the Dominican Third Order. All were actively engaged in pastoral work with women, and together they produced an enormous quantity and variety of works for women, ranging from saints' lives and treatises on mystical theology to letters of spiritual counsel and a handbook on child rearing and household management. The prominence of these authors and influence of their works would be enough to command attention. But what makes them especially pertinent to the problem posed here is the existence of writings by the very women who were the targets of their efforts. We are not forced to listen in frustration to one half of a conversation, scrutinizing texts addressed to women for hints of how they were shaped by their intended audience and guessing at the audience's likely response.[2] We can actually see how women – from the cloistered

1. Roberto Rusconi, 'St Bernardino of Siena, the wife, and possessions', in Daniel Bornstein and Roberto Rusconi, eds, *Women and Religion in Medieval and Renaissance Italy* (Chicago, 1996), pp. 182–96.
2. This method has been used with notable success by Katherine Gill, 'Women and the production of religious literature in the vernacular, 1300–1500', in E. Ann Matter and John Coakley, eds, *Creative Women in Medieval and Early Modern Italy: A Religious and Artistic Renaissance* (Philadelphia, 1994), pp. 64–104.

nuns of Corpus Domini in Venice to the Florentine housewife and mother Bartolomea degli Obizzi – assimilated or modified the messages directed at them by male authors, how *they* viewed their role in the family and in the Church.

The dear bride in the bed of fire and blood

It is fitting that these thinkers drew their inspiration from that most peculiar saint, Catherine of Siena. Catherine was born in 1347, and so belonged to the first generation that grew up in the shadow of the Black Death. She was a survivor whose sense of self and spiritual direction were shaped by the deaths of those around her.[3] Catherine's twin sister was entrusted to a wet nurse and died in infancy, while Catherine sucked her mother's milk – and with it her mother's reminders that she had been the chosen one. When Catherine reached adolescence, her mother began to prepare her for marriage. Under the tutelage of her married older sister Buonaventura, Catherine learned to do her hair and make herself attractive to a potential suitor. But then her beloved Buonaventura died in childbirth. Stricken with guilt and fear, Catherine resolved to renounce marriage. She stubbornly resisted her parents' plans to have her marry, yet refused to enter a convent, choosing instead to become a Dominican tertiary. The Third Order offered a non-cloistered religious role for women – usually widows – who made non-binding promises (rather than formal vows) to live chastely, perform certain devotions and engage in charitable activities. The Dominican tertiaries of Siena hesitated to admit young Catherine to their ranks: their non-cloistered way of life would leave her exposed to the perils of the world, and them to the risk of a blemished reputation if something should happen to her. But in the end her resolute insistence overcame their reluctance and her family's. She lived at home as a Dominican tertiary and in so doing transformed both family and convent. She turned her family home into a sacred place of prayer and contemplation, bodily austerities and spiritual combat; and she gathered around herself a spiritual *famiglia* even more numerous than her mother Lapa's ample progeny, a throng of devout followers who called this young virgin their 'mamma' – as she addressed the pope himself as 'Daddy'.

After several years spent in prayer, contemplation and care for the sick, Catherine embarked on an extraordinary public apostolate.[4]

3. Rudolph M. Bell, *Holy Anorexia* (Chicago, 1985), pp. 22–53.
4. On this aspect of Catherine's activities, see Karen Scott, 'Catherine of Siena, *Apostola*', *Church History*, 61 (1992), pp. 34–46; and Scott, 'Urban spaces, women's

She addressed letters to prelates and princes, the mercenary captain John Hawkwood and the disreputable Queen Joanna of Naples. She called sinners to repentance and warring states to peace. Critics accused her of spiritual pride and suspected her of being a witch; her own order, suspicious of her activities, placed her under the direction of the able and experienced Raymond of Capua. But he soon fell under the sway of her forceful personality, and with his support she widened the range of her activities, even travelling to the papal court at Avignon to urge the pope to return to Rome.

Catherine's charismatic authority rested on her flamboyant asceticism and visionary experiences, and both of these were linked with her gender. A modern scholar might suggest that prolonged fasting and vigils, the simple lack of food and sleep, could induce hallucinations, and that the content of those hallucinations would be shaped by the religious images which women were urged to take as the focus of their devotions.[5] But Renaissance physicians offered their own physiological explanation for women's observed propensity for visions. Females were held to be softer in character than males, and because of their moist and cool bodily humours they (like wax and similar substances) received impressions more easily and retained them better.[6] The Dominican authors of the notorious witch-hunting manual *Malleus Maleficarum* explained that 'women are naturally more impressionable, and more ready to receive the influence of a disembodied spirit; and . . . when they use this quality well they are very good, but when they use it ill they are very evil'.[7] In short, the imagination, or image-generating faculty, was more active in women than in men, at the same time that women's weaker intellects rendered them less able to evaluate critically the spiritual impressions they registered so sensitively. The very qualities that rendered women so susceptible to demonic temptations also made them privileged conduits for divine revelation.[8]

---

networks, and the lay apostolate in the Siena of Catherine Benincasa', in Matter and Coakley, eds, *Creative Women*, pp. 105–119.

5. Chiara Frugoni, 'Female mystics, visions, and iconography', in Bornstein and Rusconi, eds, *Women and Religion*, pp. 130–64.

6. Ian Maclean, *The Renaissance Notion of Woman: A Study in the Fortunes of Scholasticism and Medical Science in European Intellectual Life* (Cambridge, UK, 1980), p. 42.

7. *The Malleus Maleficarum of Heinrich Kramer and James Sprenger*, trans. Montague Summers (New York, 1971), p. 44.

8. Daniel Bornstein, 'The shrine of Santa Maria a Cigoli: female visionaries and clerical promoters', *Mélanges de l'Ecole Française de Rome, Moyen Age-Temps Modernes*, 98 (1986), pp. 224–8.

Extreme fasting, extended periods of reclusion, flagellation, self-mutilation and other austerities also figure more prominently in the lives of female saints than those of their male counterparts. This may simply reflect the limited options available to women, the restricted arenas in which they could compete as athletes of God. As Donald Weinstein and Rudolph Bell observe, 'penitence and austerity were forms of religious expression easily accessible to women who aspired to holiness'.[9] But it may also express a holy hatred of the flesh, and especially their own flesh, which was more marked in women than men, and which turned on a cultural identification of the female body with food, flesh and sexual desire.[10]

Blood, food and blazing love suffuse the words and visions of Catherine of Siena, as she wrestles with the squirming hydra of spiritual and biological kinship. Her most notorious letter, a rapt account of the execution of a young nobleman, opens (as her letters commonly do) with greetings 'in the precious blood of God's Son' and the wish that she might see the recipient of the letter – her new spiritual director, Raymond of Capua – 'engulfed and drowned in the sweet blood of God's Son, which is permeated with the fire of his blazing charity. This is what my soul desires,' continues Catherine:

> to see you in this blood. . . . Son, I see no other way of our attaining the most basic virtues we need. No, dearest father, your soul could not attain them – this soul of yours that has become my food. Not a moment passes that I am not eating this food at the table of the gentle Lamb who was slain in such blazing love. I am saying that unless you are drowned in the blood you will not attain the little virtue of true humility, which is born from hatred as hatred is from love. . . . So I want you to shut yourself up in the open side of God's Son, that open hostelry so full of fragrance that sin itself is made fragrant. There the dear bride rests in the bed of fire and blood.[11]

Catherine proceeds to play with these paired terms as she describes the execution and the visionary experience it triggered.

9. Donald Weinstein and Rudolph M. Bell, *Saints and Society: The Two Worlds of Western Christendom, 1000–1700* (Chicago, 1982), p. 234.

10. See, in general, Caroline Walker Bynum, *Holy Feast and Holy Fast: The Religious Significance of Food to Medieval Women* (Berkeley and Los Angeles, CA, 1987), and *Fragmentation and Redemption: Essays on Gender and the Human Body in Medieval Religion* (New York, 1991).

11. Eugenio Dupré Theseider, *Epistolario di S. Caterina da Siena*, Vol. 1 (Rome, 1940), letter 31, pp. 126–32; trans. from *The Letters of St. Catherine of Siena*, Vol. 1, trans. Suzanne Noffke (Binghamton, NY, 1988), pp. 108–11. On this much-discussed letter, see most recently, Joan P. Del Pozzo, 'The apotheosis of Niccolò Toldo: an execution "Love Story"', *Modern Language Notes*, 110 (1995), pp. 164–77.

Catherine visited the condemned man, comforted and consoled him, and convinced him to confess and receive communion. He worried that he would weaken at the last moment and begged her:

> 'Stay with me; don't leave me alone. That way I can't help but be all right, and I'll die happy!' His head was resting on my breast. I sensed an intense joy, a fragrance of his blood – and it wasn't separate from the fragrance of my own, which I am waiting to shed for my gentle Spouse Jesus. With my soul's desire growing, and sensing his fear, I said, 'Courage, my dear brother, for soon we shall reach the wedding feast. You will go forth to it bathed in the sweet blood of God's Son, with the sweet name of Jesus, which I don't want ever to leave your memory. I shall wait for you at the place of execution.'

Catherine was as good as her word; and while she waited for him she played at taking his place, placing her neck on the axe-man's block. When he arrived she said:

> 'Down for the wedding, my dear brother, for soon you will be in everlasting life!' He knelt down very meekly; I placed his head [on the block] and bent down and reminded him of the blood of the Lamb. His mouth said nothing but 'Gesù!' and 'Caterina!' and as he said this, I received his head into my hands, saying 'I will!' with my eyes fixed on divine Goodness.

At this point the heavens opened and Catherine saw 'the God-Man as one sees the brilliance of the sun. [His side] was open and received blood into his own blood'. And then Jesus tenderly received the soul of this youth 'and placed it all-mercifully into the open hostelry of his side'. As he did so, the young man

> made a gesture sweet enough to charm a thousand hearts. . . . He turned as does a bride when, having reached her husband's threshold, she turns her head and looks back, nods to those who have attended her, and so expresses her thanks. Now that he was hidden away where he belonged, my soul rested in peace and quiet in such a fragrance of blood that I couldn't bear to wash away his blood that had splashed on me. . . . So don't be surprised if I impose on you only my desire to see you drowned in the blood and fire pouring out from the side of God's Son. No more apathy now, my sweetest children, because the blood has begun to flow and to receive life!

The execution becomes a marriage; the bridegroom becomes a bride; Catherine's father confessor becomes her dear son – and perhaps her spouse – as she longs to see him closed in the open hostelry of Christ's fragrant wound, where the young man's soul has been received and 'the dear bride waits in the bed of fire and blood'. Male and female, self and other, life and death, all melt and run together in the powerful solvent of blood and desire.

The blood-soaked imagery and delirious eroticism of this letter could not help but make an indelible impression on its recipient, yet Raymond of Capua made no mention of it or of this entire episode in his biography of Catherine. Of course, his silence may have been due to general reservations about the propriety of such lurid imaginings: he was, after all, recounting the life of someone he considered a saint.[12] But I believe his reticence was motivated by more personal considerations. So far as we know, this letter was the first that Raymond of Capua received from Catherine, and in that context it reads all the more like a provocation and a seduction. It was this and the troubling memory of his emotional response, his own entanglement with its author, that Raymond wished to efface when, a decade or more later, he drafted her biography. No such memories bothered Tommaso d'Antonio of Siena (known as 'Caffarini'), an associate of Raymond's and, like him, a promoter of Catherine's canonization but without Raymond's intimate involvement with the saint. Tommaso thus did not hesitate to testify about this episode at the first canonization proceedings for Catherine, in 1411, where he identified himself as an eyewitness, or to insert it in the *Legenda minor*, the abridgement and adaptation of Raymond's *Legenda maior* which he prepared in 1416–17, in which he referred explicitly to Catherine's 'beautiful letter' about the event.[13]

The consolation and edification of devout women

Although he certainly admired Catherine and devoted himself to promoting her canonization, Tommaso d'Antonio did not believe that her flamboyant spirituality could or should be imitated. In order for Catherine to become a suitable model for pious women,

12. Raymond may have toned down other passages in Catherine's writings and experience that he found excessively graphic. When Catherine alludes to mystical marriage, she speaks of receiving a circlet of flesh, the foreskin of Jesus; in Raymond's biography, this wedding ring is transformed into the standard gold band, elaborately and symbolically set with four pearls and a splendid diamond. *Letters of St. Catherine*, p. 128; Raymond of Capua, *The Life of Catherine of Siena*, trans. Conleth Kearns (Dublin, 1980), p. 107.

13. *Sanctae Catharinae Senensis Legenda minor*, Ezio Franceschini, ed. (Siena, 1942), p. 92.

she had to be domesticated and declawed; and when in 1396 Raymond of Capua entrusted to Tommaso the task of organizing and directing the Dominican tertiaries in Venice, he immediately set to work crafting hagiographical texts that would serve for the spiritual direction of his charges.[14] By August of 1400 he had prepared 'for the consolation and edification of common devout persons' vernacular translations of the Latin biographies of two Dominican holy women. Vanna of Orvieto (1264–1306) was orphaned when she was just a child; she was still a child when she rejected any thought of marriage and embarked on a life of penitence, scorning all worldly goods and pleasures, devoting herself to a constant round of prayer and devotions, and being rewarded with visions and mystical raptures. Margherita of Città di Castello (1287–1320), born blind and deformed, was abandoned by her parents at the age of six; she passed through a foster home and a nunnery before donning the black mantle of a lay penitent affiliated with the Dominican order and giving herself to a life of fasting and mortification of the flesh. Though neither had yet been canonized, Tommaso urged his readers to imitate their virginity, humility and patience, and held them up for admiration as workers of miracles and objects of reverence in their native cities.

In the first two decades of the fifteenth century, Tommaso turned his hand to the far more challenging figure of Catherine of Siena herself, whose *Legenda maior* had been brought to Venice in 1395 by its author, Raymond of Capua. That unusually ample biography was both too long and not comprehensive enough: at roughly 400 pages in its modern editions, the *Legenda maior* was dauntingly bulky; and yet Raymond's refusal to include reports that he could not verify led him to exclude many of the stories about Catherine then in circulation. Tommaso solved these problems by preparing two texts. His *Legenda minor* abridged Raymond's text in order to facilitate its circulation among the faithful, while his *Libellus de supplemento* gathered information that Raymond had left out. In both works, Tommaso's emphasis was on Catherine's more striking deeds and dramatic miracles: gripping episodes that preachers could elaborate into sermons that would inspire the amazed wonderment

---

14. Tommaso was born in Siena around 1350 and died in Venice between 1430 and 1434; it was in Venice, where he settled in 1394, that he was most active as a spiritual director and most productive as a writer. See Fernanda Sorelli, 'La produzione agiografica del domenicano Tommaso d'Antonio da Siena: esempi di santità ed intenti di propaganda', in Daniel Bornstein and Roberto Rusconi, eds, *Mistiche e devote nell'Italia tardomedievale* (Naples, 1992), pp. 157–69.

of their hearers. As a result, the Catherine that emerges from Tommaso's writings is even more astonishing and inimitable than the saint portrayed by Raymond.

Tommaso had succeeded in furnishing proof that the lay penitents affiliated with the Dominican order were as worthy of reverence as any saint. Vanna of Orvieto, Margherita of Città di Castello and Catherine of Siena tower as mystics and visionaries, heroic ascetics and virgin brides of Christ. Vanna and Catherine had resolutely refused marriage. All three had rejected any care for worldly goods. All had laid waste their own bodies, conforming themselves to the suffering object of their love, Christ on the cross. As a result, the orphaned Vanna, the crippled Margherita and the illiterate Catherine all emerged as potent workers of miracles and patrons to the communities that once had scorned them. But though they surely enhanced the stature of the Dominican order, they could hardly serve as models for the devout wives and widows who were Tommaso's immediate charges.

Casting about for a model of sanctity that would be not just admirable in his readers' eyes but applicable in their lives, Tommaso fastened on a young Venetian tertiary, Maria Sturion.[15] Maria, who died of plague in 1399 at the age of twenty, appears to have been a rather ordinary young woman. She was an upper-class Venetian who made a bad marriage, was abandoned by her husband, returned to her parents' household, and found solace (and perhaps relief from boredom) in the religious services of the Dominican friars. She was pious, but not heroically so: one of the greatest signs of her holiness, according to Tommaso, was that she always arrived early at the church where he was to preach and stayed awake throughout his interminable sermons. She was modest and humble, chaste and obedient; she stripped her clothing of every vain and superfluous ornament and devoted herself to charitable activities, though with the moderation counselled by her spiritual adviser. He warned Maria against going about the city to tend the sick, since that would expose an attractive young woman like her to slander and scandal – or worse. And he persuaded her to turn over all her possessions to her mother, so that the family patrimony would be safeguarded against impulsive excesses of pious generosity.

15. Fernanda Sorelli, 'Imitable sanctity: the legend of Maria of Venice', in Bornstein and Rusconi, eds, *Women and Religion*, pp. 165–81. Sorelli edited Tommaso's biography of Maria as *La santità imitabile: 'Leggenda di Maria di Venezia' di Tommaso da Siena*, Deputazione di storia patria per le Venezie, 'Miscellanea di studi e memorie', 23 (Venice, 1984).

In Tommaso's carefully crafted biography, Maria served a dual purpose. She transmuted into imitable form the inimitable sanctity of her own model, Catherine of Siena. In the place of Catherine's extravagant self-mortifications, Maria performed measured austerities; instead of being rapt in ecstatic visions, she walked to church with modestly downcast eyes. In short – and this was Tommaso's second point – she exemplified the way in which any pious woman could live by the rules governing the Order of Penance.[16] Anyone who wanted to know what the rule's precepts meant in practice could turn to Tommaso d'Antonio's *Life* of Maria and find there a living model of decent, well-bred and non-disruptive piety. In Tommaso's hands, this sad relic of a broken marriage became the very embodiment of the primly devout young lady.

As daughters go to a good father

A far more demanding and controversial model of piety was promoted by Tommaso's colleague, Giovanni Dominici. Giovanni was born in 1355 or 1356, the son of a Venetian noblewoman and a Florentine silk merchant.[17] His father died before Giovanni was born, leaving a pregnant seventeen-year-old widow and two orphans. The two older children died shortly thereafter, so Giovanni grew up as the sole surviving child of his widowed mother, who doted on him and smothered him with affection. When he was fourteen she sent him to Venice to learn commerce, but upon his return to Florence two years later he promptly entered the Dominican order. His distraught mother berated him for taking the habit and depriving her of her only son: in effect, his election of the religious life doomed the family to extinction. However, she soon acquiesced in his decision and eventually followed her son into the Dominican order.

After studying in Florence, Pisa and Paris, Giovanni returned to Venice in 1388, sent by Raymond of Capua to lecture in theology

16. It was Tommaso himself who translated into Italian the rule of the Dominican Order of Penance, originally promulgated in 1285 by the master general Muñoz da Zamora, and won for it papal approval from Innocent VII in 1405. See Fernanda Sorelli, 'Per la storia religiosa di Venezia nella prima metà del Quattrocento: inizi e sviluppi del terz'ordine domenicano', in Maria Chiara Billanovich, Giorgio Cracco and Antonio Rigon, eds, *Viridarium Floridum: Studi di storia veneta offerti dagli allievi a Paolo Sambin* (Padua, 1984), pp. 89–114.

17. Stefano Orlandi, *Necrologio di S. Maria Novella* (Florence, 1955), Vol. 2, pp. 77–126; Giorgio Cracco, entry 'Giovanni di Domenico Banchini', *Dizionario biografico degli italiani*, 5 (Rome, 1963), pp. 657–64.

at the Dominican church of San Zanipolo. He quickly established himself as one of the religious leaders of Venice and an important figure in the Dominican order. Acting as Raymond's vicar, he reformed to the strict observance the houses of San Domenico of Castello, San Domenico of Chioggia and San Zanipolo. Nor was his reforming zeal limited to the Dominican order: he acted as spiritual adviser to doge Antonio Venier and preached for the doge's wife on feast days. Indeed, he strove to transform Venetian society by preaching as many as four times a day, engaging in pastoral care, acting as confessor and spiritual guide to the Venetian patriciate, and caring for those stricken by the plague in 1397. To aid him in this work, he assembled from throughout Italy the group of eager followers and dedicated collaborators (such as Tommaso d'Antonio of Siena) that made Venice for a time the spiritual centre of Italy.[18]

The centrepiece of Giovanni's work in Venice was the convent of Corpus Domini, an institution that was particularly dear to him for both personal and spiritual reasons. His mother, Paola Zorzi, was one of the first women to enter it, and it was here that his promotion of the Dominican observance and his evangelization of the Venetian patriciate were most fully united.[19] Members of the doge's family participated in the convent's consecration on 29 June 1394, and the twenty-seven women who took the Dominican habit that day, like the nearly fifty more who joined over the next two years, sprang in large part from the leading families of Venice. They formed one of the largest religious communities in the city, a gathering place for spiritually minded Venetians and an inspiration for convents as far away as Rome and Pisa. So fervent were the sisters of Corpus Domini that they had to be restrained from harming

18. Giorgio Cracco, 'Des saints aux sanctuaires: hypothèse d'une évolution en terre vénitienne', in *Faire Croire*, pp. 281–3; on the principal spiritual tendencies and tensions at this moment, see Cracco, 'La spiritualità italiana del Tre-Quattrocento: linee interpretative', *Studia Patavina*, 18 (1971), pp. 74–116; and Venturino Alce, 'La riforma dell'ordine domenicano nel '400 e nel '500 veneto', in Giovanni B. Francesco Trolese, ed., *Riforma della chiesa, cultura e spiritualità nel Quattrocento veneto* (Cesena, 1984), pp. 333–43.

19. On Corpus Domini, see the *Cronaca del Corpus Domini* and the *Necrologio del Corpus Domini* written by Bartolomea Riccoboni, in Giovanni Dominici, *Lettere spirituali*, Maria-Teresa Casella and Giovanni Pozzi, eds, *Spicilegium Friburgense*, 51 (Turin, 1981), pp. 257–330; and Pawel Dobrowolski, 'Piety and death in Venice: a reading of the fifteenth-century chronicle and the necrology of Corpus Domini', *Bullettino dell'Istituto Storico Italiano per il Medio Evo*, 92 (1985–86), pp. 295–324. For Giovanni's letters to the sisters of Corpus Domini, see Lia Sbriziolo, 'Note su Giovanni Dominici, I: la "spiritualità" del Dominici nelle lettere alle suore veneziane del Corpus Christi', *Rivista di storia della chiesa in Italia*, 24 (1970), pp. 4–30.

themselves through excessive fasting, vigils and self-mortification. As the convent's chronicler, Sister Bartolomea Riccoboni, noted with just a hint of spiritual pride, 'When our father [Giovanni Dominici] observed that many women were falling ill because of their numerous penances and abstinences, he commanded that all the whips and chains be brought to him; and when he saw how many there were, he remained utterly dumbfounded. He ordered that no one could scourge herself without permission from the vicaress or himself. He did this because he knew they would refrain from asking for this permission; and he likewise ordered them to take food according to their needs, because many rose from table having eaten little.'[20]

The triple lock on their portal, with each of the three keys held by a different sister, guaranteed the strict observance of cloister. Living together in this closed community, the sisters shared the daily chores as they shared in daily worship, yet also often continued the roles they had played outside its walls. Sister Domenica Moro looked after her brother for five years after their mother's death; she then entered the convent 'and acted like everyone's mother, serving both healthy and sick with great charity'.[21] Margarita Paruta and her husband had been financial supporters of Corpus Domini since its inception. 'When her husband died, she offered herself to the order, giving both herself and all her possessions, which amounted to more than two thousand ducats.' Accustomed as she was to managing a large patrician household, she fell naturally into the role of vicaress, repairing and improving the buildings and running the convent on behalf of the elderly prioress.[22]

Like most convents, Corpus Domini functioned as a place of refuge for the bereft. It offered shelter to widows and orphans, the elderly and infirm. Franceschina da Noale entered the convent as a forty-nine-year-old widow, bringing with her a seven-year-old daughter; Cristina dalla Terra was a widow of fifty-five when she entered, and she was constantly ill for the eight years she lived in the convent. Some of these widows were startlingly young: Onesta dei Marchesi, who entered the convent at the age of twenty-three, was already a widow; Beruzza Ziroldi was only thirteen when she was widowed and decided she wanted nothing more to do with the world. Those sisters who joined as young women or children tended to be in poor health: Gabriella of Siena was twenty-six when she

20. Bartolomea Riccoboni, *Cronaca*, p. 268.
21. Bartolomea Riccoboni, *Necrologio*, p. 303. Domenica's brother joined the convent with her, as a servant to the sisters.
22. Ibid., pp. 303–6.

entered, and was ill for most of the fifteen years she spent in Corpus Domini; Benedetta Rosso entered the convent at the age of ten, and was sick with consumption for twenty-three of the twenty-seven years she lived there; Eufraxia Minio was only seven when she joined, and she too was consumptive for more than half of the thirty-five years she spent in Corpus Domini.

The presence of these children afflicted with chronic illnesses raises the possibility that the convent may have been used as a dumping ground for unmarriageable girls. Yet the religious fervour of the sisters of Corpus Domini also suggests that they very much wanted to be there. At least one of the women, Piera of Città di Castello, said that she had married against her wishes; once she was widowed, she happily embraced the religious life, first as a Dominican tertiary in her native city and then as a cloistered nun in Corpus Domini. Marina Ogniben 'was a young woman of holy life and great fervour, and entered the convent with a younger sister, without the permission of her mother and her relatives'.[23] In most cases, the decision to enter the religious life was made by the woman herself, whether she was a mature and independent widow like Piera or a seventeen-year-old adolescent like Marina.

The strict cloister they observed did not remove the sisters of Corpus Domini from all contact with their families or with the rest of the outside world. In fact, as we have seen, entering the convent did not necessarily mean leaving one's family behind. There are a number of cases in which pairs of sisters or mothers and daughters joined the convent together. The younger girls, in particular, often entered along with a sibling, so that they would not feel totally deprived of family. The convent could also accommodate kin at the other end of life's journey: Corpus Domini provided the final resting place for one ill and elderly Franciscan tertiary, who was taken in to pass her last three weeks of life with her daughter Franceschina, two granddaughters and great-niece, all of them members of this Dominican community.[24]

The convent community did, however, tend to supplant the family as the primary focus of the sisters' affections. The widow Zanetta dalle Boccole 'was 22 years old when she converted, and with great fervor she left two children to God's keeping and entered as a nun here inside, where she lived for 32 years and four months.'[25] Franceschina da Noale instead brought her seven-year-old daughter into the convent with her, but she then entrusted her to the care of the novice mistress and deliberately refrained from interfering

23. Ibid., p. 296.   24. Ibid., p. 299.   25. Ibid., p. 325.

in her upbringing. The convent encouraged the sort of coolness towards close kin that Sister Bartolomea found so admirable in Lucia Da Canal, who died at the age of twenty-eight after having spent fully half of her short life within the walls of Corpus Domini: 'When her relatives visited her, she sent them away as soon as she could. Her father, mother, brothers, and sisters died, and she was never seen to weep. Her mother and sisters were buried here with us; she did not stir to touch them, but sang with the rest just as if they had no connection with her.'[26]

This reorientation of the sisters' affections was consciously sought by Giovanni Dominici, who strove to replace the ties of biological kinship with a new spiritual kinship. Giovanni, like Jesus, declared that he had come not to bring peace but a sword, and to set a son against his father and a daughter against her mother.[27] He himself took the place of both father and mother, provided for the material support of Corpus Domini and the sustenance of its inhabitants, and served as the exclusive conduit for all charitable contributions. Sister Bartolomea said of Giovanni:

> Our father was our procurator and kept us supplied with everything that was needed; all the officials [of the convent] went to him as daughters go to a good father, and like a good father he provided everything with great charity. ... There was no need to ask our relatives, since he provided us with everything. ... In short, we were like a child at its mother's breast, without the slightest care or thought.[28]

The result was a profound material, spiritual and affective dependence on Giovanni, the fatherless child who found in Corpus Domini a bevy of doting daughters – one that included his biological mother.

Giovanni's radical reorientation of his spiritual daughters' affections was not always appreciated by their biological families, whose feelings for these women did not die when they entered the convent. Lucia Da Canal's relatives came to visit her; her mother and sisters elected burial in Corpus Domini with her. They clearly tried to maintain their ties with her, and they surely did not enjoy being received with the aloofness and emotional distance that Sister Bartolomea found so admirable. As a result, resentment of Giovanni Dominici flourished in the same patrician circles in which he was

26. Ibid., pp. 304–5, with the corrections indicated in Maria Teresa Casella and Giovanni Pozzi, 'Giunta al Dominici', *Italia Medioevale e Umanistica*, 14 (1971), p. 178.
27. Bartolomea Riccoboni, *Necrologio*, p. 317; Matthew 10:34–5.
28. Bartolomea Riccoboni, *Cronaca*, p. 269, with the corrections indicated in Casella and Pozzi, 'Giunta al Dominici', p. 173. See also Bartolomea Riccoboni, *Necrologio*, p. 315.

so respected. What is more, Giovanni's encouragement of chastity threatened the preservation and continuation of the patrician family, as his personal choice to enter the religious life made amply clear. 'Many men and women left their relatives and their children to become friars and nuns', wrote Sister Bartolomea, 'and for this reason their relatives grew angry with him [Giovanni], saying: "This traitor is leading our children astray; let us remove him from the world".' There is no hard evidence that anyone actually tried to kill Giovanni, despite Sister Bartolomea's claim that his enemies plotted to murder him when he came to say mass. But there were undoubtedly more than a few concerned parents who were relieved when a clash with the Venetian government resulted in Giovanni's exile from Venice in 1399.[29]

O blessed house, foretaste of life eternal

Giovanni's not altogether successful attempts to infuse a convent with a sense of family, where he himself was the spiritual father of its spiritual sisterhood, were parallelled by his efforts to introduce monastic models into the domestic devotions of a patrician household. After his expulsion from Venice late in 1399, Giovanni returned to his native Florence. There he came into contact with a Florentine laywoman, Bartolomea degli Obizzi, to whom he addressed letters of spiritual counsel, a treatise on household management and child rearing, and a response to a series of questions on the perfection of the soul and its union with God.[30] Bartolomea was a mother of four, left in charge of the household and saddled with responsibility for managing the family property after the exile of her husband, Antonio degli Alberti, in 1400.[31] She evidently was interested in theology and drawn to the monastic life – or perhaps driven towards it by the domestic burdens that had fallen on her shoulders. Giovanni answered her yearning for the quiet of the cloister with the remark that there are many different ways to

29. Bartolomea Riccoboni, *Necrologio*, p. 317. On Giovanni's arrest and exile, see Daniel Bornstein, 'Giovanni Dominici, the Bianchi, and Venice: symbolic action and interpretive grids', *Journal of Medieval and Renaissance Studies*, 23 (1993), pp. 143–71.

30. Giovanni Dominici, *Lettere spirituali*, pp. 196–217; *Regola del governo di cura familiare*, Donato Salvi, ed. (Florence, 1860); and *Trattato delle dieci questioni e lettere a Madonna Bartolomea*, Arrigo Levasti, ed. (Florence, 1957). In addition, Bartolomea was possibly – according to Levasti (p. 5), probably – the person to whom Giovanni dedicated his major work of spiritual theology, the *Libro d'amor di carità*, A. Cerruti, ed. (Bologna, 1889).

31. On the effect of exile on the domestic strategies of the Alberti, see Susannah Foster Baxendale, 'Exile in practice: the Alberti family in and out of Florence, 1401–1428', *Renaissance Quarterly*, 44 (1991), pp. 720–56.

approach God; one should not worry about what one's state in life ought to be, but simply dedicate oneself – in whatever state – to doing God's will.[32] Since Bartolomea's state was that of a housewife, she should manage her property well – and dedicate some of it to supporting preachers of God's word (though not in a way that would draw them away from their vows of poverty).[33]

Above all, Bartolomea was called to rear her children properly, since God had given parents nothing so dear to Him as children. From the moment that they learned to speak, infants should be taught to utter holy words. They should be raised to be pious little girls and boys, surrounded by images of the saints and the Christ child. Little girls should draw inspiration from virgins like Agnes with her lamb, Cecilia crowned with roses, and Elizabeth with roses on her robe; while boys should observe the priest in church and imitate him at home, officiating at their toy altars. Boys should also be encouraged to play at preaching before their attentive and appreciative families. And Bartolomea should accustom her children to confess their faults while still young, giving them as 'penance' nuts, figs or other fruit so that confession would be a pleasure, and only when they grew older replace the sweet reward with real penances. In this way, religious models and priestly devotions could enter the domestic space, mould the child's character and transform the home into a place of worship. Even more than a place of worship, exclaimed Giovanni, the blessed home founded on such principles offered a foretaste and beginning of life eternal.[34]

The varied writings Giovanni addressed to Bartolomea degli Obizzi find their echo and response in a most unusual text: a handful of letters of spiritual advice attributed to Bartolomea herself. These fifteen letters, introduced with the heading 'These are Madonna Bartolomea replies to various persons', cover twenty-seven folios at the end of a collection of Giovanni Dominici's writings for women, copied in 1518 for the use of the Dominican convent of Santa Lucia.[35] Reading these letters, one is immediately struck by the thought that they belong more to the world of the convent where they were copied than to that of the patrician laywoman who supposedly wrote them. Their concerns are exclusively spiritual.

32. Giovanni Dominici, *Lettere spirituali*, pp. 207 and 214.
33. Giovanni Dominici, *Regola del governo di cura familiare*, pp. 114–21.
34. Ibid., pp. 131–2, 146–7, 149, 153–4, and 173.
35. 'Queste sono risposte di Madonna Bartolomea fatte ad più persone', Biblioteca Riccardiana 1414, ff. 245v–272r. This manuscript was copied at least in part by one of the sisters of the convent.

They contain nothing personal, nothing domestic, nothing familial.[36] The content of Bartolomea's letters is so unexpected that it is hard to believe that a laywoman could have written them. However, I can think of no reason why the copyist would have falsely ascribed them to a long-dead person of no particular prestige in ecclesiastical circles, and so I have chosen (provisionally and with some considerable reservations) to accept the manuscript's attribution.

In these letters Bartolomea offers guidance on the spiritual life, teaching other devout women with calm assurance. She refers to the great figures of Christian spirituality, such as Augustine, Jerome, Benedict, Bernard and Paul; she cites the canon of the mass (specifically, the *Miserere mei deus*) in support of her assertion that God cares more for interior devotions than exterior sacrifices; she offers a spiritualized reading of Jesus's instruction to his disciples to eat whatever food is set before them, turning it into a general injunction to accept the divine disposition of our lives. Bartolomea moves easily through the technical terminology of contrition and compunction, *substantia* and *potentia*. She draws models of prayer and purification from the life of Jesus, weighs the pursuit of one's own spiritual perfection against the virtue to be gained from teaching others, assesses the value of spiritual tears, warns against a longing for rapture that takes one away from devotional reading, offers comfort during spells of spiritual dryness, and points out the way to achieve 'a true annihilation of our selves'.

This interest in mystical theology is entirely in keeping with the several *spiritual* treatises Giovanni wrote for her, rather than his domestic manual. But instead of speaking as the disciple of her Dominican master (who is never mentioned), Bartolomea offers advice on her own authority – and on a subject of which she had no direct personal experience.[37] Bartolomea had clearly longed

36. One could hardly imagine a sharper contrast to the letters of another Florentine matriarch, left (like Bartolomea) in charge of the household during her menfolks' exile: Alessandra Macinghi Strozzi, *Tempo di affetti e di mercanti: Lettere ai figli esuli,* Angela Bianchini, ed. (Milan, 1987); *Selected Letters of Alessandra Strozzi,* translated with introduction and notes by Heather Gregory (Berkeley and Los Angeles, CA, 1996).

37. Bartolomea's letters are shot through with phrases like 'but I say', 'my understanding is', 'but it seems to me', 'to your question, I respond that', 'if you do not know how to gain other reward out of it than that which I can comprehend for myself, I would judge that . . .' – all cited from a single manuscript page (f. 255v). In answer to her correspondent's question about spiritual tears, Bartolomea acknowledges that 'I know nothing of them from experience, and so should hardly know how to discuss them. But nonetheless I will try to tell you something of what I think of them' (f. 254r). She then proceeds confidently to deliver her opinion despite her admitted lack of experience.

for the cloistered life, though she let Giovanni dissuade her from a monastic vocation. In her letters, however, she is able to take the other side and guide a friend through the decision to enter a convent, the commitment to the religious life that she herself never made. Several of the letters, in fact, form a connected series, a little drama enacted in one half of an epistolary exchange. The drama opens with a letter in which Bartolomea responds to a question about the manner in which someone who is committed to marriage, the care of children and other such responsibilities should perform her duties. Her correspondent clearly feels burdened – as Bartolomea had been – by her domestic and familial cares. But Bartolomea cautions her against rushing to seek a higher state, because a life with higher expectations also carries greater dangers. Ill-health evidently aggravated her friend's burdens, since in the next letter Bartolomea comforts her sick friend with the thought that physical infirmity is not inimical to spiritual well-being: on the contrary, bodily illness often *leads to* spiritual health.[38] The afflictions continue in the following letter, which reveals that Bartolomea's friend is now 'mutando stato', changing her status. Is she now at the point of her consecration as a nun, or is she considering becoming a tertiary? In either case, for the moment Bartolomea's advice is to avoid going out in public: it is better to stay secluded at home, except for the days when public attendance at church is required. In the following letter, she responds to her friend's query on how to make restitution for her wrongdoing. Bartolomea replies that restitution is not within our power; we can only pray to God for his grace. Such prayer, however, is difficult if not impossible amidst a crowd: withdrawal to a cell is preferred, if not absolutely required. Was Bartolomea thinking of a cell like that in which so many thirteenth-century anchoresses lived 'as if in a tomb', the interior cell to which Catherine of Siena retired for meditation in the fourteenth century, or the regularized groups into which most solitary *cellane* had been swept by the fifteenth century?[39] The

38. The striking prominence of illness as a component of female sanctity is noted by Weinstein and Bell, *Saints and Society*, pp. 234–5: fortitude in illness is 'the one category of activity in which women were not merely statistically overrepresented but constituted an absolute majority'.

39. On female hermits and anchoresses who lived *velut in sepulchro*, see Anna Benvenuti Papi, '*In Castro Poenitentiae': Santità e società femminile nell'Italia medievale* (Rome, 1990); on the reorganization of these solitary anchoresses into female communities, see Mario Sensi, 'Anchoresses and penitents in thirteenth- and fourteenth-century Umbria', in Bornstein and Rusconi, eds, *Women and Religion*, pp. 56–83.

answer becomes clear in the following letter, in which Bartolomea rejoices over her friend's entrance into a religious community. The remaining letters cheer her on the long and often discouraging path to spiritual perfection and warn of dangers on the way – dangers such as that perennial problem of cloistered life, 'special friend-ships'. Bartolomea's vicarious pleasure at guiding her friend into and through the monastic life is as palpable as Giovanni's delight in the playfulness of children and sensitivity to their emotional needs.

My decorated altar that I have at home

The writings examined here have invoked the language of kin-ship to charge the religious life with emotional force and drawn on clerical models to endow family life with spiritual meaning. Household and cloister overlapped, in ways that are not always pre-dictable. One might expect that young girls who were entrusted to convents for their early education would absorb monastic models and bring monastic modes of comportment into their households when they married.[40] But who would guess that devotional paint-ings and domestic altars had become such a commonplace furnish-ing in patrician homes that laywomen would donate their household altars to convents? Yet that is precisely what Margarita, the widow of Bartolomeo Luciani, did in 1396 when she bequeathed to Corpus Domini 'a decorated altar of mine that I have at home'.[41]

We have heard voices raised in a conversation that sometimes took surprising turns: a celibate friar provided practical suggestions on child rearing, while a Florentine housewife and mother offered spiritual guidance on the religious life. I have tried to keep in mind the fact that these voices are not disembodied. The people who spoke out on gendered issues lived in gendered bodies. They were themselves involved in gendered relationships; they were mothers and sons, fathers and daughters, sisters and spouses. And those relationships were further complicated by the perduring tension between spiritual and biological kinship, which posed a constant

40. Anthony Molho, '*Tamquam vere mortua*: le professioni religiose femminili nella Firenze del tardo medioevo', *Società e storia*, 12 (1986), pp. 16–17.
41. ASV, Corporazioni religiose, Corpus Domini, pergamene 1, 23 January 1396. On the spread of domestic altars in fourteenth-century Italy, see Frugoni, 'Female mystics, visions, and iconography', p. 149.

and disturbing challenge to the most deeply rooted of human sentiments. Giovanni Dominici urged Bartolomea degli Obizzi to dedicate herself to bringing up her children and instilling in them true piety, while insisting that 'properly religious children should no longer obey the flesh, but their spiritual father or mother. And so, let such children not call those who generated their flesh father or mother, but merely man or woman.'[42]

42. Giovanni Dominici, *Regola del governo di cura familiare*, p. 160.

CHAPTER NINE

Gender, Religious Institutions and Social Discipline: The Reform of the Regulars*

GABRIELLA ZARRI

This chapter seeks to encourage reflection on the relationship between gender, religious institutions and social discipline. My point of reference is the recent book, *Disciplina dell'anima, disciplina del corpo e disciplina della società tra medioevo ed età moderna*, edited by Paolo Prodi and Carla Penuti, in which the concept of social discipline is examined both for its theoretical value and for its usefulness in specific empirical applications. From the outset, however, I wish to emphasize the dynamic and diversified nature of the process of social discipline, as Prodi has already done.[1] Social disciplining produced a remarkable quantity of prescriptive norms, which at the ecclesiastical level primarily involved institutions; it pursued its aims by shrewdly balancing imposition and persuasion, discipline and doctrine. The new norms, or the renewal and reform of existing ones, were aimed especially at three institutions characteristic of medieval Christianity that were radically contested by the Protestant Reformation: religious orders, marriage and the cult of saints. In addition to institutional reform and new regulations, discipline focused on religious acculturation, with the goal of instilling 'good behaviours' and 'Christian beliefs' in the wake of the civilizing process initiated by the Renaissance, and was aimed at a new cultural

* Translated from the Italian by Michael Rocke.
1. See especially Prodi's introduction to *Disciplina dell'anima, disciplina del corpo, disciplina della società tra medioevo ed età moderna* (Bologna, 1994). On the concept of disciplining, see also William V. Hudon, 'Religion and society in early modern Italy: old questions, new insights', *American Historical Review*, 101 (1996), pp. 783–804.

subject, childhood and youth.[2] Another institution that cannot be ignored is confession and the control of conscience, which played a basic role in repairing the ecclesiastical fabric after the Protestant crisis and in fashioning the new, disciplined individual of Tridentine Catholicism.[3] Inquisitors and confessors contributed together to this process through a complex ensemble of new theological and juridical definitions and of practices that formed part of a politics of control and persuasion.

Here I will explore the differences between male and female roles in pre- and post-Tridentine ecclesiastical prescriptions and ideology, specifically in the reform of the regulars, that is, religious orders that observe a rule. I will also draw attention to those novel elements that escaped this process of adaptation, and indeed were encouraged by a disciplining that was apparently not at odds with modernization.

The disciplining of the regulars

The need to reform the regulars became clear from at least the late fourteenth century, when an impulse for renewal that began in a few convents and with a few prominent individuals soon came to involve all of the major orders, giving birth to the Observant movements. This reform 'from below', quickly found support from princes, urban ruling classes and the papacy itself, all interested in encouraging monasteries and convents to return to stricter discipline. From the mid-fifteenth century, however, this aim also became linked to a social transformation in which the religious profession was considered a necessary container for the excess male and female population.[4] Those involved were, above all, the urban ruling classes, caught up in a process of aristocratization and of stabilizing the

---

2. Ottavia Niccoli, *Il seme della violenza: Putti, fanciulli e mammoli nell'Italia tra Cinque e Seicento* (Rome and Bari, 1995); Angelo Turchini, *Sotto l'occhio del padre: Società confessionale e istruzione primaria nello Stato di Milano* (Bologna, 1996).

3. Paolo Prodi, 'Discorso conclusivo', in *Dalla penitenza all'ascolto delle confessioni: Il ruolo dei frati mendicanti*, Atti del XXIII Convegno internazionale, Assisi, 12–14 ottobre 1995 (Spoleto, 1996), pp. 289–306; Adriano Prosperi, *Tribunali della coscienza. Inquisitori, confessori, missionari* (Torino, 1996).

4. Gabriella Zarri, 'Aspetti dello sviluppo degli Ordini religiosi in Italia tra Quattro e Cinquecento: Studi e problemi', in Paolo Prodi and Peter Johanek, eds, *Strutture ecclesiastiche in Italia e Germania prima della Riforma* (Bologna, 1983), pp. 207–57; Zarri, 'Monasteri femminili e città (secoli XV–XVIII)', in Giorgio Chittolini and Giovanni Miccoli, eds, *La Chiesa e il potere politico dal Medioevo all'età contemporanea* (*Storia d'Italia, Annali 9*) (Turin, 1986), pp. 359–429.

norms of primogeniture, which reserved the inheritance to the eldest son and excluded other children. In varying ways, between the mid-fifteenth and the mid-sixteenth centuries this social process involved all the Italian cities.[5]

Episodes of the breakdown of monastic discipline – especially among nuns – emerge from chronicles and from literary and inquisitorial sources; some have inspired fictional accounts that are significant for the history of the family or of customs, while others have led to studies in the history of sexuality. A newly published source now furnishes first-hand evidence on monastic deviance.[6] The petitions (*suppliche*) sent to the Roman office of the Sacra Penitenzieria to obtain absolution for censures or reserved sins, or dispensations from the obligations of monastic vows, present in unmediated form a broad range of violations of the vow of chastity committed by religious in the fifteenth and sixteenth centuries. These transgressions confirm and delineate the permeable relations that existed between ecclesiastical structures and city life, for monasteries had not yet been defined as places separate from the social body and the urban context, and their perimeters could be traversed in both directions. Nuns came in contact with priests, laymen and other religious, with whom they sometimes had amorous or sexual relations that then might result in a request for absolution from the sin of apostasy or the annulment of monastic vows. Two different examples show that in the later fifteenth century, clergymen and laymen had similar opportunities to enter convents and that nuns were not subject to particularly severe norms.

In 1476, both protagonists of an illicit love affair petitioned the Sacra Penitenzieria for absolution from the censures and excommunications that had been imposed on them, seeking to return to their previous status. The apparently unmarried Milanese layman Giovannangelo Mantegazza, had entered the convent of Poor Clares in Voghera, where he slept overnight and had relations with suor Battistina, later convincing her to leave the convent and go with him to his home; for some time they then lived together in concubinage. Confirming Mantegazza's story, suor Battistina declared:

5. Most recently, Gérard Delille, 'Strategie di alleanza e demografia del matrimonio', in De Giorgio and Klapisch-Zuber, *Storia del matrimonio*, (Bari, 1996), pp. 283–303. On the demography of female convents, see Luigi Tittarelli, 'Monacazioni, matrimoni e fecondità a Perugia nel Seicento', *Bollettino di Demografia Storica*, S.I.DE.S 20 (1994), pp. 157–71; Judith C. Brown, 'Monache a Firenze all'inizio dell'età moderna: Un'analisi demografica', *Quaderni storici*, 29 (1994), pp. 117–52.

6. Filippo Tamburini, *Santi e peccatori: Confessioni e suppliche dai Registri della Penitenzieria dell'Archivio Segreto Vaticano (1451–1586)* (Milan, 1995).

Both inside and outside the walls of the said convent she was carnally known in the act of fornication by that layman, and was taken by him from the said convent, and she permitted him to keep her for many days in concubinage, later having children.[7]

The nun's petition also stated that after abandoning the convent in Voghera, she later returned to the religious life, entering a convent in Tortona. She thus asked to be absolved by special grace from excommunication and from the crime of apostasy.

In 1486, fra' Paolo de Mangonibus, the provost of the monastery of San Pietro e Paolo degli Umiliati in Correggio, asked the Sacra Penitenziaria for absolution from his excommunication for sacrilege. Exploiting his office and power, he had induced two nuns of his order to have sexual relations with him:

He stated that many times he carnally knew suor Cherubina, professed nun in the convent of the said Order in Milan, and also a suor Benetina, also a professed nun in the convent of San Bernaba in Tortona, of the same Order, both inside and outside of the walls of the said houses, and he procreated offspring by them.[8]

Two different stories – in which cloistered nuns became involved with a layman and a cleric, and which reveal the close relations that existed between society and religious orders. The resulting ties between individuals could be deep, or at the least have social consequences for offspring; they could temporarily break the separation from the world postulated by monastic vows, although in these cases attempts to escape these vows were evidently unachievable or denied.

On the other hand, religious vows contracted under coercion (*per vim et metum*) could be annulled. This was the case with two young women who were forced to become nuns in the convent of Poor Clares of Santa Maria del Pionto near Arezzo. Margherita della Scarpa, an Aretine, was placed in the convent while still a minor. When she reached her majority, she was persuaded 'by threats, [harsh] words, and terror' to make her profession. Afterwords she remained in the convent, even though she continued to declare 'openly and publicly', that she in no way wanted to be a nun. When the opportunity arose, she left the convent, abandoned the religious habit, and returned 'to the secular world', where she intended to remain. Later she wanted to marry, but on hearing that her preceding vow made this impossible, she petitioned the Sacra Penitenzieria on 12 January 1481 for the annulment of her vows and permission

7. Ibid., pp. 151–3; passage cited, p. 152.
8. Ibid., pp. 173–4; passage cited, p. 173.

to marry. After the Bishop of Arezzo verified the truthfulness of Margherita's claims, the Penitenzieria declared that her profession was invalid. Four years later, a petition sent directly to the pope to obtain the annulment of monastic vows revealed a similar but more complicated situation. Antonia Castiglione of Arezzo, placed in the convent in Pionto at the age of three, had also been forced to take vows. She lived as a nun for twelve years, but, like Margherita, as soon as the opportunity arose to leave the nunnery, she returned to her family and married. When she petitioned to clarify her situation legally, she had already been married for two years, something possible only because of the nature of marriage practice before Trent. In this case, too, the former nun's petition was approved.[9]

It is striking that in both these cases it was not paternal authority that forced the monachization of these two girls, but rather a female figure: her mother in Margherita's case, and a paternal aunt in Antonia's. Both nuns left their convent soon after the deaths of these relatives who had impeded their return home. Considering their lack of willingness, the ecclesiastical authorities had no difficulty in granting each woman an annulment.

The lack of discipline among regulars, however, must not be identified only or mainly with forbidden sexuality or forced monachization. Belonging to an ancient religious order, with its substantial landed estates, and holding important monastic governing offices conferred prestige and power in civil society. It was not by chance that one of the basic aims of the fifteenth-century Observant reforms was to abolish the custom of perpetually re-electing the same monastic officers and to replace this with temporary tenures. Reformers considered it contrary to the spirit of conventual self-rule and conducive to authoritarian governance that the same individual should repeatedly hold the office of prior or prioress. The reform, however, encouraged the formation of groups and factions within monasteries, especially when the office of prior or prioress was up for renewal.[10] Such factions were useful for gaining positions of prestige or power within the monastery: for example, the groups in female communities that supported the singers or organists against the professed nuns who had no particular gifts for music or singing,[11]

9. Ibid., pp. 159–60 and p. 160, n. 1.
10. Examples in Massimo Marcocchi, *La riforma dei monasteri femminili a Cremona: Gli atti inediti della visita del vescovo Cesare Speciano (1599–1606)* (Cremona, 1966).
11. See in Craig Monson, *Disembodied Voices: Music and Culture in an Early Modern Italian Convent* (Berkeley, CA, 1995); also Robert Kendrick, *Celestial Sirens: Nuns and their Music in Early Modern Milan* (Oxford, 1996).

or more strongly rooted familial factions that mirrored citizen groups that opposed each other in struggles for political supremacy.[12]

Citizens' interest in the good government of monasteries was motivated above all by the desire to control the management of ecclesiastical properties, both to prevent their dispersal or private use by individual clans, and to avoid having these properties, with their tax exemptions, expand even further. Great attention was also devoted to the discipline and moral behaviours of monasteries to protect the honour of both local families and the community, for which reason cities such as Genoa, Venice and Florence instituted special magistracies for the good government of nunneries in the fifteenth and early sixteenth centuries.[13] But the papacy and the Church hierarchy also became actively committed to the reform of the regulars, in part as a response to the Lutheran opposition to monasticism.

Male and female religious

Being forced to make a religious profession was not purely a feminine fate.[14] True, the large dowries required to find a girl a good marriage were the reason many families chose the convent for their daughters. Yet men too were also often coerced into an ecclesiastical career, as an alternative to the military, by the demands of primogeniture: in the requests they made for the annulment of vows, men also claimed to have been driven into a religious profession *per vim et metum*. Still, regulars who were dissatisfied with their condition could at least seek dispensation from the obligation to live in a monastery, taking advantage of the *licentiae extra standi*. Between the fifteenth and sixteenth centuries, one did not have to be an intellectual like Erasmus, with a European-wide reputation, to obtain such a licence: the Roman curia granted them easily for

12. Letizia Arcangeli, 'Ragioni politiche della disciplina monastica: il caso di Parma tra Quattro e Cinquecento', in Gabriella Zarri, ed., *Donna, disciplina, creanza cristiana dal XV al XVII secolo: Studi e testi a stampa* (Rome, 1996), pp. 165–87.

13. Romano Canosa, *Il velo e il cappuccio: Monacazioni forzate e sessualita' nei conventi femminili in Italia tra Quattrocento e Settecento* (Rome, 1991).

14. Enrico Cattaneo, 'Le monacazioni forzate fra Cinque e Seicento', in G. Farinelli and E. Paccagnini eds. *Vita e processo di suor Virginia Maria de Leyva monaca di Monza* (Milan, 1985), pp. 145–95; Paola Vismara Chiappa, *'Per vim et metum': Il caso di Paola Teresa Pietra* (Como, 1991); Francesca Medioli, 'Monacazioni forzate: donne ribelli al proprio destino', *Clio*, 30 (1994), pp. 431–54; Paolo Fontana, 'Monacazioni forzate e letteratura clandestina: note da un documento genovese', *Rivista di storia e letteratura religiosa*, 32 (1996), pp. 127–32.

purposes of study, for sickness, or for going to the aid of relatives. Such flights from monastic discipline often had economic and social causes: an 'ex-monk' generally did not return to his family (which had probably opposed his decision); rather, those who had been ordained priests tried to find financial autonomy and a place within the diocese by obtaining a benefice. With the often dramatic, initial spread of Lutheran ideas, however, such apostasy began to assume ideological overtones, as more and more regulars abandoned their monasteries without authorization. By the 1530s, the relative tolerance that had once permitted ex-monks and apostates to be reinserted into the Church was coming to an end, and in the following decades coercive and repressive measures were taken against them, by ecclesiastical authorities who suspected them of heresy.

In his study of mid-sixteenth-century monastic discipline in the diocese of Bologna, Guido Dall'Olio uncovers the continued coercion that forced many men to take religious vows.[15] Thus, don Evangelista de Mucia, born the second of three children of an arrogant and overbearing carpenter, had not wanted to follow his father's trade; rather, he had intellectual inclinations (and was described as 'devoted to letters'). Three times he had run away, until his father was finally heard to shout at him, 'Get out of my house, you loafing good-for-nothing, and go become a friar!' Under the circumstances, the monastic profession was an obligatory route, and not until his father died in 1551 did don Evangelista ask for dispensation to leave his Augustinian monastery of San Giacomo.[16] The Augustinian Giulio della Volpe, in 1549, likewise declared that he had been forced to become a monk, as did the Servite Guglielmo Grandi, who obtained the annulment of his vows and licence to live outside the monastery as a priest.[17]

With his bull *Postquam divina bonitas* (also called *Contra apostatas*) of 1558, Paul IV aimed to induce all such former monks to return to their monasteries, placing even those with dispensations from the curia on the same level as non-regular apostates and depriving them of Church benefices. Recalcitrants were to be singled out and forced to wear a beret of black cloth encircled by two white bands, and Christians, on penalty of excommunication, were forbidden to offer them hospitality.[18]

---

15. Guido Dall'Olio, 'La disciplina dei religiosi all'epoca del Concilio di Trento: sondaggi bolognesi', *Annali dell'Istituto storico italo-germanico in Trento*, 21 (1995), pp. 93–140.

16. Ibid., p. 117.   17. Ibid., pp. 116–17.   18. Ibid., p. 121.

Bologna, the most important city in the papal state after Rome, had already instituted restrictive measures against ex-monks dedicated to the care of souls. Armed with the papal bull and supported by secular authorities, in 1558 the bishop warned all apostates to return to their monasteries within twelve days, or face the prescribed penalties. Some saw the Church as taking over from the family, in this implicitly violent attempt to force men to embrace an unwanted and unaccepted status. Don Pietro da Bassa, granted a dispensation to leave the order because he had been forced to take vows as a boy, obeyed the decree out of fear of the penalties, but he had a public declaration drawn up about the imposition he had suffered:

> I, don Pietro Bassa, in the presence of you witnesses and the notary written herewithin, state ... that should I in any way or form, and once or more times, return to the monastery, and should I there take the habit and live and cloister myself for certain days, months or years, that in any of the said cases I expressly protest and protest anew, and declare that all this is and will always be done out of fear, force, and violence, and out of the doubt that my superiors' disdain will cause even worse to befall me. For this reason I do not by any means intend be a friar.[19]

Other ex-monks also probably obeyed the pope's bull out of fear of prison or the galleys. In the Bolognese diocese, thirty-three apostates from various orders turned themselves in: ten Franciscans (including seven Conventuals and three Observants), six Servites, four regular Augustinian canons, four Augustinian eremites, four Carmelites, three Celestines and two Dominicans.

The number of apostates in Bologna was not large compared with all of those with professed vows in the various monasteries. But it is still significant, considering the limited possibilities and inclinations to declare openly that one had been coerced to profess monastic vows. The economic and social motives that led parents to steer their children into the monastery are summarized well in one of the most widely circulated texts of the Reformation, *Il Sommario della Santa Scrittura e l'ordinario dei cristiani*, published in Italy in the mid-1530s. Written in the Netherlands and translated into the major European languages, the text denounces a situation that was common to all of Catholic Europe. Aimed above all at *negoziatori*, or workers, the religious meaning of whose work is re-evaluated, *Il Sommario* was both a theological treatise and a moral guide for the various 'states' of life. In Italy it helped spread widely the message

19. Ibid., pp. 122–3.

of evangelical freedom.[20] The anonymous author exhorts fathers and mothers not to place 'their children in religion without caution', and summarizes the motives that led parents to monachize their children by force:

> Some do it because they have many offspring; so that they might be able to marry the others more richly, they put one or two who have some bodily imperfection in religion. Others do it to obtain honour from their sons, because they have become monks, priests or prelates. And finally, some do it in the hope of being helped and succoured by their sons.[21]

There were few religious, the author claimed, who dared to abandon the monastery. Even though they made an effort to observe their vows faithfully, they lived in 'hypocrisy'.

> Nowadays we see that many monks and nuns live in monasteries against their wills, and everything they do proceeds from a forced soul and unwillingly. They are discouraged from leaving because of the world's shame, because they have promised to stay. Often they curse those who persuaded and advised them to enter the monastery, and they wish that their cloisters would be burned down. Their hearts are never content, and their consciences are unable to find rest. They are more alienated from God than they were when they were laypersons. . . . In the whole world there is no more dangerous sin than this perversity and hypocrisy. It would be much better for such people to leave the cloister.[22]

These statements were made in a context of criticism of monastic vows that was clearly related to Erasmus's and later Luther's position that the religious profession and life were mere ceremony, an institution that added nothing to the consecration of baptism. But beyond the ulterior goal of furnishing ideological justification for abandoning monasteries, *Il Sommario* reveals the motives that led parents to monachize both their male and female children by force. It explores the reasons why the religious – who made a monastic profession in order to conduct a more perfect life than that of simple Christians – did not 'improve in their spiritual lives'. It also stigmatizes different male and female defects. Monks entered religion for considerations of convenience or prestige:

---

20. Cesare Bianco, ed., *Il sommario della Santa Scrittura e l'ordinario dei cristiani*, with an introduction by Johannes Trapman (Turin, 1988).
21. Ibid., p. 137.   22. Ibid., p. 129.

One enters out of need, to have his expenses covered; another to become a great prelate; a third to live in idleness and to have a good time; and many out of vanity, to be reputed saints and devout and to be honoured by common people, or to demonstrate by preaching that they are intelligent.[23]

Nuns spent their time reading and singing texts whose meaning they did not comprehend because they no longer understood Latin, and they led idle lives contrary to the poverty they had promised:

There is another thing in the life of nuns that is extremely blame-worthy and contrary to the Gospels: that is, they are so sumptuously dressed, so refined and richly ornamented, with veils, vestments, belts, knives, slippers, so much so that I don't know what holiness there is in the life of nuns, since it conforms so much now to the world.[24]

The *Sommario*'s denunciation of the economic and social motives that were at the root of monastic recruitment accompanied an explicit criticism of the institution of monasticism, which had distanced itself from the tradition of the early Church. Then monks and nuns did not take vows, they were not cloistered, they did not have to recite 'certain Masses, or have canonical hours to sing every day'. The corruption of monasticism began with the protection of 'princes and great lords' who founded and gave donations to monasteries, and 'due to wealth, good discipline and good living were gradually destroyed and corrupted'.[25]

This schematic identification of the reasons for monastic indis-cipline and of the different forms of male and female deviation from the ideal did not include a possible differentiation in the 'status' of monks and nuns. The institution's goals were the same for both, and its origins equally recent. But who were monks and nuns, and how were their identities and roles perceived in the early modern period?

In the sixteenth century, the condition of the male or female religious was definable above all in relation to marriage. While the prevailing perception regarding males was that of the absence of conjugal bonds, or celibacy, for nuns it was that of a particular mar-ital state, the marriage contract with Christ. Although in religious thought mystical marriage was a metaphor for the Christian life common to both males and females, in liturgy, hagiography, religious literature and iconography the concept and image of the 'sponsa Christi' assumed so great a significance that it can be considered

23. Ibid., p. 132.   24. Ibid., pp. 140–1.   25. Ibid., p. 123.

gender specific. The nun was the wife of Christ *par excellence*. The male religious did not receive any particular meaning from the mystical marriage, and his status was defined more by his separation from the world and by his belonging to the Army of Christ (*militia Christi*). A brief review of the terminology and rites of monastic profession will be useful for clarifying these differences.

The Greek term *monachos* and the Latin *monachus*, which entered into the universal use of the Church with the *Life of Anthony* written by Athanasius, basically mean a 'solitary person'. Etymologically, the term indicates isolation and simplicity of heart, but with the *Life of Anthony* the first meaning came to prevail. The word monk first served to designate those who left the world for religious reasons, without distinguishing among eremites, anchorites, and cenobites, but after the spread of cenobitism in the West, it ended up meaning exclusively those who lived in a community and observed the Benedictine rule.[26]

The meaning of the term *religiosus* is broader. From the first centuries of the Christian era it indicated those categories of persons who made profession to an especially strict observance, such as a life of celibacy, penitence and poverty, even though they did not submit to a specific rule. But even then the various monastic rules came to use the adjective *religiosus* widely, to indicate a spiritual quality characteristic of monastic persons and things, so that the word was given virtually a technical meaning. Finally, in the thirteenth century, on the basis of the gradual identification of the term with a life consecrated to God according to the observance of a rule, Thomas Aquinas codified the meaning of *religiosus* thus: 'the name of religious is given antonomastically to those who consecrate themselves entirely to God, offering themselves to God as in a burnt sacrifice'. From then on the meaning of the term *religiosus* was greatly expanded. It became linked to stable and controllable institutions such as religious orders, and encompassed various forms of consecrated life (monks and nuns, military orders and mendicants), becoming synonymous with the regular clergy.[27]

Monachus and *religiosus* indicate a status that is common to both males and females, distinguished by separation from the world and by obedience to a rule. It is possible, however, to identify a gender difference in the monastic state by starting with an examination of religious consecration and profession ceremonies that spread and

---

26. Jean Gribomont, 'Monaco', in *DIP*, 6 (1973), columns 45–6.
27. Thomas Aquinas, *Summa Theologica* (II/II, q. 186, art. 1); Jean Gribomont and Jean-Marie-Roger Tillard, 'Religio (Religiosus)', *DIP*, 7 (1973), columns 1628–36.

acquired juridical character beginning in the seventh and eighth centuries. For virgin females there was a very ancient form of con-secration, which applied to nuns as well as devout women, includ-ing widows, who desired to dedicate themselves to God. From the fourth century on, the intention of females to take the path of virginity was confirmed, with a liturgical benediction. The ceremony for consecrating women to a virginal life which, in its ritual ele-ments and prayers, was inspired by and resembled a nuptial pact, can be dated from that moment on.[28] No ancient liturgical rite, in contrast, distinguished men's intention to dedicate themselves to the religious life or, better, to the *militia* and *sequela Christi*, images that synthesize the status of the early anchorites. Although the decision to renounce marriage and to dedicate themselves to prayer and penitence was common to both men and women who chose a particular form of service to God, a rite of consecration for males was codified only with the monastic profession. Unlike the *consecratio virginum*, the monastic profession, in its various forms, did not place primary emphasis on the *propositum verginitatis*, but rather on membership in a community and obedience to a rule of life. In any case, the ceremonies for female and male monastic profession were profoundly different. While in the early modern period the former still preserved ritual elements of the *consecratio virginum* and thus re-called nuptial symbolism,[29] the latter recalled the values of military service and of vassal-like obedience to the community's superior.[30] Although they shared the same life status, nuns and monks identi-fied with two different metaphors of the Christian life – one marital, the other military.

The reforms of Trent, between tradition and innovation

In the first half of the sixteenth century, around the time of the publication of *Il Sommario della Sacra Scrittura* and the spread of reformed ideas in Italy, two religious institutions clearly expressed the different symbolism to which female and male monastic life

28. Andrea Boni and Matias Augé, 'Consacrazione delle vergini', *DIP*, 2 (1973), columns 1613–27.

29. Gabriella Zarri, 'Ursula and Catherine: the marriage of the virgins in the sixteenth century', in E. Ann Matter and John Coakley, eds, *Creative Women in Medieval and Early Modern Italy* (Philadelphia, 1994), esp. pp. 262–7.

30. A.H. Thomas, 'La profession religieuse des Dominicains: formule, cérémonies, histoire', *Archivum Fratrum Praedicatorum*, 39 (1969), pp. 5–52.

referred: the Company of Saint Ursula and the Company of Jesus. Founded with the aim of making the religious life available to women of humble origin who lacked a dowry and thus had no access to convents, the Company founded by Angela Merici returned to the tradition of the primitive Church. The Ursulines elaborated a form of adherence to the institution that in part revived the ritual of the *consecratio virginum*, long fallen into disuse in favour of the monastic profession. Nuns and Ursuline virgins were thus defined by the shared metaphor of the *sponsa Christi*.[31] In contrast, Ignatius Loyola and his early disciples in the Company of Jesus derived their inspiration from the Christian militia; abandoning the primitive missionary ideal, they presented their institution as a military squadron. Marshalled around the standard of Christ, they followed the lead of a general and swore obedience to the pope.[32]

In returning to the most ancient traditions of the Church, the Ursulines and the Jesuits represented an innovation with respect to existing religious institutions. Not coincidently, Angela Merici's chancellor, Gabriele Cozzano, was forced to write a defence of the new institution against those who criticized the moral danger in which the virgins lived in their own houses, compared with the greater protection offered by convents. He vigorously upheld the legitimacy and novelty of the Ursulines' *status vitae*, describing the course of religious life from apostolic times to the institution of monasteries in terms similar to the criticisms expressed by the author of the *Sommario*:

> First the Church in its earliest and golden state of life was without cloisters or confined convents. Later, as it declined, monasteries developed. So that those who preferred the cloistered life to any other came to abase the very perfection and primitive golden state of the holy Church, which this company of ours resembles.[33]

The Fathers who met in council at Trent were not of the same opinion. After decades of failed attempts to reform the regulars, in the final phase of the Tridentine assembly they confronted the problem of the religious orders.

The Protestant condemnation of monastic vows encouraged the ecclesiastical authorities to move decisively to extirpate the abuses of the religious orders by returning to the traditional discipline of

31. Zarri, 'Ursula and Catherine', pp. 237–78.
32. John W. O'Malley, *The First Jesuits* (Cambridge and London, 1993), chapter 1.
33. 'Risposta contro quelli persuadono la clausura alle Vergini di Sant'Orsola', ms of the Biblioteca Queriniana published in Luciana Mariani, Elisa Tarolli and Marie Seynaeve, *Angela Merici: Contributo per una biografia* (Milan, 1986), p. 575.

the regulars and by extinguishing the ferments of novelty that came from the new female and male congregations formed in the 1520s and 1530s. While the Ursulines and Jesuits were allowed to conserve some of the main prerogatives of their institutions, the Angelics and Barnabites, who had organized along similar principles, had to adapt their constitutions to the Conciliar regulations.[34]

The Council of Trent entrusted the discussion of the religious to a reform decree and did not confront dogmatic questions on this subject. The *Decretum de regularibus et monialibus*, approved after a five-day discussion in November 1563, imposed as conditions for monastic discipline the renewal of the rules, the observance of vows and the renunciation of property.[35] It set a minimum age of sixteen for the profession of vows, and required at least one year of probation after investiture. Moreover, it prohibited superiors of monasteries to accept gifts or transfers of property from the families of the religious prior to their profession. Although these norms were directed indifferently at both male and female religious, there was nonetheless a significant difference regarding the proper means for encouraging their application and observance. The necessary condition for female observance was enclosure, which was hereafter imposed rigorously. For males, observance required stable residence in a monastic house and the obligation to request licence from the superior to leave the monastery for reasons related to their office. This norm, intended to limit apostasy and the avoidance of conventual obligations, in fact assumed a different assessment of the vow of chastity, which for women was considered a more precious good that required greater protection. Of course, the connection between modesty as a typically feminine virtue and seclusion as the means for preserving it was a central element of the culture of the period, and was not limited exclusively to the monastic condition. It is enough to recall that the widely disseminated treatise, the *Nova iconologia* by Cesare Ripa, portrays 'Modesty' as a young girl, veiled and dressed in white, with a tortoise as her attribute, 'to show that modest women should stay assiduously at home, just like the turtle in the house given her by Nature'.[36]

34. Giuseppe Cagni, 'Carlo Bascapè e le costituzioni dei Barnabiti e delle Angeliche', *Barnabiti studi*, 10 (1993), pp. 137–245. On the Angelics' first foundation, the convent of San Paolo in Milan, see René Baerstein, 'In widow's habit: women between convent and family in sixteenth-century Milan', *Sixteenth Century Journal*, 25 (1994), pp. 787–807.

35. Giuseppe Alberigo, Giuseppe Dossetti, Perikles P. Joannou, Claudio Leonardi and Paolo Prodi, eds, *Conciliorum Oecumenicorum Decreta*, bilingual edition (Bologna, 1991), pp. 776–84.

36. *Nova iconologia del Cavalier Cesare Ripa Perugino* (Padua, 1618), pp. 430–1.

Surprisingly, the Council of Trent did not discuss monastic vows and chastity in connection with the decree on the regulars, but it did reconfirm their validity in the canons on the sacrament of marriage. From the early sixteenth century certain theologians, such as Ambrogio Catarino Politi, had opposed the Erasmian doctrine that devalued chastity and conferred greater dignity on marriage.[37] And in 1562 Manuzio came out with an edition of the booklets *De virginitate* by Ambrose, Jerome and Augustine.[38] In March 1563, during the Council's debate on the sacrament of marriage, Giovanni Ludena held a disputation on the theme of marriage and priestly celibacy. Pretending to hold a dialogue with Calvin, he argued that the obligation of celibacy was not in contrast with the precept on matrimony, for 'the Church, by forbidding the marriage of priests, honours marriage'. In fact, the Church forbade marriage to those who, because of other commitments, could not dedicate themselves completely to wife and family:

> For Christian husbands can leave their wives and family temporarily to perform their prayers, but priests must always attend to praying and to divine affairs. Thus, if they were married, they would necessarily be deficient in their duties both toward God and toward their wives.[39]

In the post-Conciliar period, Basilio Gradi wrote a treatise for nuns, the *Trattato della verginità et dello stato verginale*, in which he attempted to lay a theological foundation for the superiority of virginity to marriage, and for the difference between female and male virginity. Drawing on patristic sources, he declared that virginity was the condition of man before sin, while marriage was the consequence of sin itself.[40] Virginity, as Augustine had stated, represented the way of life of Adam and Eve in the terrestrial paradise, and the chaste life was worthy of all praise, 'especially in women, inasmuch as it is more fitting for them since Adam was created outside of Paradise, and Eve inside'.[41] According to Jerome, the difference between virginity and matrimony was as great as that

---

37. F. Ambrosii Catharini Politi Senen. O.P. *Opusculum De Coelibatu, adversus impium Erasmum* (Siena, 1581).

38. S. Ambrosius, S. Hieronymus, S. Augustinus, *De virginitate opuscula* (Rome, 1562).

39. *Ioannis Ludegnani de matrimonio et sacerdotum coelibatu disputatio, 16 martii 1563,* in *Concilium Tridentinum. Diariorum, actorum, epistolarum, tractatuum nova collectio,* Societas Goerresiana ed. tomus IX, pars VI (Friburgi-Brisgoviae, 1924), pp. 446–58, cit. 458.

40. Basilio Gradi, *Trattato della verginità e dello stato verginale* (Rome, 1584), p. 4.

41. Ibid., p. 6; cf. the passage by Ambrose in *De Paradiso*, 4, 24, *Patrologia Latina*, 14, col. 300b, which Gradi arbitrarily interprets in a way that is favourable to women.

between the terrestrial paradise and the rest of the world, between heaven and earth, 'because marriage was ordained for the world, and virginity for heaven'.[42]

In the absence of specific sixteenth-century reflections on virginity, its positive value still had to be located in biblical and patristic texts that assimilated this state of life to the conjugal relationship between Christ and the Church or between Christ and the soul.[43] It was on the basis of this principle that nuns' violation of the vow of chastity was punished as adultery, as is specified in the famous catechism of Pietro Canisio, citing Jerome and Augustine:

> Moreover, a woman who pledges herself to God and accepts the holy veil is now married, married to the immortal man, and if she were to marry according to the common law of spouses, she commits adultery, and becomes the maidservant of death.[44]

The marital metaphor, with everything it meant in terms of relationships and submission to men, constituted the unifying status of woman, whatever her condition of life. If virginity continued to be considered the state of greatest perfection, marriage was the exemplary model for relations. Although she was a virgin, the *sponsa Christi* was subject to male authority: her father, her bishop, her spiritual father. The priest, in contrast, as the bridegroom of the Church in his qualification as bishop or parish priest, was essentially the father and 'economist' of the community. The male religious, finally, as a *miles Christi*, achieved his greatest distinction as a missionary.[45]

Female convents and social disciplining

The Tridentine decree on the regulars was merely a first step towards the reform of the religious orders. The Conciliar fathers did not ignore the economic and social reasons for the excessive growth in monastic professions, but the measures they took against forced monachization – such as raising the minimum age of profession

---

42. Ibid., p. 6.

43. E. Ann Matter, *The Voice of My Beloved: The Song of Songs in Western Medieval Christianity* (Philadelphia, 1990).

44. Pietro Canisio, *Summa doctrinae christianae* (Salmanticae, 1570), fol. 70v.

45. Roberto Rusconi, 'Gli ordini religiosi maschili dalla controriforma alle soppressioni settecentesche: cultura, predicazione, missioni', in Rosa ed., *Cultura e società nell'Italia moderna* (Rome and Bari, 1992), pp. 207–74; Adriano Prosperi, 'Il missionario', in Rosario Villari ed., *L'uomo barocco* (Rome and Bari, 1991), pp. 179–218; Prosperi, *Tribunali della coscienza*, pp. 549 ff.

and, for women, an examination of the postulant's free will – were not very decisive. The bishops attending the Council were of the same social class that imposed the convent on daughters, and they shared its mentality and culture. This is shown by a letter sent in May 1549 by the bishop of Feltre, the Bolognese Tommaso Campeggi, to the bishop of Maiorca, his relative Giovanni Battista Campeggi. The subject of the letter is a possible marriage of a relative, Madonna Laura, with a suitor of lower social rank. After stating the reasons why he did not want Laura to marry this man, Tommaso Campeggi wrote:

> [Laura] is very near to being drowned just as if she were to be thrown into the Reno [the river that runs through Bologna]. For this reason it would be better to make her a nun than to marry her so poorly and infelicitously, with so much pain and displeasure of those who love her.[46]

The Conciliar fathers also shared the concerns of urban ruling classes about too rigorous a reform. They did not suggest specific measures, but limited themselves to imposing enclosure with a formulation that was so generic that it later required further interpretation. The most important disposition regarding nuns, however, gave bishops the responsibility of maintaining vigil over enclosure in all the convents of their diocese, even those that were directly dependent on a religious order. The discipline of female convents was thus removed from the immediate responsibility of the generals and superiors of the orders, and became primarily the task of the secular clergy, even personally involving the pope and bishops.

The first to act were the pope and the Sacra Congregazione of the Council (later renamed the Congregation of Bishops and Regulars), to whom fell the task of clarifying the meaning of Conciliar deliberations on cloister. Pius V interpreted the deliberations restrictively by suppressing the houses of tertiaries living in community and convents that had never adopted strict cloister. He thus aligned himself against the legal norm whereby religious could not be obligated to observe a rule that was stricter than the one they accepted when making their profession.[47] This initiated a legal controversy

46. ASB, Archivio Malvezzi Campeggi, ser. III, Lettere 1548–49, vol. 9: Lettere del vescovo di Feltre al vescovo di Maiorca, 22 maggio 1549.

47. As discussed in the unpublished pamphlet of the Dominican controversialist theologian, Tommaso Elisio, conserved in the Concilio series of the Archivio Segreto Vaticano. On the character and contents of the text, see Michele Miele, 'La riforma dei conventi nel Cinquecento: osservazioni e istanze di un teologo napoletano dell'epoca', *Memorie domenicane*, n.s. 3 (1972), pp. 76–113.

that left open various possibilities for mediation, recomposition and disregard of the apostolic constitutions themselves, as happened with tertiaries living in communities. After a period in which they partially adapted to the norms of cloister, they were able to reconstitute their open houses. But what needs to be stressed is rather the multi-layered and hierarchical interventions that characterized the discipline of female convents.

The reception of the Tridentine reforms, and thus the imposition of cloister, had a different character and happened at different times in various European countries and regions of Italy. But everywhere the obligation of cloister was tenaciously pursued and overseen by the ecclesiastical authorities. This resulted in a clear reduction of the nuns' autonomy, their powers of management, their implicit relations with the outside world and relatives, and of their convents' prestige, based on their musical and singing ability and on the splendour of investiture ceremonies and patronal feasts. With the obligation of cloister, dependence on male authority became complete. Not that a perfect observance of monastic vows was achieved, or that relations with relatives and with the society were completely interrupted, but henceforth the networks of relations would be mediated exclusively by male authority.[48] The nuns' fathers and male relatives supervised the convents' economic affairs; the bishop signed the licences that gave access to the cloister; even visits by superiors of the religious orders were regulated.

When bishops acquired specific authority to control the enclosure of free convents, nuns who were subject to the jurisdiction of a religious order found that the levels of hierarchies to which they owed obedience were suddenly expanded. Should there be suspicions of heresy, even the Tribunal of the Inquisition might interrogate nuns and impose spiritual penances on them, as happened in 1583 at the convent of San Lorenzo in Bologna, when the cannonesses were implicated in a trial for the use of magical practices to find a lost musical instrument.[49] In such conditions, the orders' superiors sometimes became allies to whom the nuns could turn to attenuate the strict discipline imposed by the Ordinaries. The cardinal protectors of the orders became intermediaries with

48. The Venetian nun Arcangela Tarabotti, for example, corresponded with intellectuals and met the city's nobility and cultural leaders in parlatory: Francesca Medioli, *L'Inferno monacale' di Arcangela Tarabotti* (Turin, 1990); also Silvia Evangelisti, '"Farne quello che pare e piace . . .": L'uso e la trasmissione delle celle nel monastero di Santa Giulia di Brescia (1597–1688)', *Quaderni storici*, 30 (1995), pp. 85–110.

49. Biblioteca Comunale Archiginnasio di Bologna, ms B 1877, Processo contro Angela Tossignani.

the pope or the Sacred Congregation of the Bishops and Regulars to obtain mitigations of the regulations on enclosure or of the prohibitions against playing certain musical instruments.[50] At times even influential laymen acted as informers and bearers of petitions to Rome.[51] In short, an entire network of men, from lay protectors to religious superiors, was now charged with watching over monastic discipline and was requested to render it less rigorous.

Although political motives and state protection sometimes made it difficult even for papal visitors to apply the strict Tridentine norms, these reforms clearly imposed a new discipline on convents, and this was accomplished above all through male control.[52] The imposition of new and more rigorous repressive norms was accompanied by an effort on the part of confessors, preachers and devotional books to enhance the spiritual acculturation and methodical prayer practices, which helped add spiritual meaning to the discipline transmitted from above.[53] But the complex apparatus established to ensure enclosure had the dual result of reducing the network of female relations and of diminishing nuns' autonomy in favour of convents' male intercessors. Even spiritual power, which could be acquired through a sometimes heroic self-construction of sainthood, did not escape the control of confessors and inquisitors.[54] The disciplining of monasteries did not in fact interrupt relations between male religious and nuns, but rather oriented them towards a greater hierarchical dependence.

Female religious life, however, was not limited to the monastic profession, and the imposition of enclosure did not extend to those female groups, inspired by the Company of Saint Ursula, which in the sixteenth century revived a special form of consecration that

50. ASB, *Demaniale. San Giovanni in Monte* 120/1460, *Notizie diverse*, Letter of don Cherubino da Cremona to the abbot, 1 December 1584; letter of Donna Battista Dolfi to don Arcangelo de' Rossi, 7 August 1578; letter of cardinal Rusticucci to the nuns, 3 December 1588; letter of cardinal Montalto the nuns, 7 December 1588.

51. Ibid., Letter of Paolo Ghiselli to the Prioress Donna Battista Dolfi, 3 May 1578.

52. Michele Miele, 'Sisto V e la riforma dei monasteri femminili di Napoli', *Campania Sacra*, 21 (1990), pp. 123–209; on Neapolitan convents, see Elisa Novi Chavarria, 'Nobiltà di seggio, nobiltà nuova e monasteri femminili a Napoli in età moderna', *Dimensioni e problemi della ricerca storica*, 2 (1993), pp. 84–111.

53. On female behavioural and devotional readings, see the various essays in G. Zarri, ed., *Donna, disciplina, creanza cristiana dal XV al XVII secolo. Studi e testi a stampa* (Rome, 1996); on culture in convents, see the case of Bascapè in Danilo Zardin, *Donna e religiosa di rara eccellenza: Prospera Corona Bascapè, i libri e la cultura nei monasteri milanesi del Cinque e Seicento* (Florence, 1993).

54. Ottavia Niccoli, 'Il confessore e l'inquisitore: a proposito di un manoscritto bolognese del Seicento', in G. Zarri ed., *Finzione e santità tra medioevo ed età moderna* (Turin, 1991), pp. 412–34; Prosperi, *Tribunali della coscienza*, esp. chapters 21 and 26.

required only the vow of chastity.[55] Through this route, more modern forms of female religious commitment found expression after Trent, and as has already been mentioned, the traditional regular third orders acquired renewed vigour.[56] The social disciplining of female religious, based above all on enclosure, did not translate into total assent by existing institutions. Moreover, after the early Tridentine period, even the theory and practice of enclosure had to come to terms with new cultural and social demands.[57]

The impulse given by the Council of Trent to the reform of the religious and of nuns was inseparable from the process of disciplining that invested other ecclesiastical institutions, such as marriage, confession and the cult of the saints, subjects too vast to examine here. One can raise questions about which elements tended to reinforce traditional culture and about the possible modernity of the Tridentine decisions and deliberations, but undeniably the single norms and their application were part of a process of religious and social transformation that can be effectively categorized as 'modern'.[58] Regarding male regulars, strict norms against apostasy and inquisitorial repression would clearly have been ineffective in renewing discipline had they not been accompanied by the creation of a new identity for the religious – that of the missionary who fulfilled his service to God in preaching and in converting infidels, taking as his model the martyrs who died in the struggles with Protestants or in the New World. For nuns, the discipline imposed with enclosure in effect privileged a method that ran counter to women's aspirations for a more active commitment in society and in the Church, reduced the spaces for freedom, and restricted networks of social relations; yet it also helped exalt the civic prestige of convents, conferring on nuns the specific role of safeguarding and protecting the city. The *miles Christi* and the *sponsa Christi* gained new meaning in a society that enthusiastically assumed as behavioural models the figures most representative of their condition – those men and women who the Church elevated to the honour of the altars.

55. Gabriella Zarri, 'Disciplina regolare e pratica di coscienza: le virtù e i comportamenti sociali in comunità femminili (secc. XVI–XVIII)', in Prodi, ed., *Disciplina dell'anima*, pp. 257–78.

56. Lucetta Scaraffia and Gabriella Zarri, eds, *Donne e fede: Santità e vita religiosa* (Rome and Bari, 1994), especially the chapters by Zarri and Marina Caffiero.

57. Francesca Medioli, 'La clausura delle monache nell'amministrazione della congregazione romana sopra i regolari', in G. Zarri, ed., *Il monachesimo femminile in Italia dall'alto medioevo al secolo XVII: A confronto con l'oggi* (Verona, 1997), pp. 249–82. On seventeenth-century convents, see Mario Rosa, 'La religiosa', in Villari, *L'uomo barocco*, pp. 219–67.

58. Paolo Prodi and Wolfgang Reinhard, eds, *Il Concilio di Trento e il moderno* (Bologna, 1996).

CHAPTER TEN

Gender, Religious Representation and Cultural Production in Early Modern Italy[1]

KAREN-EDIS BARZMAN

It is when one really starts thinking about the implications of 'Why have there been no great women artists?' that one begins to realize to what extent our consciousness of how things are in the world has been conditioned – and often falsified – by the way the most important questions are posed.[2]

The development of the field of study (a selected survey)

The critical analysis of narratives about gender and artistic production in early modern Italy may be said to have begun with Linda Nochlin's 'Why have there been no great women artists?' (1971). Nochlin did not write as an Italianist when she took up this insinuating question, nor did she limit her narrative to the early modern period. Yet she located the origins of the modern myth of the artist of 'genius' (always given as male) in Giorgio Vasari's *Lives of the Artists*, citing, among others, his biography of Giotto, in which an untutored youth springs to preeminence: 'bearing within his

1. An earlier version of the material on Maria Maddalena de' Pazzi appears in *Annali d'italianistica* (1995). I would like to thank the following for their comments and advice prior to publication: Lorraine Berry, Judith Brown, Roger Crum, Steven Levine, Marilena Mosco, Charles Reeve, Patricia Rucidlo, Melinda Schlitt, Nina Serebrennikov, Malcolm Stimson, John Tagg, and the members of the graduate seminar on gender and cultural production in early modern Italy, which I offered at UCLA in 1996.
2. Linda Nochlin, 'Why have there been no great women artists?', special issue of *Art News*, entitled 'Women's Liberation, Women Artists, and Art History', (1971), pp. 22–39; see p. 25.

person since birth a mysterious essence . . . called Genius or Talent, which, like murder, must always out, no matter how unlikely or unpromising the circumstances'.[3] In her discussion, Nochlin implicated the institutions that structured and regulated the lives of Renaissance artists (family, workshop, guild, academy), exposing the asymmetries of gender and power within them that enabled men to excel in the production of art. Thus she concluded that women's 'lack of artistic genius' was nothing more than the effect of internalized desires and affects that rendered women submissive in their institutionalized exclusion from basic practices of training and production.

Studies of women and art in early modern Italy had appeared before Nochlin's article but, in the main, they reflected and reinforced a tendency to celebrate an essentialized femininity as it was thought to manifest itself in various practices. Walter Shaw Sparrow's 1905 description of Elisabetta Sirani at work is a case in point:

> Elisabetta was little more than twenty . . . and the clergy who had been sent to order the work . . . looked on whilst she, radiant with inspiration, made her first impulsive sketch in pen-and-ink. The beholders were enchanted, and the huge picture, differing little in essentials from the sketch, was painted [with great rapidity]. In brief, Elisabetta Sirani, like all women of genius, worked under an intuitive rather than technical guidance; and in her art, consequently, . . . we find those blemishes and beauties which belong to a native habit of spontaneous workmanship.[4]

Studies like Sparrow's sought to add a number of women to the artistic canon, on the assumption that they had some share of 'genius', if only intuitive, on a par with the 'Old Masters' themselves. At this level, these studies had some success – those women now widely cited in textbooks and surveys today include Sofonisba Anguisola, Lavinia Fontana, Artemisia Gentileschi and Elisabetta Sirani – but early work on female artists remained largely anecdotal and, by the time Nochlin exposed the masculinist myth of 'genius', scholars were on the way to a more rigorous practice in the recovery of female artists. In his study of Artemisia Gentileschi, for example, Ward Bissell set a precedent for archival research on female artists and for serious connoisseurship of their work.[5] This kind of

3. Ibid., p. 26.
4. Walter Shaw Sparrow, *Women Painters of the World: From the Times of Caterina Vigri (1413–63) to Rosa Bonheur and the Present Day* (London, 1905), p. 29.
5. Ward Bissell, 'Artemisia Gentileschi – A new documented chronology', *Art Bulletin*, 50:2 (1968), pp. 153–68.

scholarship still lays the foundation for other interpretative approaches in the field. Liana Cheney's articles on Lavinia Fontana and Barbara Longhi similarly provided useful models, combining formal and stylistic analyses with iconographic research.[6]

Even so, Nochlin's challenge was of a different cast, calling for a radical shift in practice and procedure in gender studies in Italian Renaissance and Baroque art history. Nochlin began by purposively *conceding* the negligible number of 'great' women artists – 'There *are* no women equivalents for Michelangelo'[7] – precisely to open the door to alternatives to the recovery of female artists. Moreover, by underscoring that art historical knowledge itself is contingent upon procedures of investigation defined by convention and embraced by habit, she invited a critical re-assessment of the assumptions driving the discipline. It merits noting that discussions in Italian studies of women and patronage, iconography, semiotics (the study of signs), reception, and the role of visual and material culture in the construction of gender all postdate Nochlin's essay.

To take the example of patronage, as late as 1975 David Wilkins was still able to assert that 'no study has been undertaken on the specific roles women may have played as patrons'.[8] Indeed he was right, for the study of 'Old Masters' inevitably constituted the subtext of previous studies of women who commissioned art in the Italian Renaissance, as in the case of Erwin Panofsky's study of the *camera di San Paolo*, in which Panofsky's concern with the iconography of Correggio's fresco overshadowed his interest in Giovanna Piacenza as the fresco's patron.[9] Wilkins himself countered by drawing attention to the role of such women as Giovanna de' Piacenza and Isabella d'Este as patrons, analysing material from secondary sources. Subsequent work on female patronage in Italy, much of it based on archival research, has gone on to widen the social scope of studies in this area. In addition to reviewing secondary literature, Marilyn

6. Liana Cheney, 'Lavinia Fontana, Boston *Holy Family*', *Woman's Art Journal*, 5:1 (1984), pp. 12–15; 'Barbara Longhi of Ravenna', *Woman's Art Journal*, 9:1 (1988), pp. 16–20.

7. Nochlin, 'Why have there been no great women artists?', p. 25.

8. David Wilkins, 'Woman as artist and patron in the Middle Ages and the Renaissance', in Douglas Radcliff-Umstead, ed., *The Roles and Images of Women in the Middle Ages and Renaissance* (Pittsburgh, PA, 1975), pp. 107–31, and p. 115 in particular.

9. Erwin Panofsky, *The Iconography of Correggio's* Camera di San Paolo (London, 1961). Also see Egon Verheyen, *The Paintings in the 'Studiolo' of Isabella d'Este at Mantua* (New York, 1971), in which the author concentrated on the formal and iconographic concerns of Renaissance masters whose work adorned the *studiolo*, despite his intention to 'throw light on the personality of the patron', p. 3.

Dunn, for instance, used unpublished documents in her article on the patronage of the nuns of Santa Marta al Collegio Romano.[10] Her focus, on 'matters of attribution and chronology' pertaining to the 'leading artists' involved in the church decoration, still reflects the tentative and ambivalent embrace of gender studies in Italian art history, even as late as the late 1980s. Nonetheless, Dunn opened the study of female religious as patrons. It was only subsequently that Catherine King traced emergent patterns of middle-class and elite 'matronage' in Renaissance Italy, explaining the social and economic constraints that limited such patronage to widows or nuns commissioning altarpieces, devotional images, funerary monuments and architecture.[11] Architectural commissions, according to King, were primarily the product of corporate patronage by nuns and tertiaries, but this has recently been challenged by the work of Carolyn Valone, who has discussed the self-fashioning of Roman widows as pious patrons of architecture (hospitals, convents, monasteries and churches) following the precedent of early Christian and medieval women, upon whom the Roman 'matrons' modelled their activities.[12] Valone has also argued the role of women as promoters of post-Tridentine Church reform (primarily under the influence of Filippo Neri), adding to our understanding of the avenues of agency embraced by aristocratic women of the period.

An alternative to the study of women as producers and patrons of art was the exploration of the field of meanings within which images of women circulated in Renaissance Italy. In the 1970s and 1980s, Elizabeth Cropper used the writings of poets to develop this theme in a specialized vein, drawing connections between Petrarchan conventions of expression and painters' concerns with ideal female beauty.[13] Implicitly, she raised issues that are timely in gender studies today, for example, the importance of historicizing the reception of works of art, so as to situate the viewer's reading within a

10. Marilyn Dunn, 'Nuns as art patrons: the decoration of S. Marta al Collegio Romano', *Art Bulletin*, 70:3 (1988), pp. 451–77.

11. Catherine King, 'Medieval and Renaissance matrons, Italian-style', *Zeitschrift für Kunstgeschichte*, 55:3 (1992), pp. 372–93.

12. Carolyn Valone, 'Roman matrons as patrons: various views of the cloister wall', in Craig Monson, ed., *The Crannied Wall. Women, Religion, and the Arts in Early Modern Europe* (Ann Arbor, MI, 1992), pp. 49–72; idem, 'Women on the Quirinal Hill: patronage in Rome, 1560–1630', *Art Bulletin*, 76:1 (1994), pp. 129–46.

13. Elizabeth Cropper, 'On beautiful women: Parmigianino, Petrarchismo, and the vernacular style', *Art Bulletin*, 58:3 (1976), pp. 374–94; idem, 'The beauty of woman: problems in the rhetoric of Renaissance portraiture', in Margaret Ferguson et al., eds, *Rewriting the Renaissance. The Discourses of Sexual Difference in Early Modern Europe* (Chicago, 1986), pp. 175–90.

particular historical moment and culture. Cropper's work also suggested epistemological questions about the ways human subjects are defined in the historical moment in which they live and about the role cultural representations, including works of art, played in these processes. Few have adopted Cropper's approach, which calls for erudition in art history as well as in Italian literary studies. Significant for women's studies, however, is that her work ultimately allows the question of gender to slip away, returning to the traditional concerns of Italian Renaissance art history, specifically to the comparison (*paragone*) of painting and poetry, and to the genius of artists of the 'High Renaissance' who are said to have 'opposed the *natural, universal language of painting* to the conventions of poetry' and thus to have achieved 'a perfect illusion of natural beauty' (emphasis mine). The assumption that a pictorial language could be 'universal' or 'natural' has repeatedly been challenged from the perspective of new theories of representation.

Mary Rogers extended the terms of the debate opened by Cropper, turning to prose texts on feminine decorum to investigate the codes that regulated femininity in the realm of social exchange as well as that of artistic convention.[14] Rogers's work presents an interesting model for those concerned with the relationship between representation (textual and pictorial) and human subjects. By contrast, most other studies have seen images of women in early modern Italy simply as effects of pre-established social relations, particularly within the family. Patricia Simons, for example, has argued that the value of fifteenth-century profile portraits of women was determined, in their own day, by their circulation as signs of the wealth and honour of the women's husbands, in a 'display culture' of masculine power and privilege.[15] At the same time, she insisted on a disjunction between social and representational levels: 'Profile portraits . . . are not simply reflections of a pre-existent social or visual reality.'[16] While she thus refused a traditional iconographic and iconological model of interpretation and its assumption that social relations and historical events are not informed by works of art, she did not go on to develop a discussion of the *relation*

14. Mary Rogers, 'The decorum of women's beauty: Trissino, Firenzuola, Luigini and the representation of women in sixteenth-century painting', *Renaissance Studies*, 2:1 (1988), pp. 47–88.

15. Patricia Simons, 'Women in frames: the gaze, the eye, the profile in Renaissance portraiture', *History Workshop. A Journal of Socialist and Feminist Historians*, 25 (1988), pp. 4–30.

16. Ibid., p. 15.

between representation and social processes (which may be seen as a subset of the processes of representation).[17] Nevertheless, by casting the eye of the contemporary viewer as a 'performing agent' and by emphasizing the culturally specific context within which viewing takes place, Simons did insist on the importance of historicizing the reception of images.

Cristelle Baskins also attempted to address the limits of standard procedures in social history and the history of art, with their shared impulse to fix the meaning of images. In her essay on the naked figure of Griselda – a Boccaccesque peasant of virtue, publicly stripped and re-costumed by a nobleman at their marriage – Baskins analysed the cultural construction of ideal femininity in matrimony.[18] She pointed to competing meanings that attached to 'Griselda' as *sign* in Renaissance culture and insisted that the work of art is not a re-presentation of a prior 'social reality': 'Nobles were unlikely to link themselves with a *contadina* [peasant woman] for more than illegitimate pleasure. Furthermore, no real husband would tolerate the public stripping of his bride. ... Griselda's nuptial disrobing belongs neither to the standard iconography of marriage nor to the illustration of social history or actual marriage practice.'[19] However, the *work* of representation in these images – the way, for example, they framed the form and meaning of matrimonial relations – remains to be explored.

Other scholars have moved away from questions of women and 'art' and have focused instead on questions about the objectifying aspects of the representation of women, including the role of representations as models for women's active and contemplative lives.[20] Studies of furnishings in domestic interiors and of objects associated with gender-specific practices have contributed to this shift and to a concern with broader questions regarding the engagement of women with images and material culture in early modern Italy, particularly in Florence, Rome and Venice.[21]

17. Erwin Panofsky, 'The history of art as a humanistic discipline' and 'Iconography and iconology: an introduction to the study of Renaissance art', in idem, *Meaning in the Visual Arts* (Garden City, NY, 1955), pp. 1–25, 26–54.

18. Cristelle Baskins, 'Griselda, or the Renaissance bride stripped bare by her bachelor in Tuscan *cassone* painting', *Stanford Italian Review*, 10:2 (1991), pp. 153–75.

19. Ibid., p. 173.

20. Simons, 'Women in frames'; Cropper, 'The beauty of woman'; Karen-edis Barzman, 'Devotion and desire. The reliquary chapel of Maria Maddalena de' Pazzi', *Art History*, 15:2 (1992), pp. 170–96.

21. Diane Ahl, 'Renaissance birth salvers and the Richmond *Judgment of Solomon*', *Studies in Iconography*, 7–8 (1981/82), pp. 157–74; Baskins, 'Griselda'.

Already from the 1970s on, a veritable industry had developed around the topic of women and erotic imagery. Even in contributions by feminist scholars, however, few commentators addressed the representation of *women's*, rather than men's, desires and delights. While Rona Goffen has discussed female auto-eroticism in the content of Giorgione's *Dresden Venus* and Titian's *Venus of Urbino*, she continued to assume a heterosexual male viewing audience and did not address the relation of the images to the pleasure of the female viewer.[22] Moreover, her collapse of cultural differences between 'then' and 'now' and her assumption of the universal value of our own models of interpretation illustrate the pitfalls of neglecting to historicize reception or to acknowledge that cultural differences condition the way subjects construe meaning in historically specific and often radically divergent ways.

In discussions of early modern Italian art, only Simons has considered women's viewing and bodily pleasures outside a heterosexual frame of reference, using text and image to address the possibilities of lesbian relations in the period.[23] Here again, she implicitly took up Nochlin's call to re-think art historical methods and procedures, asking new questions of various sources (legal, medical and religious texts as well as paintings and prints) to render sensuality and desire visible within 'female-female relations'. Refusing notions of an authentic or essential lesbian identity, Simons stressed the historically specific character of Renaissance patriarchal culture and, thus, the contingent nature of Renaissance women's sexual practices in association with other women (framed as they were by the admonitory and repressive discourses of the day). In the process, mindful of the culturally-conditioned nature of sex as a social practice, she reflected on the determining role of representation in the world of social exchange, in the present and the past.

Simons's work stands alone. A much more extensive literature has been produced on the display of the female figure in a heterosexual, *male* economy of pleasure.[24] Such studies, along with the majority of art historical works focused on male artists and male

22. Rona Goffen, 'Renaissance Dreams', *Renaissance Quarterly*, 40:4 (1987), pp. 682–706.

23. Patricia Simons, 'Lesbian (in)visibility in Italian Renaissance culture: Diana and other cases of *donna con donna*', *Journal of Homosexuality*, 27:1–2 (1994), pp. 81–122.

24. Charles Hope, 'Titian's erotic paintings', and David Rosand, 'Ermeneutica amorosa: observations on the interpretation of Titian's Venuses', in *Tiziano e Venezia: Convegno internazionale di studi* (Vicenza, 1980), pp. 111–24 and 375–81 respectively; Goffen, 'Renaissance Dreams'.

patrons in this period, might be said to contribute to an understanding of masculine subjectivity, even if only implicitly. Few, however, have explicitly taken up this subject of the relations between
art and patterns of identity formation for Renaissance men, either
from the perspective of production *or* of the audience. The exceptions deal with male sexual behaviour, particularly homoeroticism.
Even in such studies, however, scholars have assumed that, rather
than playing a determining role, art simply *reflects* the proclivities
of individual artists and their patrons, or the habits of thought
and practice typical of their era. Donald Posner's early article on
Caravaggio's 'homoerotic' works, for example, saw Caravaggio's
paintings as expressions of the artist's sexuality, which, in a display
of trenchant homophobism, Posner described as 'unnatural', especially in the taste for 'overfed', 'depraved' and 'indecent' youths.[25]
Similarly, if more sympathetically, James Saslow has examined
images of Ganymede as 'vehicle[s] for explicitly erotic or sexual
concerns [of the period] . . . , [correlating] changes in [Ganymede's]
popularity, form, and iconography . . . with shifting attitudes
towards . . . homoeroticism'.[26]

Avenues for future research

The works I have been discussing must, of course, themselves be
considered historically as moments in the development of gender
studies and queer theory, as they have influenced art history. All
serve as unprecedented or noteworthy examples of new approaches
in the field of Renaissance studies, or as important models for work
that followed. At this point, however, it would be useful to return
to Nochlin, who implied that epistemological shifts in the discipline can be signalled by new sets of questions – questions that may
well be timely for particular communities at specific moments.[27] As
we have seen, over the past ten years, articles and essays have appeared that implicitly point to such new sets of questions – Simons's
and Baskins's work belongs in this category. Other scholars have
focused more explicitly on the agency of gendered subjects and the

25. Donald Posner, 'Caravaggio's homo-erotic works', *Art Quarterly*, 34:3 (1971),
pp. 301–24, pp. 302–3 in particular.
26. James Saslow, *Ganymede in the Renaissance. Homosexuality in Art and Society* (New
Haven, CT, 1985), pp. 2–3.
27. On forms of thought that have become pressing for feminist enquiry at
particular moments in time, see Jane Flax, 'Postmodernism and gender relations
in feminist theory', *Signs*, 12:4 (1987), pp. 621–2.

production of meaning. Production of meaning here involves both the making and viewing, not only of 'art' (that is, objects and images traditionally falling within the purview of art history), but also of what we might term, more broadly, 'cultural production', beyond architecture, sculpture, painting, and even *cassoni* (clothing chests) and *deschi da parto* (birth trays). Such a focus must include social subjects themselves, caught up in the world of visual, material and textual culture. 'Art' certainly played a role in the construction of gendered identities in early modern Italy. However, the production of historical subjects involved the entry of the subjects themselves, from birth, into broader cultural frameworks of language, gesture, costume, ritual, familial roles and other regulated practices constituting complex forms of representation.

Scholars outside art history have begun to analyse this process using pictorial imagery and crafted objects as points of departure or source material. Such studies suggest new and appealing approaches for the discipline. Diane Hughes, for instance, charted over a period of 250 years the shifts in the meaning of cloth and jewelled accessories prescribed to mark and isolate Jewish women and prostitutes.[28] She began with the ways such cultural signs absorb multiple and even competing meanings through time, but she was also interested in the space for resistance. Bodies are shown to take their place within the fields of visual and material culture, but they are not devoid of agency. Hughes emphasized, for example, the ways power could be contested by the donning or refusing of specific forms of dress. She thus provided a complex picture of the relation between systems of meaning and other social processes.

The broader world of material culture within which women moved has also become a focus of enquiry. For example, Christiane Klapisch-Zuber has explained the centrality of wood, terracotta and papier mâché *bambini* (child-like dolls) in the ways women actively participated in and identified with their devotional and domestic roles.[29] Her work has emphasized *ritual, customs* of play, and the normalizing effects of the 'fantasized manipulation' of objects within fixed and coherent frameworks of practice, all reinforced by preaching and the disciplining of the family and the convent. Subsequent work in this area has shifted the focus to perverse or deviant forms

28. Diane Hughes, 'Distinguishing signs. Ear-rings, Jews and Franciscan rhetoric in the Italian Renaissance city', *Past and Present*, 112 (1986), pp. 3–59.
29. Christiane Klapisch-Zuber, 'Holy dolls: play and piety in Florence in the Quattrocento', in her *Women, Family, and Ritual in Renaissance Italy* (Chicago, 1985), pp. 310–29.

of 'play' and to the possibilities of exceeding normative and normalizing models and of transgressing their social codes. In contrast to Klapisch-Zuber's emphasis, such a move is informed by a stress on the complexity and inherent instability of meanings that attach to representations, including representations of the self. In this context, sixteenth- and seventeenth-century usages of the image of Mary Magdalen will serve as an example of the way patterns of representation and the deployment and reception of images and cultural objects in institutional settings work together to construct gendered identities, without ever being able to render them stable.

Religious practice and the use of devotional images in a sixteenth-century convent

In 1583, a young woman, baptized Caterina de' Pazzi, entered a Carmelite convent in Florence, made her profession and assumed the name 'Maria Maddalena' (Mary Magdalen). Three weeks later, the Carmelite sisters found her running from room to room, clutching a small carving of Jesus that she had detached from a crucifix. She spoke fervently about the sacrifice of Jesus and the need for the observance of religious vows, admonishing the sisters for their laxity. Though she spoke for hours, she refused water. However, she would put her mouth to the right hand of the crucified figure, swallowing as though she were drinking from the mark representing a wound.[30] Four years later, in 1587, the sisters once more found 'Maria Maddalena' in rapture, this time with a clay doll of the Virgin Mary in her arms. 'And with this doll', they recorded, 'she performed many beautiful gestures and actions', extolling the veneration of Mary.[31] In 1592, Maria Maddalena removed a life-sized figure of Jesus from a cross high on the wall of the Carmelites' choir, intoning a hymn in which the sisters spontaneously joined. They followed her through the convent and its gardens, as she carried the effigy in her arms – like Mary in a *Pietà*, they claimed. On this occasion, too, she spoke for hours about salvation and the sacrifice of Jesus, as if in colloquy with God.[32]

It may seem strange to have moved to a narrative of mystical 'ecstasy' in the midst of a discussion of gender and representation

---

30. Maria Maddalena de' Pazzi, *The Complete Works* (Fatima, Portugal, 1973), Vol. 1, pp. 50–61.
31. Ibid., Vol. 4, p. 267.   32. Ibid., Vol. 5, pp. 203–7.

in early modern Italy. The narrative comes from the transcriptions of Maria Maddalena's speech made, at the direction of the convent's confessors, by teams of Carmelite nuns, who recorded the mystic's words and gestures as best as time and circumstance allowed.[33] These transcriptions suggest rich possibilities for the study of the *reception*, as well as the *production*, of devotional images by women. Maria Maddalena de' Pazzi's demonstrative physical engagement with devotional objects indicates the need for art historians to re-evaluate the limited status and the place they have assigned images and crafted objects in the lives of women and men in early modern Italy.[34] More importantly in this context, however, the transcriptions also raise the issue of Maria Maddalena's performance as a complex form of representation in itself, through which she produced herself as a subject. While it may be conceded that these transcriptions, like all texts, are in themselves representations, the seven volumes of records still give us access to the woman's *unauthorized* acts of representing herself, in her theatrical use of sacred objects and distinctive forms of religious and theological speech. These particular forms of expression began after Caterina de' Pazzi assumed the name 'Mary Magdalen', which may be seen as more than a mere coincidence.

Like all subjects, the early modern mystic moved in culture as 'a citational self', performing social representations already partially scripted prior to each and every rehearsal.[35] Caterina de' Pazzi spoke in the name of Mary Magdalen; she gestured like the Virgin Mary. Performing in 'a place that oscillates between ritual and theatre', she moved within a grid of names and a social frame of reference that the culture offered her.[36] The concept of theatre is literally appropriate here. Carved effigies were frequently carried in religious plays and feastday celebrations, while figures of Jesus were detached from crosses and used in re-enactments of the Deposition and Lamentation on Good Friday. Thus, even the mystic's use of sculpture had its analogue in what was a codified form of public

33. For the transcriptions, see Maria Maddalena de' Pazzi, *Tutte le opere di Santa Maria Maddalena de' Pazzi, dai manoscritti originali*, 7 vols (Florence, 1960). The *Complete Works* cited above are the English translation.

34. See John T. Paoletti, 'Wooden sculpture in Italy as sacral experience', *Artibus et Historiae*, 26 (1992), pp. 85–100. My work on Maria Maddalena de' Pazzi also emphasizes non-liturgical contexts within which devotional objects and images were taken up by the faithful, in this case, specifically women. For a similar emphasis, see Klapisch-Zuber, 'Holy dolls'.

35. Judith Butler, 'Performative acts and gender construction: an essay in phenomenology and feminist theory', *Theatre Journal*, 40 (1988), pp. 519–31.

36. Michel de Certeau, *The Writing of History* (New York, 1988), pp. 261–4.

performance (liturgical drama) with which she must have been familiar. It was within a given 'network of symbolization',[37] and within received and recognizable (or, at least, interpretable) categories of identity, then, that Maria Maddalena and her contemporaries inscribed themselves in culture. And it was within the same given network of symbolization that they experienced their own subjectivity and that of others.

The Magdalen as sign in early modern Italy

In attempting to explain the possible connections between the name 'Mary Magdalen' and the actions of a woman in late-sixteenth-century Florence, it would be useful to turn to semiotics, the study of signs that circulate in culture.[38] In semiotic terms, 'Mary Magdalen' circulated as a sign in the society of early modern Italy. Like all signs, it had the potential for multiple meanings within the mystic's social world. Its most common associations, 'sinner' and 'penitent', had their origins in the canonical Gospels – for example, in Luke 7:37–50, where a female sinner washes the feet of Jesus with her tears, dries them with her hair, and anoints them with oil at the house of Simon the Pharisee. By the time of Gregory the Great at the turn of the seventh century, Church Fathers had already associated the sins of the woman in this passage with prostitution, based in part on the ambiguous phrase in Luke 7:47, 'for she loved much'. Moreover, they had linked her with 'Mary Magdalen', a name appearing fourteen times in *other* narrative contexts in Matthew, Mark, Luke and John.[39] Thus 'The Magdalen' acquired the valence of 'whore', although the early sources do not *name* her as such.[40] Her association with penitence also originates in scripture, although, again, not in passages identifying her by name. The sins for which she repented eventually multiplied in texts over the centuries to include avarice and lust. These associations do not *essentially* define

37. Certeau, *Writing History*, p. 264.
38. My semiotic approach, which is based on the notion of the instability of meaning, the open-ended nature of interpretation and the connections between signs and their referents in the material and social world, approaches Charles Sanders Peirce's concept of infinite or endless semiosis.
39. Marjorie M. Malvern, *Venus in Sackcloth. The Magdalen's Origins and Metamorphoses* (Carbondale, IL, 1975), pp. 16–29, 55.
40. 'Magdalen' was originally a place-name and refers to a village in antiquity near Tiberias, on the north-west bank of the lake of Galilee; see Susan Haskins, *Mary Magdalen. Myth and Metaphor* (New York and London, 1993), p. 15.

any woman called 'Mary Magdalen', not even the Magdalen named in scripture, who may or may not have 'loved much', and who was said (by Matthew, Mark and John) to have wept at the foot of the cross. The concepts and the words that convey them (the signs) belong to an order of encoded language and representation, and the movements and affects of any subject may be interpreted in various ways within this order (even by the subject herself).

In the medieval and early modern periods, painting, sculpture, sermons, passion plays and other forms of cultural production reinforced the identification of the Magdalen as 'whore' and/or 'penitent' at the level of popular Christian thought. To ensure her identification *as* 'The Magdalen', artists frequently included an oinment jar, which was the saint's most common attribute, alluding to her anointing of Jesus.[41] A good example is Francesco Morandini's Florentine painting of 1580 – with its excessive rouging of the Magdalen's cheek, the sheer garment through which her nipples protrude, and the jewels and pearls that stud her fabric – marking her as 'ideal courtesan' at a time when government authorities repeatedly promulgated sumptuary laws in an attempt to regulate dress and adornment for men and women, according to elaborate social codes.[42] The elites of Italian cities frequently violated these laws. But contemporary portraits of women of high social standing typically included heavy brocaded or textured garments, which constrict and *conceal* the sitters' sexed anatomy, unlike the thin, transparent material worn by Morandini's figure.

The writer Pietro Aretino both reflected and reinforced associations of the Magdalen with prostitution in his *Sei Giornate* or *Ragionamento* of 1534, a comic dialogue about three estates of womanhood – prostitutes, nuns and married women – in which a courtesan identifies the Magdalen as the patron saint of her profession: 'today is the day of Magdalen, our advocate', she states, 'and so, we do not work',[43] The humour implicit in this assertion (indeed, Aretino seems to have intended it as a joke) depended on widespread knowledge that religious houses for penitent prostitutes and 'fallen women' typically designated the Magdalen as their patron saint. Scores of such houses existed in Italy alone by the

---

41. Marilena Mosco, ed., *La Maddalena tra sacro e profano* (Milan, 1986), pp. 66–72. For reproductions of the images discussed below, see Karen-edis Barzman, 'Cultural production, religious devotion, and subjectivity in early modern Italy: the case study of Maria Maddalena de' Pazzi', in *Annali d'Italianistica: Women Mystic Writers*, Vol. 13 (1995), pp. 283–305.

42. On sumptuary laws, see Hughes, 'Distinguishing Signs'.

43. Pietro Aretino, *Sei Giornate* (Turin, 1975), p. 11.

mid-sixteenth century.[44] It might seem a contradiction that the Magdalen could serve as advocate and protectress of both courtesans and *convertite*. In fact, 'prostitute' and 'penitent' operated as paired opposites in early modern Europe. As with all signs, the signification of each term depended on its antithesis, which always lurks behind manifest meaning in any representation.[45] 'Mary Magdalen' had an especially strong and *explicit* double valence in the dominant codes of the period, for the dramatic personal reform of the woman in the sources called forth the latent, inverse meaning assigned to her initially as 'prostitute'.

As with language in general, however, the name could not be tamed to one or two meanings, and, within the paired alternatives ('prostitute' and 'penitent'), images of the Magdalen increasingly acquired an additional, *erotic* content. Indeed, a new pictorial tradition emerged in the early sixteenth century in which the Magdalen became the vehicle for some of the most titillating images circulating in early modern Italy. Catholic reformers denounced erotic images as indecent and inconsistent with the ends of representation in the service of Christian faith, which was to instruct in orthodoxy and to present models for imitation. The control of bishops, who were responsible for approving images for public devotion, however, did not extend to private spheres of patronage, within which the taste for sexually charged imagery played itself out, particularly at elite levels of society. 'Mary Magdalen' was ideal in this context, for the Magdalen who had once moved in the social world was not a figure from contemporary culture, but a woman from the early Christian past, whose antiquity and associations with prostitution provided the kind of temporal and social distance for elites that made her eroticization licit. Titian's *Penitent Magdalen* of the 1530s, which pre-dated the Council of Trent, and Francesco Furini's painting of the same subject of *circa* 1633, which was the product of Tridentine reform, both belong to this tradition. They both also depend on the identification of the saint as 'ascetic hermit', an aspect of her persona developed exclusively in apocryphal and medieval sources, which ascribed to her an isolated existence for thirty years in a grotto or rustic setting.[46] In addition to 'ascetic hermit',

44. Sherrill Cohen, *The Evolution of Women's Asylums since 1500. From Refuges for Ex-Prostitutes to Shelters for Battered Women* (New York and Oxford, 1992), p. 18.

45. Judith Butler, *Bodies That Matter* (New York, 1993), p. 12. Here I depend on a relational or structural view of language and other forms of representation, in which nothing has significance in itself, but derives meaning from its relation to other things.

46. For a summary of these sources, see Sarah Wilk, 'The cult of Mary Magdalen in fifteenth-century Florence and its iconography', *Studi medievali*, 26 (1985), p. 686.

Titian and Furini coded her as 'penitent', with reddened eyes and tear-stained face. To a viewing audience steeped in Counter-Reformation theology, the tears would have been particularly important. The Tridentine Church cast tears as the very image of confession and penitence, with theologians invoking the tears of saints (including those of Mary Magdalen) in their defence of penance[47] – a sacrament whose validity was contested by Protestant reformers. Thus, weeping saints, who were widely deployed in text and image, were read metaphorically by many as exemplary penitents.[48]

Cristofano Allori's *Magdalen in the Desert* of 1612 casts Mary Magdalen as a hermit and a *contemplative*, rather than as a penitent. The figure gazes heavenward without shedding tears. This identification of the Magdalen ultimately depends upon her conflation with a woman called Mary in Luke 10:38–42, who listened quietly at the feet of Jesus while her sister, Martha, served.[49] The salient point here is that the Magdalen's eremitic retreat, whether interpreted as ascetic, penitent or contemplative, provided an iconographic rationale for the depiction of her naked body.

In medieval representations of the Magdalen as a hermit saint, artists had veiled her nakedness with hair. Her exposed face, forearms and feet functioned as a trope, signalling her nakedness even as the hair concealed most of her body.[50] By the fifteenth century, this type of representation had become traditional, although artists began to expose more of the limbs and even an emaciated chest, to signal food deprivation and abstinence in general. Fifteenth-century polychrome sculptures of the Magdalen by Desiderio da Settignano and Donatello are well-known examples.[51]

47. On the weeping of saints in the defence of the sacrament of penance, see Haskins, *Mary Magdalen*, pp. 255–6.

48. Even before Tridentine reforms, the fifteenth-century Archbishop Antoninus secured the Magdalen as a model of penance in Florence. His treatise on confession (*Specchio di coscienza*), which circulated widely in early sixteenth-century Florence, even contains a five-page 'transcription' of the Magdalen's purported confession, which was to precede penance; see Wilk, 'The cult of Mary Magdalen', p. 693. Devotional paintings and sculptures from this period that isolate the figure of the saint, however, do not portray her weeping. Her tears were reserved primarily for Crucifixion and Lamentation scenes.

49. Mary and Martha enact the two models of Christian life, contemplative and active, for which see Victor Saxer, *Le culte de Marie Madeleine en occident des origines à la fin du moyen âge* (Paris, 1959), pp. 335 ff.; Malvern, *Venus in Sackcloth*, pp. 27–8.

50. Daniel Russo, 'Entre Christ et Marie. La Madeleine dans l'art italien des XIIIe–XVe siècles', in Georges Duby and Charles Pietri, eds., *Marie Madeleine dans la mystique, les arts et les lettres. Actes du colloque international, 1988* (Paris, 1989), pp. 173–90, p. 185 in particular.

51. For illustrations of the sculptures, see Mosco, *La Maddalena*, pp. 35 and 51.

Beginning around the time of Titian, however, artists broke with these protocols for the depiction of the Magdalen as a hermit (contemplative *or* penitent). Emphasizing her state of undress, they coded her as a sensual nude with voluptuous proportions and colourful modelling of the flesh – from Titian's ruddy browns, to Furini's shades of pink and blue, which invite careful inspection of the bodies and were clearly intended to induce pleasure in the viewer. Thus, they cast the Magdalen into the realm of the erotic, setting up contradictions or tensions that are internal to their works and that do not come into play in earlier representations of the reclusive saint.

The fashioning of an erotic Magdalen already represents an excess of meaning with respect to the Magdalen as whore-turned-penitent, for the erotic does not have any obvious or necessary connection with penitence, or even with prostitution, for that matter. The play of several sometimes arbitrarily connected or competing meanings at a single moment in culture indicates the complexity of the name as signifier. This multiplicity of meaning was compounded by another association, that of the Magdalen as a woman authorized to speak – perhaps less prominent than the others in pictorial imagery but nonetheless present in the collective imagination of the early modern period. It is this association that brings us back to the performed representations of Maria Maddalena de' Pazzi.

In the canonical Gospels, divine authority stands behind the speech of the Magdalen. After the Crucifixion in the Gospel of Matthew (28:9–10), Jesus addresses the Magdalen directly, in the presence of another Mary. In Mark 16:9 and John 20:14, he appears to her alone, and in John 20:15–17 he directs her to speak on his behalf, to explain to the apostles the significance of the resurrection and the imminence of his ascent. These passages implicitly assign her first place among the disciples of Jesus, the *Apostola Apostolorum* ('Apostle of the Apostles'). Thus, it is scripture that ultimately affirms her authority to inform and to instruct as well as to speak. It also implicitly establishes her as the prototypical Christian mystic, who received immediate knowledge of God through visions of, and verbal exchanges with, the divine. Maria Maddalena de' Pazzi, with her multiple visions and 'colloquies with God', falls into this category.

Although the Gospels comprise the texts most widely known throughout Christian history, the Magdalen's pronouncement to the Apostles, which is integral to their narrative, rarely appears in devotional art from any period.[52] Nonetheless, the sanctioning of

52. Mosco, *La Maddalena*, p. 126.

her speech seems significant in the context of Maria Maddalena's attempts to speak authoritatively herself, despite protocols of silence within cloistered communities. This woman had gestured like the Virgin Mary, and had spoken like the Magdalen, within the walls of an institution that sanctioned silence. Moreover, she had admonished and instructed in her speech and gestures, in a world that granted few women voices of authority.

Simple procedures of artistic invention are all it takes to effect a normative image of the subject who transgresses social conventions. Official representations of Maria Maddalena de' Pazzi from the time of her canonization in 1669 omitted her fantasized play and theatrical interaction with statuary and sacred objects, which are given so clearly in the Carmelites' transcriptions of her unauthorized speech.[53] Moreover, they erased all signs of her evangelizing, securing her normalization posthumously, in paint, bronze and stone. The paintings and sculptures in the reliquary chapel of *Santa Maria Maddalena de' Pazzi* in Florence indicate this rehabilitation of her image after her death. For example, Luca Giordano's painting in this chapel, depicting *Maria Maddalena Reaching for the Infant Jesus from the Arms of the Virgin*, could well have represented the mystic's preaching, but it did not. The Carmelite sisters had reported that the mystic frequently cuddled a doll of Jesus, giving them to understand that the infant Son had descended to her 'from the breast of God the Father', when they could see nothing other than the solitary woman's gestures. On these occasions, she would speak for hours in the sisters' presence about theological matters, Church reform, moral transgression and the means to salvation. Allegorizing, she would often condemn religious who broke their vows and would then lapse into silence, appearing to comprehend great things, in an attitude of adoration. None of this appears in Giordano's painted image of Maria Maddalena with the infant Jesus. Here Giordano omitted references to reform and to Maria Maddalena's preaching in the presence of the nuns. He also modified her peculiar coupling of the infant with God the Father, substituting Mary according to convention. The painter's authority in these instances probably derived from a biography of the mystic, written by one of her confessors two years after her death in 1609, as part of the campaign to promote her beatification and

---

53. On images of Maria Maddalena as *beata*, *prior* to her canonization, see Piero Pacini, 'I "depositi" di Santa Maria Maddalena de' Pazzi e la diffusione delle sue immagini, 1607–1668', *Mitteilungen des kunsthistorisches Institutes in Florenz*, 32 (1988), pp. 171–252.

canonization.[54] This biography, which the Carmelite order had authorized, contains many of the same narrative elements as Giordano's
painting.[55] It neutralizes the political tenor of the woman's voice
and, significantly, enjoyed a much wider circulation in early modern Italy than the transcriptions of Maria Maddalena's speech. The
biography went into a second printing in 1611; the sisters' transcriptions were not published until the second half of the twentieth
century.

Artists other than Giordano contributed to the decorations in
the church in Florence that bears Maria Maddalena's name. Their
work, however, remained consonant with his, erasing the mystic's
speech and gestures and encoding her as '*Santa* Maria Maddalena
de' Pazzi' in terms that conformed to established hagiographic
models. Not surprisingly, imagery of the Magdalen herself conformed to the same normative type.

Representation and the formation of the self

Speech and gesture are often taken as unproblematic forms of
representation granting access to a coherent and stable subject –
the Enlightenment subject of reason and self-determining thought.
Representation is often presumed to function instrumentally, allowing for the autonomous creation of meaning as an expression of
uniquely individual experience. Subjectivity, however, may also be
understood as the *effect* of language and of representation in general. Within this critical framework one could argue that there was
no stable referent in the social world attached to the name 'Maria
Maddalena de' Pazzi'. There was no identity, there was no self,
prior to the formation of her self in and through a range of practices that carried specific meanings.[56]

54. Vincenzo Puccini, *Vita della Madre Suor Maria Maddalena de' Pazzi Fiorentina*
(Florence, 1609).

55. Barzman, 'Devotion and desire'.

56. In his lucid introduction to Lacanian psychoanalysis in *The Politics of Psychoanalysis* (New Haven and London, 1987), Stephen Frosh asserts: '[T]here is [no]
particular pre-existent subjectivity which learns to express itself in the words made
available by language ... but rather ... the initially "absent" subject becomes concrete through its positioning in a meaning system which is ontologically prior to it.
... The subject, the pronominal "I", is created through an order that originates
outside it [and is more extensive than it].' p. 130. Frosh is arguing here that, in
certain respects, we are possessed and 'spoken' by language we do not own ourselves; we construct ourselves, to a large extent, according to the possibilities offered
within a pre-existent semiotic field.

The representational practices employed by Maria Maddalena involved spoken language and a complex language of the body that incorporated material objects – devotional objects and works of sacred 'art'. Any discussion of the formation of her gendered self has to take into account the location of the woman's actions in the semiotic field, within which she, and all of her contemporaries, had to assume positions that pre-existed their interventions as users of language and representation. The signs within this field, and the various subject-positions they seem to offer, are never fixed themselves. Nonetheless, to begin to use language at all means to assume a place within pre-established structures of relations, and to take on identities established within institutions (family, Church, state) prior to one's own entry into culture. Far from a fixed or stable self, Caterina de' Pazzi shifted as she moved through relations that structured her world of experience. 'Child' to her 'parents' throughout her life, she moved as 'professed nun' within the confines of the convent. 'Caterina' or 'Maria Maddalena' de' Pazzi performed within a matrix of identities already scripted by the time she gave them voice. Her 'profession' as nun opened up possibilities yet also set limits on her movements within the social world, even as normative protocols governed her actions as 'mystic'. These actions constituted a citational practice based on models and precedents that were partly codified in texts and works of art, which positioned her as mystic, and enabled others to recognize (that is, to 'read') her, and to acknowledge her as such.[57]

Citation in any context is a process of rehearsal or repetition. It is a complex operation that unfolds in time as well as in space. Maria Maddalena gestured like the Virgin after venerating her image in paint and stone, or while reading about her in devotional texts and listening to her praises sung in the choir. She also took the place of the grieving Madonna while embracing a carved statue of her dying son, leading a procession of those who began by watching and who felt inspired on more than one occasion to join in. With the example of these interventions in the culture of conventual life, distinctions between production and reception begin to fall

57. A similar degree of complexity pertained to Maria Maddalena's baptized name. 'Caterina' or 'Catherine' did not represent an act of naming on *her* part, yet it, too, presented a set of coordinates in the field of meaning, and carried multiple associations and expectations in the social world. For a typology of Caterina Benincasa (Saint Catherine of Siena) as a hagiographical model for pious comportment in the sixteenth century, see Gabriella Zarri, 'Le sante vive. Per una tipologia della santità femminile nel primo Cinquecento', *Annali dell'Istituto storico italo-germanico in Trento*, 6 (1980), pp. 371–445.

apart, for they appear to be attendant upon each other. The performative self, the citational self, the textual and spectacular self – this self cannot be categorized as produced *or* received representation, for it constitutes both, diachronically (*through* time) but it does so in one and the same event or procedure.

Conclusion

I have explored one direction within which we might further the shift in the study of gender and cultural production in early modern Italy, from women and 'art' to women and performed representation – to the signifying practices through which individuals themselves entered visual, material and textual culture as gendered subjects. My intention is not to remove paintings and other works of art from the field of study. Rather, it is to acknowledge the historically conditioned status of things *as* 'works of art', and to integrate them in gender studies with other objects and representations, which include performative subjects themselves. At the very least, this allows for a more expansive discussion of women's interventions in culture than the traditional boundaries of art history permit, which is particularly important for those of us working on a period with relatively few female painters or sculptors. Many interventions by women, as I have argued, depended on procedures that collapse distinctions between 'artist' and 'audience', or, more generally, between 'production' and 'reception'. Implicitly, then, this approach calls for a reconsideration of the usefulness or desirability of a particular vision of art history that regards these activities as radically different from each other and mutually exclusive.

The desire to reform, to revise or to intervene in culture in a meaningful way has never been the exclusive prerogative of an intellectual elite or of 'artists' – male or female. Here I have offered the performing subject within conventual life as an integral aspect of cultural production, attempting in the process not to essentialize feminine subjectivity. This refusal to essentialize stems from doubts about the epistemological status of representation, including representations of the self, and from questions about subjectivity and what might be termed today 'the politics of identity'. Implicit in the study of the Carmelite mystic, above, are the following questions: Is identity coherent and fixed? Is it self-styled or self-determined? Are representations expressions of 'individuality'? Or are individuals actually constituted in and through their use of language, gesture and other forms of representation?

Maria Maddalena de' Pazzi provides a useful case study for the investigation of these questions in early modern Italy.[58] Her 'ecstasies', incorporating props that included 'works of art' and sacred imagery, formed part of a pattern of activity that constituted *her* as the focal point of spectacle, in which she commanded an audience of listeners, viewers and those moved to participate. Despite the appearance of spontaneity and individual expression, they were the effect of elaborate forms of representation based on received models that circulated in painting, sculpture and other media, which she and her contemporaries encountered within a variety of liturgical and devotional contexts. Maria Maddalena was *herself* a work of 'art'.

Moving in a similar direction as Simons, Baskins and Hughes, I have considered the complexity of meaning that attached to signs, which, in turn, imparted an instability to meaning. It is the porousness of signs like 'Mary Magdalen', their ability to absorb multiple and even competing meanings, that laid the foundation for subjective manoeuvring, as individuals positioned themselves in coded systems, entering the world of human society through representations. It is here that we can say with certitude, all subjects enter the field of cultural production.

58. The emphasis in women's history on female religious and women's devotional practices, which my work also reflects, is due in part to the relative abundance of extant textual sources about them, many of which were produced to document their activities and their discourses in orchestrated programmes of surveillance and containment.

Suggested Further Readings

ROBERT C. DAVIS

Chapter 1: The Geography of Gender in the Renaissance

Besides its obvious links to the current flourishing of women's studies, the recent interest in the gendering of space in Renaissance Italian cities also owes much to a rising appreciation of the ritual and symbolic importance of public space generally during the Renaissance. Much of this new awareness among scholars is due to the work of Richard Trexler and Edward Muir, whose monographic studies, on Florence and Venice respectively, are cited elsewhere in this section, but who are also responsible for a number of shorter, equally vital pieces that focus on both specific and comparative aspects of ritual and place in the Renaissance. Thus, for Richard Trexler see, 'Florentine religious experience: the sacred image', in *Studies in the Renaissance*, 19 (1972), pp. 7–41; and '*Correre la terra*: collective insults in the late Middle Ages', in *Mélanges de L'École Française de Rome, Moyen Age-Temps Modernes*, 96 (1984), pp. 845–902. For Edward Muir, see 'Images of power: art and pageantry in Renaissance Venice', in *American Historical Review*, 84 (1979), pp. 16–52; 'The virgin on the street corner: the place of the sacred in Italian cities', in *Religion and Culture in the Renaissance and Reformation*, S. Ozment, ed. (Kirksville, MO, 1989); and together with Ronald F.E. Weissman, 'Social and symbolic places in Renaissance Venice and Florence', in *The Power of Place: Bringing together Geographical and Sociological Imaginations*, J.A. Agnew and J.S. Duncan, eds (Boston, 1989), pp. 81–103.

Although the most succinct treatment in English of the question of gendered geography in Renaissance Italy remains Dennis Romano, 'Gender and the urban geography of Renaissance Venice', in *Journal of Social History*, 23 (1989), pp. 339–53, a broader study of the impact of urban topography on a society and its mores is available in Elisabeth Crouzet-Pavan, *'Sopra le acque salse': espaces, pouvoirs, et société à Venise, à la fin du Moyen Age* (Rome, 1992). On unsafe and tumultuous conditions in the streets of Italian cities generally, see Steven Hughes, 'Fear and loathing in Bologna and Rome: the papal police in perspective', in *Journal of Social History*, 21 (1987), pp. 97–116; Christiane Klapisch-Zuber, 'The "Mattinata" in Medieval Italy', in her *Women, Family, and Ritual in Renaissance Italy* (Chicago, 1985), pp. 261–82; and David Herlihy, 'Some psychological and social roots of violence in the Tuscan cities', in *Violence and Civil Disorder in Italian Cities, 1200–1500,* L. Martines, ed. (Berkeley, 1972), pp. 129–54.

Scholarly and popular interest in the Grand Tour of the seventeenth and (especially) eighteenth centuries has been strong and continuous at least since the beginning of the 1900s. The result has been a number of luxurious picture books and exhibition catalogues, most recently those of Andrew Wilton and Ilaria Bignani, *Grand Tour: The Lure of Italy in the Eighteenth Century* (London, 1996); and Cesare de Seta, *L'Italia del Grand Tour: Da Montaigne a Goethe* (Naples, 1992); see also, Bruce Redford, *Venice and the Grand Tour* (New Haven, 1996). Specifically on English Grand Tourists, see the many works of Jeremy Black, culminating with *The Grand Tour of the Eighteenth Century* (New York, 1992). The best exploration of the Grand Tour as a social phenomenon marked by the meeting and often mutual incomprehension of different cultures, however, perhaps still remains R.S. Pine-Coffin's lengthy introduction to his *Bibliography of British and American Travel in Italy to 1860* (Florence, 1974). Nearly all of the hundreds of travel accounts cited in this monumental reference work can be found in *Early English Books on Microfilm*, which itself can now be accessed and searched on-line.

Chapter 2: Gender and the Rites of Honour in Italian Renaissance Cities

The centrality of personal and group honour to Renaissance Italians is a concept whose fortunes have fluctuated widely over the last century and a half. Burckhardt identified its pursuit by princes as one of the driving forces of the era in his *Civilization of the Renaissance in Italy*, but just as succeeding historians largely shifted the period's cultural centre of gravity from the petty despotisms to

Florence and Venice, so they also tended to downplay the drive for honour as too chivalric and medieval for these bourgeois, merchant republics. Honour is currently enjoying a renaissance of its own, however, largely thanks to a new crop of ethno-historians, who have adapted this cultural concept so dear to anthropologists, not only as a key to understanding the Renaissance mentality, but also as a way to access the less visible parts of Renaissance society, such as women, workers and the poor. The broad outlines of the possibilities and implications of an ethnographic approach to the Renaissance have been sketched out by Peter Burke, in his *The Historical Anthropology of Early Modern Italy: Essays on Perception and Communication* (Cambridge, UK, 1987). Honour-based interpretations of more specific facets of Italian society, with their almost inevitable linkages to questions of gender, are to be found in: Sandra Cavallo and Simona Cerutti, 'Female honor and the social control of reproduction in Piedmont between 1600 and 1800', and Lucia Ferrante, 'Honor regained: women in the Casa del Soccorso di San Paolo in sixteenth-century Bologna', both in *Sex and Gender in Historical Perspective*, Edward Muir and Guido Ruggiero, eds (Baltimore, 1990), pp. 46–72 and 73–109; Robert C. Davis, *The War of the Fists: Popular Culture and Public Violence in Late Renaissance Venice* (New York, 1994); and Edward Muir, 'The double binds of manly revenge in Renaissance Italy', in *Gender Rhetorics: Postures of Dominance and Submission in History*, Richard A. Trexler, ed. (Binghamton, NY, 1994), pp. 65–82.

A quarter-century ago, Natalie Z. Davis signalled a new scholarly awareness in the tight interplay between honour and ritual in her collected essays, *Society and Culture in Early Modern France* (Stanford, CA, 1975). This understanding was made explicit for the Italian Renaissance not long after, particularly in Edward Muir, *Civic Ritual in Renaissance Venice* (Princeton, 1981); and Richard C. Trexler, *Public Life in Renaissance Florence* (Ithaca, NY, and London, 1980). Their largely political and religious interest in ritual has more recently been extended to the personal realm, especially with regards to rites of passage, by James R. Banker, *Death in the Community: Memorialization and Confraternities in an Italian Commune of the Late Middle Ages* (Athens, GA, and London, 1988); Louis Haas, ' "Il mio buono compare": choosing godparents and the uses of baptismal kinship in Renaissance Florence', in *Journal of Social History*, 29 (1995), pp. 341–56; Christiane Klapisch-Zuber, *Women, Family, and Ritual in Renaissance Italy* (Chicago and London, 1985); and Sharon T. Strocchia, *Death and Ritual in Renaissance Florence* (Baltimore, 1992).

Even as the study of ritual behavior has become more personalized, it has also become more broadly based, as scholars have reached the inevitable conclusion that, if working or dispossessed men and women in Renaissance Italy had honour, so too must they have had ritual forms with which to express it. Recent works such as Elizabeth S. Cohen, 'Honor and gender in the streets of early modern Rome', *Journal of Interdisciplinary History*, 22 (1992), pp. 597–625; Thomas V. Cohen, 'The lay liturgy of affront in sixteenth-century Italy', *Journal of Social History*, 25 (1992), pp. 857–77; Daniel R. Lesnick, 'Insults and threats in medieval Todi', *Journal of Medieval History*, 17 (1991), pp. 71–89; and Guido Ruggiero, *Binding Passions: Tales of Magic, Marriage, and Power at the End of the Renaissance* (New York, 1993), all not only explore the implications of ritual behaviour at all social levels, but also offer promising approaches for expanding the study of gender in Renaissance Italy beyond the relatively restricted circle of ruling elites.

Chapter 3: Daughters and Oligarchs: Gender and the Early Renaissance State

'Did women have a Renaissance?', the late Joan Kelly-Gadol's provocative essay that so effectively shifted the paradigm of Renaissance historiography, can be found in Renate Bridenthal and Claudia Koonz, eds, *Becoming Visible: Women in European History* (Boston, 1977), pp. 137–64; and has since been reprinted in *Women, History, and Theory: The Essays of Joan Kelly* (Chicago, 1984), pp. 19–50; and reviewed by Judith C. Brown in *American Historical Review*, 92 (1987), pp. 938–40. For the background context in which this essay was originally written, see Lauro Martines, 'A way of looking at women in Renaissance Florence', in *Journal of Medieval and Renaissance Studies*, 4 (1974), pp. 15–28; and Stanley Chojnacki, 'Patrician women in early Renaissance Venice', in *Studies in the Renaissance*, 21 (1974), pp. 176–203. The debate on the extent to which Italian women of all classes were involved in or benefited from social developments in the Renaissance was given new depth in terms of sources and analysis by Christiane Klapisch-Zuber, in particular in 'The cruel mother: maternity, widowhood, and dowry in Florence in the fourteenth and fifteenth centuries' and 'The Griselda complex: Dowry and marriage gifts in the Quattrocento', in her *Women, Family, and Ritual in Renaissance Italy* (Chicago, 1985) pp. 117–31 and 213–46 respectively. Reactions against these scholars' generally negative assessments of female prospects during the Renaissance have sought to bring new sources to bear on the question. See especially, Elaine G. Rosenthal, 'The position of women in Renaissance Florence: neither autonomy nor subjection', in *Florence and Italy: Renaissance Studies in Honour of Nicolai Rubinstein*, Peter Denley and Caroline Elam, eds (London, 1988), pp. 369–81; and Donald E. Queller and Thomas F. Madden, 'Father of the bride: fathers, daughters, and dowries in late medieval and early Renaissance Venice', in *Renaissance Quarterly*, 46 (1993), pp. 685–711.

The formation of the Renaissance state, with its attendant intrusion into individual and family lives, has been most recently explored by Giorgio Chittolini, Antony Molho, Trevor Dean, Elena Fasano Guarini and others in *The Origins of the State in Italy, 1300–1600*, a supplement issue of *Journal of Modern History*, 67 (1995) which is the English translation of G. Chittolini, A. Molho and P. Schiera, eds, *Origini dello stato. Processi di formazione statale in Italia fra medioevo ed età moderna* (Bologna, 1994). Earlier works of note on the topic include Marvin B. Becker, *Florence in Transition*, II, *Studies in the Rise of the Territorial State* (Baltimore, 1968); James S. Grubb, *Firstborn of Venice: Vicenza in the Early Renaissance State* (Baltimore, 1988); Dennis Romano, *Patricians and Popolani: The Social Foundations of the Venetian Renaissance State* (Baltimore, 1987); and Trevor Dean, *Land and Power in Late Medieval Ferrara: The Rule of the Este, 1350–1450* (Cambridge, 1988).

Two works which have been fundamental in sparking scholarly interest in Renaissance Italian nuns and convents are Richard C. Trexler, 'Celibacy in the Renaissance: the nuns of Florence', in *Power and Dependence in Renaissance Florence*, 3 vols (Binghamton, NY, 1993), Vol. II, *The Women of Renaissance Florence*, pp. 6–30; and Judith C. Brown, *Immodest Acts. The Life of a Lesbian Nun in Renaissance Italy* (New York, 1986). Further important works on the social place of the convent in Renaissance urban life include Jutta Sperling, 'Convents and the body politic in late Renaissance Venice' (PhD dissertation, Stanford University, CA, 1995); Gabriella Zarri, *Le sante vive: profezie di corte e devozione femminile tra '400 e '500* (Turin, 1990); Sharon Strocchia, 'Learning the virtues: convent schools and female culture in Renaissance Florence', in *Women's Education in Early Modern Europe: A History, 1500–1800*, Barbara Whitehead, ed. (New York, forthcoming); Gene Brucker, 'Monasteries, friaries, and nunneries in Quattrocento Florence', in *Christianity and the Renaissance: Image and Religious Imagination in the Quattrocento*, Timothy Verdon and John Henderson, eds (Syracuse, NY, 1990).

Dowries, which are studied in legal and economic terms elsewhere in this volume, also provide a significant benchmark of the degree and success of government intervention in Renaissance family politics – a facet of this institution that has been explored by Heather Gregory, 'Daughters, dowries and the family in fifteenth-century Florence', in *Rinascimento*, 2nd ser., 27 (1987), pp. 215–37; Julius Kirshner and Anthony Molho, 'The dowry fund and the marriage market in early quattrocento Florence', in *Journal of Modern History*, 50 (1978), pp. 403–38; Anthony Molho, *Marriage Alliance in Late Medieval Florence* (Cambridge, MA, 1994); and in numerous articles by Stanley Chojnacki, including 'Nobility, women, and the state: marriage regulation in Venice, 1420–1535', in *Marriage in Renaissance Italy*, Trevor Dean and K.J.P. Lowe, eds (Cambridge, UK, 1997); 'The power of love: wives and husbands in late medieval Venice', in *Women and Power in the Middle Ages*, Mary Erler and Maryanne Kowaleski, eds (Athens, GA, 1988), pp. 126–48; and 'Social identity in Renaissance Venice: the second serrata', in *Renaissance Studies*, 8 (1994), pp. 341–58.

Chapter 4: Person and Gender in the Laws

Law and legal culture, although fundamental to all levels of Medieval and Renaissance society, have for the most part proven too arcane a field to attract many scholars in either Renaissance or gender studies. Two of the best recent historical overviews that are now available in English translation are, R.C. van Caenegem, *An Historical Introduction to Private Law*, trans. by D.E.L. Johnston from the original French of 1988) (Cambridge, UK, 1992); and Manlio Bellomo, *The Common Legal Past of Europe, 1000–1800*, trans. from 2nd edn by Lydia G. Cochrane (Washington, DC, 1995). The 'deep background' intermingling of Roman and Lombard law that finally produced Renaissance communal law, and the evolving legal notions of women that resulted, are still best covered in several large-scale studies in Italian, however. See Maria Teresa Guerra Medici, *I diritti delle donne nella società altomedievale*, Ius Nostrum, Studi e Testi, 2nd ser., (Rome, 1986); and Manlio Bellomo, *La condizione giuridica della donna in Italia* (Turin, 1970). For an elegant discussion (in Italian) of the whole question of *ius commune* and *ius proprium*, see Paolo Grossi, *L'Ordine giuridico medievale* (Bari, 1995).

The issue of personhood and the individual has been approached from both a legal and an anthropological standpoint. Particularly worth mentioning is Aaron Gurevich, 'The "persona" in search of the individual', in *The Origins of European Individualism*, Aaron Gurevich, trans. Katherine Judleson, in *The Making of Europe*, Jacques LeGoff, ed. (Oxford, 1995), pp. 89–99; see also J.S. LaFontaine, 'Person and individual: some anthropological reflections', in *The Category of the Person: Anthropology, Philosophy, History*, M. Carrithers, S. Collins and S. Lukes, eds (Cambridge, 1985). The legal problems presented by property, specifically in the context of Renaissance Italy and especially in the form of inheritence and dowries, have been succinctly treated in several recent articles: Samuel K. Cohn, Jr, 'Le ultime volontà: famiglia, donne e peste nera nell'Italia centrale', *Studi storici*, 32 (1991), pp. 858–75; Thomas Kuehn, 'Law, death, and heirs in the Renaissance: repudiation of inheritance in Florence', *Renaissance Quarterly*, 45 (1991), pp. 484–516; and idem, 'Social processes and legal processes in the Renaissance: a Florentine inheritance case from 1452', *Quaderni fiorentini per la storia del pensiero giuridico moderno*, 23 (1995), pp. 365–96.

The nature of Renaissance gender-biased law and the various constraints and protections it imposed on each sex has until now been largely explored only as it pertained to urban Italian women, in particular in Florence and Venice. As in so much else, the best general background for the legal culture's definitions of women is Ian Maclean, *The Renaissance Notion of Woman* (Cambridge, 1980), but see also Yan Thomas, 'The division of the sexes in Roman Law', in *A History of Women in the West*, Vol. 1, *From Ancient Goddesses to Christian Saints*, P. Pantel, ed. (Cambridge, MA, 1992). The most comprehensive recent study in English of late-medieval Italian women and the law is Thomas Kuehn, *Law, Family, and Women: Toward a Legal Anthropology of Renaissance Italy* (Chicago, 1991). More focused research, particularly on female wealth and its potential for empowerment, have also resulted in articles that throw a strong light on the legal cultures particular to individual Renaissance cities. For Venice, see Stanley Chojnacki, '"The most serious duty": motherhood, gender, and patrician culture in Renaissance Venice', in *Refiguring Woman: Perspectives on Gender and the Italian Renaissance*, M. Migiel and J. Schiesari, eds (Ithaca, NY, 1991), pp. 133–54. On Florence, see Julius Kirshner, 'Wives' claims against insolvent husbands in late medieval Italy', in *Women of the Medieval World*, J. Kirshner and S.F. Wempel, eds (Oxford, 1985), pp. 256–303; idem, 'Maritus lucretur dotem uxoris sue premortue in late medieval Florence', in *Zeitschrift der Savigny-Stiftung für Rechtsgeschichte, Kanonistische Abteilung*, 77 (1991), pp. 111–155; and Elaine Rosenthal,

'The position of women in Renaissance Florence: neither autonomy nor subjection', in *Florence and Italy: Renaissance Studies in Honour of Nicolai Rubinstein*, Peter Denley and Caroline Elam, eds (London, 1989), pp. 369–81. For a balancing view of some of the legal constraints on men in Renaissance Florence, see Thomas Kuehn, *Emancipation in Late Medieval Florence* (New Brunswick, NJ, 1982).

Chapter 5: Women and Work in Renaissance Italy

Although economic approaches to Italian Renaissance history held pride of place in the field as recently as a generation or two ago, scholarly activity has declined in this field in recent years. It is a decline amply reflected in the comparative scarcity of economic-based studies in women's and gender history of the Renaissance, both of which have emerged only fairly recently. For a recent overview in Italian of the literature on the economic role of women in late medieval Italy, see G. Piccini, 'Le donne nelle vita economica, sociale e politica dell'Italia medievale', and Isabelle Chabot, 'Risorse e diritti patrimoniali', both in *Il lavoro delle donne*, A. Groppi, ed. (Bari, 1996), pp. 5–46 and pp. 47–70 respectively; and Isabelle Chabot, 'La reconnaissance du travail des femmes dans la Florence du bas Moyen Age: contexte, idéologique et réalité', in *La donna nell'economia (XIII–XVIII)*, S. Cavaciocchi, ed. (Florence, 1990), pp. 563–76. For useful studies in English on women's work, see Christiane Klapisch-Zuber's introduction to *A History of Women in the West*, Vol. II: *Silences of the Middle Ages* (Cambridge, MA, 1992); also David Herlihy, *Opera Muliebria: Women and Work in Medieval Europe* (New York, 1990); and Judith Brown, 'A woman's place was in the home: women's work in Renaissance Tuscany', in *Rewriting the Renaissance: The Discourses of Sexual Difference in Early Modern Europe*, M. Ferguson, M. Quilligan and N. Vickers, eds (Chicago, 1986), pp. 206–24.

Certainly the most comprehensive introduction to the economic life of the Renaissance Italian family is David Herlihy and Christiane Klapisch-Zuber, *Les Toscans et leurs familles. Une étude du catasto florentin de 1427* (Paris, 1978), trans. as *The Tuscans and their Families* (New Haven, CT, 1985). On the economic impact of female wealth on middle- and upper-class Renaissance families, see especially Donald E. Queller and Thomas F. Madden, 'Father of the bride: fathers, daughters, and dowries in late medieval and early Renaissance Venice', in *Renaissance Quarterly*, 46 (1993), pp. 685–711; and David Herlihy, 'Family and property in Renaissance Florence', in *The Medieval City*, H.A. Miskimin, D. Herlihy and A.L. Udovitch, eds (1977), pp. 3–24. A recent family study that approaches the topic of female wealth outside the context of the northern Italian cities is Tommaso Astarita, *The Continuity of Feudal Power: The Caracciolo di Brienza in Spanish Naples* (New York, 1992).

Forming the other side of the gender equation, men's work in the Renaissance has attracted rather more attention among economic historians, especially before the field's general decline set in. Particularly useful here for the Florentine working class is Richard A. Goldthwaite, *The Building of Renaissance Florence* (Baltimore, 1980); and Samuel K. Cohn, Jr, *The Laboring Classes in Renaissance Florence* (New York, 1980). For a socio-economic study of a community of working-class men and women in late-Renaissance Venice, see Robert C. Davis, *Shipbuilders of the Venetian Arsenal: Workers and Workplace in the Preindustrial City* (Baltimore, 1991); also on Venetian workers, see Richard T. Rapp, *Industry and Economic Decline in Seventeenth-Century Venice* (Cambridge, MA, 1976).

Chapter 6: Medicine and Magic: The Healing Arts

Renaissance medicine brings together, perhaps uniquely for a single field of study, the highest intellectual aspirations of the age together with its most varied and practical concerns, including economics, popular beliefs and public policy. Offering such an ideal point of entry into Renaissance social history, medicine and health care have thus, not surprisingly, attracted considerable scholarly attention over the years, producing a huge body of literature in their own right. The best recent, general introduction to the subject in this period is Nancy G. Siraisi, *Medieval and Early Renaissance Medicine: An Introduction to Knowledge and Practice* (Chicago, 1990); see also Carlo M. Cipolla, *Public Health and the Medical Profession in the Renaissance* (Cambridge, UK, 1976); and Katharine Park, 'Medicine and society in medieval Europe, 500–1500' in *Medicine in Society*, Andrew Wear, ed. (Cambridge, UK, 1991).

Focusing more specifically on varieties of medical practitioners in Renaissance Italy are Katharine Park, *Doctors and Medicine in Early*

Renaissance Florence (Princeton, NJ, 1985); Richard Palmer, 'Physicians and surgeons in sixteenth-century Venice', in *Medical History*, 23 (1979), pp. 451–60; Vivian Nutton, 'Continuity or rediscovery? The city physician in classical antiquity and medieval Italy', in *The Town and State Physician in Europe from the Middle Ages to the Enlightenment*, Andrew W. Russell, ed. (Wolfenbüttel, 1981), pp. 9–46; and Guido Ruggiero, 'The status of physicians and surgeons in Renaissance Venice', in *Journal of the History of Medicine*, 36 (1981), pp. 168–84. For an overview of the range of healing available to Renaissance Italians, see Peter Burke, 'Rituals of healing in early modern Italy', in his *The Historical Anthropology of Early Modern Italy: Essays on Perception and Communication* (Cambridge, UK, 1987), pp. 207–20; Carlo M. Cipolla, *Fighting the Plague in Seventeenth-Century Italy* (Madison, WI, 1981); Richard Palmer, 'Pharmacy in the republic of Venice in the sixteenth century', in *The Medical Renaissance of the Sixteenth Century*, A. Wear, R.K. French and I.M. Lonie, eds (Cambridge, UK, 1985), pp. 100–17; Katharine Park, 'Healing the poor: hospitals and medical assistance in Renaissance Florence', in *Medicine and Charity before the Welfare State*, Jonathan Barry and Colin Jones, eds (London, 1991), pp. 26–45; and idem, 'Stones, bones, and hernias: surgical specialists in fourteenth- and fifteenth-century Italy', in *Medicine from the Black Death to the French Disease*, Jon Arrizabalaga, ed. (London, 1997).

As the premier science of the human body, medicine has also long held a primary place in gender, and especially women's studies. In the medical context, medieval and Renaissance misogyny, concepts of gender differences and philosophies of female anatomy receive their most authoritative treatment in Joan Cadden, *Meanings of Sex Difference in the Middle Ages: Medicine, Science, and Culture* (Cambridge, UK, 1993); see also Helen Rodnite Lemay, 'Antonius Guainerius and medieval gynecology', in *Women of the Medieval World: Essays in honor of John H. Mundy*, Julius Kirshner and Suzanne F. Wemple, eds (Oxford, 1985); on Renaissance medicine's gendered world-view and its connections to Aristotle, see Ian Maclean, *The Renaissance Notion of Woman: A Study in the Fortunes of Scholasticism and Medical Science in European Intellectual Life* (Cambridge, UK, 1980); and Gianna Pomata, *La promessa di guarigione: malati e curatori in Antico Regime* (Rome/Bari, 1994). Medicine, like all Renaissance professions, was also gendered in social terms, between male and female practitioners, for which see especially Monica Green's important article, 'Women's medical practice and health care in medieval Europe', in *Signs*, 14 (1989), pp. 434–73, reprinted in

Sisters and Workers in the Middle Ages, Judith M. Bennett, ed. (Chicago, 1989), pp. 39–78; as well as John Benton, 'Trotula, women's problems, and the professionalization of medicine in the Middle Ages', in *Bulletin of the History of Medicine,* 59 (1985), pp. 30–53; and Monica Green, *Women and Literate Medicine in Medieval Europe: Trota and the 'Trotula'* (Cambridge, UK, forthcoming).

The strong linkages between Renaissance medicine and religion and magic have also produced a number of studies. A recent overview is provided in Richard Kieckhefer, 'The specific rationality of medieval magic', in *American Historical Review,* 99 (1994), pp. 813–36; also, Giancarlo Susini, ed., *Medicina, Erbe e Magia* (Milan, 1981); and David Gentilcore, *From Bishop to Witch: The System of the Sacred in Early Modern Terra d'Otranto* (Manchester, 1992). Approaching gendered medicine from its magical side has greatly altered present-day views of the dynamics of female witchcraft in Renaissance Italy, a topic innovatively explored through Inquisition investigations held in Friuli and the Veneto during the 1500–1600s by Guido Ruggiero, in *Binding Passions: Tales of Magic, Marriage, and Power at the End of the Renaissance* (New York, 1993); also important is Claudio Bondì, *Strix: medichesse, streghe e fattucchiere nell'Italia del Rinascimento* (Rome, 1989); for an institutional study on the same, see Ruth Martin, *Witchcraft and the Inquisition in Venice, 1550–1650* (Oxford, 1989).

Chapter 7: Gender and Sexual Culture in Renaissance Italy

Despite the obvious affinities between the two fields, sexuality originally lagged behind gender in the context of Renaissance social history. Discretely ignored by such nineteenth-century scholars as Burckhardt and Molmenti, what role sex would play in Renaissance studies was long determined by students of humanism and intellectual history, most notably, Ian Maclean, in his *The Renaissance Notion of Woman: A Study in the Fortunes of Scholasticism and Medical Science in European Intellectual Life* (Cambridge, UK, 1980); and more recently, Joan Cadden, *Meanings of Sex Differences in the Middle Ages: Medicine, Science, and Culture* (Cambridge, UK, 1993). When it began to emerge as a topic a generation ago, Renaissance sexuality was still less a field in its own right than one element in the demographic, institutional and legal histories of the era that were coming increasingly into vogue. In this sense it figures prominently in:

David Herlihy and Christiane Klapisch-Zuber, *Les toscans et leurs familles. Une étude du catasto florentin de 1427* (Paris, 1978), trans. as *The Tuscans and Their Families* (New Haven, 1985); Richard C. Trexler, 'Florentine prostitution in the fifteenth century: patrons and clients', in idem, *The Women of Renaissance Florence*, vol. 2 of *Power and Dependence in Renaissance Florence* (Binghamton, NY, 1993), pp. 31–65 (originally published as 'La prostitution florentine au XVe siècle: patronages et clientèles', in *Annales, ESC*, 36 [1981], pp. 983–1015); Patricia Labalme, 'Sodomy and Venetian justice in the Renaissance', in *Legal History Review*, 52 (1984), pp. 217–54; Sherill Cohen, *The Evolution of Women's Asylums since 1500: From Refuges for Ex-prostitutes to Shelters for Battered Women* (New York, 1992); John Brackett, 'The Florentine Onestà and the Control of Prostitution, 1403–1680', in *Sixteenth-Century Journal*, 24 (1993), pp. 273–300.

Another line of approach, one that has linked sexuality and sociology, provides its own insights into the impact of the biological drive and sexual competition on the socio-politics of the Renaissance. Ground-breaking in this respect were (for France) Natalie Z. Davis, 'Women on top', in her *Society and Culture in Early Modern France: Eight Essays* (Stanford, CA, 1975), pp. 124–51; Guido Ruggiero, *Violence in Early Renaissance Venice* (New Brunswick, NJ, 1980); Christiane Klapisch-Zuber, 'Women servants in Florence during the fourteenth and fifteenth centuries', in *Women and Work in Preindustrial Europe*, B.A. Hanawalt, ed. (Bloomington, IN, 1986), pp. 56–80; Elisabeth Cohen, 'No longer virgins: self-presentation by young women in late Renaissance Rome', in *Refiguring Woman: Perspectives on Gender and the Italian Renaissance*, M. Migiel and J. Schiesari, eds (Ithaca, NY, 1991), pp. 169–91; and Stanley Chojnacki, 'Subaltern patriarchs: patrician bachelors in Renaissance Venice', in *Medieval Masculinities. Regarding Men in the Middle Ages*, C.A. Lees, ed., with the assistance of T. Fenster and J.A. McNamara (Minneapolis, 1994), pp. 73–90.

Studies of the Italian Renaissance that focused specifically on sexual issues began to emerge only in the mid-1980s, perhaps because the strong inclination of many scholars of the 1970s to see gender as a social construct had conspired to undervalue the very sexual exchanges on which this construct was ultimately based. Methodologically, these recent studies owe a great deal to the new interpretive and theoretical approaches pioneered by the Italian journal *Quaderni storici* and loosely known as *microstoria*; this approach has been made available in English, in Edward Muir and Guido Ruggiero, eds, *Sex and Gender in Historical Perspective, Selections from Quaderni storici* (Baltimore, 1990). This has especially meant using trial records from the rich Italian criminal archives as a means of reconstructing the sexual values, customs and mentalities of the Renaissance. A good overview of the world of illicit sex that emerges, as well as the theoretical framework that formed it, is to be found in Nicholas Davidson, 'Theology, nature and the law: sexual sin and sexual crime in Italy from the fourteenth to the seventeenth century', in *Crime, Society and the Law in Renaissance Italy*, T. Dean and K.J.P. Lowe, eds (Cambridge, UK, 1994), pp. 74–98. Particularly successful applications of the approach are Guido Ruggiero, *The Boundaries of Eros. Sex Crime and Sexuality in Renaissance Venice* (New York, 1985); and Judith C. Brown, *Immodest Acts. The Life of a Lesbian Nun in Renaissance Italy* (New York, 1986). These two works, although limited by their nature to illicit sexuality, have structured much of the subsequent discourse on sex in the Italian Renaissance. The authors have also combined forces to edit a multi-volume series, 'Studies in the History of Sexuality' (Oxford University Press), whose latest contribution in Italian Renaissance studies is Michael Rocke, *Forbidden Friendships: Homosexuality and Male Culture in Renaissance Florence* (New York, 1996).

Chapter 8: Spiritual Kinship and Domestic Devotions

In recent years the field of European medieval spirituality has been identified at least as much with social history and psychology as with theology or the study of religious institutions. For placing sanctity in its larger social context, the primary work in the field has certainly been Rudolph M. Bell and Donald Weinstein, *Saints and Society: The Two Worlds of Western Christendom, 1000–1700* (Chicago, 1982). The exploration of the psychological realms of spirituality, with its ready connections to women and their bodies, has effectively helped to give the topic its central place in gender studies, in particular with Rudolph M. Bell *Holy Anorexia* (Chicago, 1985); Caroline Walker Bynum, *Holy Feast and Holy Fast: The Religious Significance of Food to Medieval Women* (Berkeley and Los Angeles, 1987); and idem, *Fragmentation and Redemption: Essays on Gender and the Human Body in Medieval Religion* (New York, 1991).

By its nature both fluid and ecumenical, medieval spirituality of either sex has been more often studied in terms of the individual or religious order, rather than those of city-states or nations. Its exploration in the specific context of the Italian Renaissance has thus lagged somewhat behind larger, pan-European models, with such notable exceptions as Ronald Weissman, *Ritual Brotherhood in Renaissance Italy* (New York, 1982); Daniel Bornstein, *The Bianchi of 1399* (Ithaca, NY, 1993); and some smaller studies, such as John Martin, 'Out of the shadow: heretical and Catholic women in Renaissance Venice', in *Journal of Family History*, 10 (1985), pp. 21–33; Christiane Klapisch-Zuber, 'Holy dolls: play and piety in Florence in the quattrocento', in her *Women, Family, and Ritual in Renaissance Italy* (Chicago, 1985), pp. 310–29; Anthony Molho, '*Tamquam vere mortua*: Le professioni religiose femminili nella Firenze del tardo medioevo', in *Società e storia*, 43 (1989), pp. 1–44.

The creative and empowerment sides of female spirituality have, however, been more thoroughly explored recently, especially in two series of collected essays: E. Ann Matter and John Coakley, eds, *Creative Women in Medieval and Early Modern Italy: A Religious and Artistic Renaissance* (Philadelphia, 1994); Daniel Bornstein and Roberto Rusconi, eds, *Women and Religion in Medieval and Renaissance Italy* (Chicago, 1996).

Chapter 9: Gender, Religious Institutions and Social Discipline: The Reform of the Regulars

Questions concerning the new religious rigour introduced by the Catholic reforms of Trent have generated a vast historical literature. With regard to their impact on such institutions as convent and sacramental reform in Italy, Italian scholars have, not surprisingly, been in the forefront: perhaps nowhere more so than with Adriano Prosperi's recent *Tribunali della coscienza: inquisitori, confessori, missionari* (Turin, 1996), a fundamental book, which examines the transformation of religious life in Italy between the Protestant Reformation and the Counter-Reformation. On the Tredentine reforms more broadly, the most recent and important studies are: for France, Elisabeth Rapley, *The Dévotes: Women & Church in Seventeenth-Century France* (Kingston, London and Buffalo, 1990); for Spain, Isabelle Poutrin, *Le voile et la plume: autobiographie et sainteté féminine dans l'Espagne moderne* (Madrid, 1995); for German-speaking areas and, in general, for the Ursulines, see Anne Konrad, *Zwischen Kloster und Welt: Ursulinen und Jesuitinen in der katholischen Reformbewegung des*

16.–17. Jahrhunderts (Mainz, 1991). On the cult of saints, see Gabriella Zarri, ed., *Finzione e santità tra medioevo ed età moderna* (Turin, 1991). On the problems related to the interpretation of the Conciliar dictates, the various papal bulls and the institutional and economic consequences of the reform of the nuns, the studies by Raimondo Creytens remain essential: 'La giurisprudenza della Sacra Congregazione del Concilio nella questione della clausura delle monache (1564–1576)', in *La Sacra Congregazione del Concilio: Quarto centenario della fondazione (1564–1964). Studi e ricerche* (Città del Vaticano, 1964), pp. 563–97; 'La riforma dei monasteri femminili dopo i decreti tridentini', in *Il Concilio di Trento e la Riforma tridentina* (Rome, 1965), I, pp. 45–83.

Works dealing more specifically with problems of convent discipline include the excellent recent work by Romano Canosa, *Il velo e il cappuccio. Monacazioni forzate e sessualità nei conventi femminili in Italia tra Quattrocento e Settecento* (Rome, 1991): a general study of the breakdown of convent discipline, especially in terms of the cloistering of nuns, it also features a useful summary of the existing literature. See also, Letizia Arcangeli, 'Ragioni politiche della disciplina monastica: il caso di Parma tra Quattro e Cinquecento', in *Donna, disciplina, creanza cristiana dal XV al XVII secolo: studi e testi a stampa*, Gabriella Zarri, ed. (Rome, 1996), pp. 165–87: an excellent case study on the effects of introducing triennial abbatial elections in the Benedictine convents of Renaissance Parma, and the political motives that lay behind attempts by civic authorities to promote monastic discipline. First-rate but somewhat less recent works along similar lines in English include Judith C. Brown, *Immodest Acts* (New York, 1986); and Guido Ruggiero, *The Boundaries of Eros* (New York, 1985).

The frequent coercion exerted even on males in the profession of religious vows is illustrated in a rich case study by Guido Dall'Olio on the discipline of regulars in the diocese of Bologna in the Tridentine period, which also provides information on the number of ex-monks in the mid-sixteenth century: 'La disciplina dei religiosi all'epoca del Concilio di Trento: sondaggi bolognesi', in *Annali dell'Istituto storico italo-germanico in Trento*, 21 (1995), pp. 93–140. Still essential to the study of the regulars is also the classic work by Hubert Jedin, 'Zur Vorgeschichte der Regularenreform, Trid. Sess. XXV', in *Romische Quartalschrift*, 44 (1936), pp. 231–81; see also Gigliola Fragnito, 'Gli Ordini religiosi tra Riforma e Controriforma', in *Clero e società nell'Italia moderna*, Mario Rosa ed. (Rome and Bari, 1992), pp. 115–205.

Chapter 10: Gender, Religious Representation and Cultural Production in Early Modern Italy

The importance of gender to modern-day Renaissance art history can hardly be overstated: perhaps no other new methodology has ever had such a profound impact on the field. Certainly seminal to the historiography traced in this chapter has been Linda Nochlin's early article, 'Why have there been no great women artists?', pp. 22–39 in the special issue of *Art News*, entitled 'Women's Liberation, Women Artists, and Art History', (1971); the essay has been reprinted in the collected writings of Linda Nochlin, *Women, Art, and Power and Other Essays* (New York, 1988), pp. 145–78.

Also significant in the past decade has been the ongoing reappraisal by art historians of the interrelation of art and religion in the Renaissance. Recent works that explore the function of, or response to, sacred images and objects include Hans Belting, *Likeness and Presence. A History of the Image before the Era of Art* (Chicago, 1994); David Freedberg, *The Power of Images. Studies in the History and Theory of Response* (Chicago, 1989); and Henk van Os, ed., *The Art of Devotion in the Later Middle Ages in Europe, 1300–1500* (Princeton, NJ, 1994). For a further bibliography of those art historians of the Italian Renaissance (including historians of religious drama) whose studies have taken them in this direction, see John T. Paoletti, 'Wooden sculpture in Italy as sacral experience', in *Artibus et Historiae*, 26 (1992), pp. 85–100, especially notes 1, 6, and 41.

For an introduction to semiotics and the theory of signs, especially as they pertain to the methodology in this chapter, see Robert Scholes, *Semiotics and Interpretation* (New Haven and London, 1982). Also see the work of Ferdinand de Saussure and Charles Sanders Peirce discussed by Keith Moxey in *The Practice of Theory: Poststructuralism, Cultural Politics, and Art History* (Ithaca, NY, 1994), pp. 31–37; and Mieke Bal and Norman Bryson, 'Semiotics and art history', *Art Bulletin*, 73:2 (1991), pp. 188–94.

Index